ERROR PATTERNS IN COMPUTATION

Using Error Patterns to Improve Instruction

 EIGHTH EDITION ⅃

Robert B. Ashlock
Covenant College

Merrill
Prentice Hall

Upper Saddle River, New Jersey
Columbus, Ohio

Library of Congress Cataloging-in-Publication Data

Ashlock, Robert B.
  Error patterns in computation : using error patterns to improve instruction /
Robert B. Ashlock.—8th ed.
    p. cm.
  Includes bibliographical references.
  ISBN 0-13-027093-8
    1. Arithmetic—Study and teaching (Elementary) I. Title.
  QA135.5 .A782 2002
  372.7'2044—dc21   00-051138

Vice President and Publisher: Jeffery W. Johnston
Editor: Linda Ashe Montgomery
Production Editor: Mary M. Irvin
Design Coordinator: Diane C. Lorenzo
Project Coordination and Text Design: Carlisle Publishers Services
Cover Design: Jason Moore
Cover Art: Super Stock
Production Manager: Pamela D. Bennett
Director of Marketing: Kevin Flanagan
Marketing Manager: Krista Groshong
Marketing Coordinator: Barbara Koontz

This book was set in Bookman by Carlisle Communications, Ltd., and was printed
and bound by R. R. Donnelley & Sons Company. The cover was printed by The Lehigh
Press, Inc.

Earlier editions © 1994 by Merrill/Macmillan Publishing Company; 1990, 1986, 1982,
1976, 1972 by Merrill Publishing Company.

Prentice-Hall International (UK) Limited, *London*
Prentice-Hall of Australia Pty. Limited, *Sydney*
Prentice-Hall Canada, Inc., *Toronto*
Prentice-Hall Hispanoamericana, S.A., *Mexico*
Prentice-Hall of India Private Limited, *New Delhi*
Prentice-Hall of Japan, Inc., *Tokyo*
Prentice-Hall Singapore Pte. Ltd
Editora Prentice-Hall do Brasil, Ltda., *Rio de Janeiro*

10 9 8 7 6 5 4 3 2 1
ISBN 0-13-027093-8

Preface

⌐⌐

We want to help our students learn to think mathematically. Mere skill in computing is not our primary concern.

Even so, computation in its many forms—using estimation, mental computation, calculators and computers, and paper-and-pencil procedures—continues to have a significant role in both the learning of mathematics and in solving problems within the world around us. This is made clear in *Principles and Standards for School Mathematics,* published by the National Council of Teachers of Mathematics in 2000.

We hope all of our students will understand what they study. We want them to succeed in mathematics and to enjoy solving problems—but students sometimes learn misconceptions. As they learn about operations and methods of computation, they sometimes adopt erroneous procedures in spite of our best efforts.

This book was written for those who are willing to listen carefully to what each student says and to make thoughtful analyses of student papers—teachers who want to help each student by discovering error patterns they may be using, and to be enabled, thereby, to focus instruction more effectively. This book was written to help teachers, whatever the level, to look at *all* student work diagnostically.

Error Patterns in Computation has changed greatly through the years. The first 96 pages of this edition are devoted to instructional issues. These pages provide help with diagnosing misconceptions and error patterns in computation, and they present many ideas for teaching varied methods of computation.

Much of the book focuses on detecting the systematic errors many students make when computing with paper and pencil. Reasons students may have learned erroneous procedures are considered, and strategies for helping those students are presented. Of course, many of the instructional strategies described are useful when teaching any student—whether that student has experienced difficulty under previous instruction or not.

The erroneous patterns displayed by students are not due to carelessness alone, nor are they due to insufficient practice. Students observe patterns and make inferences during instruction. In the case of an error pattern, that which has been learned does not always produce correct answers. Interestingly, some incorrect procedures produce correct answers part of the time. When this happens, students are reinforced in their belief that they have learned the desired concepts and skills.

You will find looking for error patterns to be a very worthwhile assessment activity. You will gain more specific knowledge of each student's strengths upon which to base future instruction. Whenever you observe error patterns in your own classroom, be sure to refrain from assigning practice activities that reinforce incorrect concepts and procedures.

THE EIGHTH EDITION

This edition reflects many of the concerns of NCTM's *Principles and Standards for School Mathematics*, including emphasis on concepts as well as skills. In this edition:

- Understanding the meanings of operations is emphasized, as is knowing when to use each operation. Computation, by whatever method, is distinguished from the operation itself.
- Different methods of computation are presented with an emphasis on using each method when appropriate. Paper-and-pencil procedures are considered in the context of other methods of computation.
- Many error patterns are presented within problem-solving contexts.
- Varied means of assessment are described and illustrated; self-assessment is emphasized. Extensive material on interviewing is included.
- Instruction in computation is addressed extensively through topics such as:
    Concepts and principles
    Understanding operations
    Computational fluency
    Mental computation, estimation, using calculators
    Paper-and-pencil procedures
    Developmental and corrective instruction
    Models and concrete materials

The role of language
Understanding and recalling number combinations
Graphic organizers
Peer tutoring
Portfolios

- Instructional ideas are also included in chapters that illustrate error patterns for particular operations and areas of mathematics.
- Lists of resources for assessment and instruction, and the summary of research on error patterns (Appendix B) have been carefully updated.

NEW SECTIONS

New in the eighth edition are:

- A glossary with definitions and illustrations
- A chapter with error patterns in algebra
- A section presenting gamelike activities with pattern boards and base blocks for instruction with whole-number algorithms (Appendix C)
- A section describing and differentiating conceptual learning and procedural learning
- A section on attaining computational fluency
- Sections on involving peers in assessment and peer tutoring
- New material on developing number sense and the role of invented algorithms

ORGANIZATION OF THE TEXT

The book is organized into two parts with appendices. Part One considers the place of computation within our age of calculators and computers, then focuses on various aspects of assessment and instruction for both concepts and skills. In Part Two, sample student papers are presented in chapters that focus on a particular mathematical topic. Within each chapter you have opportunities to identify patterns of error and to suggest corrective instruction, then compare your ideas with those in this book.

Experience has shown that direct involvement through simulation, as provided in this text, helps both preservice and inservice teachers become more proficient at diagnosing and correcting computational procedures. You gain skill by actually looking for patterns, making decisions, and planning instruction. If you are to benefit, it is important that you "play the game" and actually take time to respond.

Chapters 4–12 can be read in either of two ways: a chapter can be read in sequence or, within a chapter, one error pattern at a time can be read as directed in the text. Most readers choose to focus on one pattern at a time.

Additional student papers are included in Appendix A, where you have further opportunities to practice identifying error patterns.

ACKNOWLEDGMENTS

I wish to express appreciation for the encouragement of many classroom teachers who have shown great interest in this book over the years, and to acknowledge the help of teachers, former students, and their students. These colleagues have identified many of the error patterns presented. I would also like to thank the reviewers of the manuscript for their insights and comments: Bea Babbitt, The University of Nevada–Las Vegas; Carol Larson, The University of Arizona; Donna Strand, Baruch College CUNY–New York City; and Karen A. Verbeke, The University of Maryland–Eastern Shores.

—*Robert B. Ashlock*

Contents

⌐⌐

CHAPTER 8   Fractions and Decimals: Multiplication and Division   184

CHAPTER 9   Percent Problems   202

CHAPTER 10   Geometry and Measurement   212

CHAPTER 11   Integers   238

PART ONE

⌐⌐

Diagnosis and Instruction

This book is designed to help us improve mathematics instruction in our classrooms by becoming more diagnostically oriented. Diagnosis should be continuous throughout instruction, and both are addressed within Part I. The focus is on computation, but many of the ideas presented in Part I can be applied throughout the curriculum if we wish to become more sensitive and responsive to where our students are in their development.

How important is it to teach paper-and-pencil computation procedures in our age of calculators and computers? Chapter 1 addresses this concern and the need for conceptually oriented instruction. Paper-and-pencil procedures are only one method of computation students use when solving problems; we need to make sure our students are able to use them all, and know when each is most appropriate.

Why do our students sometimes learn misconceptions and erroneous procedures when learning to compute? Chapter 2 examines the learning process and presents helpful diagnostic concepts and procedures. Tools for diagnostic teaching are also described.

Diagnostic teaching involves careful observation. It attempts to determine what individuals are actually learning, the concepts they are truly learning, and the procedures they are really employing—whether correct or not.

If we are to teach diagnostically, we must adapt our instruction to what we observe and what we learn about each of our students. As we learn more about a particular student, we tailor our instruction to the student; we observe and learn more, and adapt our instruction again. We repeat this diagnosis-instruction cycle as often as necessary. In Chapter 3 there are many ideas to help us adapt instruction to the needs of each student.

Chapter 1

Computing with Paper and Pencil in an Age of Calculators and Computers

⌐⌐

In this age of calculators and computers, do our students actually need to learn paper-and-pencil procedures? We want our students to understand mathematical concepts, but how does this relate to learning to do paper-and-pencil procedures?

As we examine these and other questions in this chapter, we will find that even in our technological age paper-and-pencil computation is required. True, paper-and-pencil procedures constitute only one alternative for computing—though it often makes sense to use such procedures. While our students are learning to compute with paper and pencil, their knowledge of number combinations and numeration concepts can be developed—knowledge needed for doing other forms of computation.

Instruction in Mathematics Today

Our society is drenched with data. We have long recognized that verbal literacy is essential to our well being as a society; now we recognize that quantitative literacy or *numeracy* is also essential. Accordingly, our goals are changing. We want to see instructional programs enable students to understand and use mathematics in a technological world. We are not interested in students just doing arithmetic in classrooms; we want to see arithmetic procedures applied in real-world contexts where students observe and organize data. We no longer assume that students must be skillful with computation before they can actually begin investigating interesting topics in mathematics.

Even so, basic computation is not being ignored. The importance of computation is made clear in *Principles and Standards for School*

Mathematics, published in 2000 by the National Council of Teachers of Mathematics.

> Knowing basic number combinations—the single-digit addition and multiplication pairs and their counterparts for subtraction and division—is essential. Equally essential is computational fluency—having and using efficient and accurate methods for computing.[1]

Number and Operation is one of the five content standards for grades pre–K through 12 in *Principles and Standards for School Mathematics.*

Number and Operations Standard

Instructional programs from prekindergarten through grade 12 should enable all students to—

- understand numbers, ways of representing numbers, relationships among numbers, and number systems;
- understand meanings of operations and how they relate to one another;
- compute fluently and make reasonable estimates.[2]

Number combinations and computation are often involved when the other four content standards—Algebra, Geometry, Measurement, and Data Analysis and Probability—are learned and applied. Moreover, application in every grade of the five process standards—Problem Solving, Reasoning and Proof, Communication, Connections, and Representation—frequently entails number combinations and computation. Number combinations and computation are very much a part of standards-based instruction in mathematics today.

INSTRUCTION IN COMPUTATION TODAY

We increasingly need to integrate arithmetic with the world of our students, including their experiences with other subject areas. In order to solve problems encountered in the world around them our students need to know not only how to compute a needed number, but also *when* to compute.

> Today's students need to learn *when* to use mathematics as much as they need to learn *how* to use it. Basic skills for the twenty-first century include more than just manual mathematics.[3]

In order for our students to know when to use specific operations, we need to emphasize the meanings of operations during instruction.

If students are to gain computational fluency, they need to learn different methods of computation to use in different problem-solving situations. The following quotation from NCTM's *Principles and Standards for School Mathematics* emphasizes this point in relation to computation.

> Part of being able to compute fluently means making smart choices about which tools to use and when. Students should have experiences that help them learn to choose among mental computation, paper-and-pencil strategies, estimation, and calculator use. The particular context, the question, and the numbers involved all play roles in those choices.[4]

If we focus on paper-and-pencil procedures but do not introduce other methods of computing, our students are apt to believe that the process of computing is limited to paper-and-pencil procedures.

When students have a problem to solve there are decisions to be made before any required computation begins. Consider these parts of a conversation overheard in a student math group led by Chi. Calculators were available and students were free to get one if they needed it, but the teacher also encouraged other methods of exact computation: mental computation and paper-and-pencil procedures.

Chi: We have three word problems to solve. Here's Problem A. *You are to help the class get ready for art class. There are 45 pounds of clay for 20 people. How many pounds do you give each person?*

Raul: We need an exact answer. Each person should get exactly the same amount.

Terry: I don't think we need to use the calculator. Each person gets a little more than two pounds . . . but how much more?

Sonja: That's easy, just divide 45 by 20.
The students proceed to divide 45 by 20 with paper and pencil.

Chi: Here's Problem B. *Wanda's scores for three games of darts are 18, 27, and 39. What is her average score?*

Raul: Another exact answer.

Chi: Shall we get the calculator?

Sonja: I can do it in my head.

Terry: I don't see how. I'm going to use paper; it's easy.

Sonja: Round each number up . . . 20 + 30 + 40 is 90 . . . divided by 3 is 30. But we need to subtract: 2 and 3 (that's 5) and one more . . . 6 divided by 3 is 2. Two from 30 is 28. Her average score is 28.

Terry: That's what I got, too.

Different methods of computation are listed in Figure 1.1. Because an approximation is often sufficient, the first decision a student must make is whether an exact number is needed. In regard to exact computation, paper-and-pencil procedures constitute only one of the methods of computation available.

The diagram in Figure 1.2 also focuses on decisions about the method of computation to be used for solving a particular problem.

FIGURE 1.1 Methods of computation

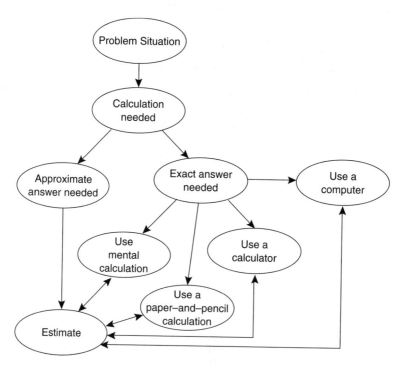

METHODS OF COMPUTATION

Approximation
• Estimation

Exact Computation
• Mental computation
• Paper-and-pencil algorithm
• Calculator or Computer

FIGURE 1.2 Decisions about calculation procedures in numerical problems. (Source: Reproduced from *Curriculum and Evaluation Standards for School Mathematics* [Reston, VA: National Council of Teachers of Mathematics, 1989], p. 9, by permission of National Council of Teachers of Mathematics.)

(Note that estimation should be involved even when an exact answer is needed.) As we teach computation we must help our students learn *when* each particular method of computation is appropriate. The actual teaching of different methods of computation is addressed in Chapter Three.

When a solution to $300 - 25 = \square$ is needed by a fourth grader, mental computation is likely the most appropriate method to use. But there are times when a paper-and-pencil strategy is the most efficient procedure for an individual. When a calculator is not immediately available and an exact answer is needed for the sum of two or three multi-digit numbers, it often makes sense to use a paper-and-pencil procedure.

Because computational procedures are tools for helping us solve problems, whenever possible the *context* for teaching different methods of computation should be a problem-solving situation; we need to keep focused on problem solving as we teach computation procedures.

The *goal* of instruction in computation today continues to be computational fluency. Students need to be able to use efficient and accurate methods for computing if they are to enjoy success in most areas of mathematics.

ALGORITHMS

It is common to speak of algorithmic *thinking* which uses specific step-by-step procedures, in contrast to thinking which is more self-referential and recursive.[5] Polya's four-step model for problem solving is an example of algorithmic thinking.[6]

An algorithm is a step-by-step procedure for accomplishing a task, such as solving a problem. In this book the term usually refers to paper-and-pencil procedures for finding a sum, difference, product or quotient. The paper-and-pencil procedures that individuals learn and use differ over time and among cultures. If a "standard" algorithm is included in your curriculum, remember that curriculum designers made a choice. If some students have already learned different algorithms (for example, a different way to subtract learned in Mexico or in Europe) remember that these students' procedures are quite acceptable if they always provide the correct number.

Usiskin lists several reasons for teaching various types of algorithms, a few of which follow. These apply to paper-and-pencil procedures as well as to the other types of algorithms he discusses.[7]

- *Power.* An algorithm applies to a class of problems (e.g., multiplication with fractions).
- *Reliability and accuracy.* Done correctly, an algorithm always provides the correct answer.

- *Speed.* An algorithm proceeds directly to the answer.
- *A record.* A paper-and-pencil algorithm provides a record of how the answer was determined.
- *Instruction.* Numeration concepts and properties of operations are applied.

CONCEPTUAL LEARNING AND PROCEDURAL LEARNING

Conceptual learning in mathematics focuses on ideas and on generalizations that make connections among ideas. In contrast, procedural learning focuses on skills and step-by-step procedures without explicit reference to mathematical ideas. Both are necessary, but procedural learning must be based on concepts already learned; procedural learning should be tied to conceptual learning and to real-life applications.[8] NCTM stresses the importance of conceptual learning in *Principles and Standards for School Mathematics*.[9]

Ideas need to be understood and woven together in order for concepts to build on one another. As a part of their increasing number sense, younger students need to understand principles and concepts associated with whole numbers and numerals. Thereby they begin to make reasonable estimates and accurate mental computations.

Our students need to understand the meaning of each operation (and not do just the computations) so they can decide which operation is needed in particular situations; otherwise they do not know which button to push on a calculator or which paper-and-pencil procedure to use.

Conceptual understanding is *so* important that some mathematics educators stress the invention of algorithms by young students; they fear that early introduction of standard algorithms may be detrimental and not lead to understanding of important concepts.[10] Understanding the concepts and reasoning involved in an algorithm does lead to a more secure mastery of that procedure.[11] It is also true that standard algorithms *can* be taught so that students understand the concepts and reasoning associated with procedures.

The paper-and-pencil procedures we teach actually involve more than procedural knowledge; they entail conceptual knowledge as well. Many of the instructional activities described in Chapter 3 and beyond in this book are included because students need to understand concepts. Students are not merely mechanical processors; they are involved conceptually as they learn—even when they are taught procedures. Research has shown that

> . . . instruction can emphasize conceptual understanding without sacrificing skill proficiency . . . understanding does not detract from skill proficiency and may even enhance it.[12]

It must be recognized that as a student uses a specific paper-and-pencil algorithm, the procedure becomes more automatic. When an algorithm is used over time, a student employs it with less conceptual knowledge and more procedural knowledge, a process that researchers sometimes call "proceduralization."

ERROR PATTERNS IN COMPUTATION

Errors are a positive thing in the process of learning—or at least they should be. In many cultures errors are regarded as an opportunity to reflect and learn.

As they learn computation procedures, many students—even students who invent their own algorithms—learn *error patterns.* Chapters 4–12 include specific examples of error patterns—systematic procedures that students learn but which most often do not provide the correct answer. Sometimes error patterns do produce the correct answer. When they do, students (and often teachers) assume that a correct procedure has been learned.

Algorithms incorporating error patterns are often called *buggy algorithms.* A buggy algorithm includes at least one erroneous step, and the procedure does not consistently accomplish the intended purpose.

As we teach computation procedures we need to remember that our students are not necessarily learning what we think we are teaching. We need to keep our eyes and ears open to find out what our students are *actually* learning. We need to be alert for error patterns!

PAPER-AND-PENCIL PROCEDURES TODAY

NCTM's *Principles and Standards for School Mathematics* clearly supports teaching computation skills:

> . . . students must become fluent in arithmetic computation—they must have efficient and accurate methods that are supported by an understanding of numbers and operations. "Standard" algorithms for arithmetic computation are one means of achieving this fluency.[13]

The required arithmetic computation skills include estimation, mental computation, and use of calculators as well as paper-and-pencil procedures. But it is noteworthy that even in an age of calculators and computers, students need to be able to use appropriate paper-and-pencil algorithms when it makes sense to do so.

As we teach our students to use paper-and-pencil algorithms we need to remember that they sometimes learn error patterns. We need to be diagnosticians, carefully observing what our students do and looking for patterns in their written work. The next chapter is designed to help us approach instruction diagnostically.

REFERENCES

1. National Council of Teachers of Mathematics. (2000). *Principles and standards for school mathematics*. Reston, VA: Author, p. 32.
2. National Council of Teachers of Mathematics. (2000). *Principles and standards for school mathematics*. Reston, VA: Author, p. 32.
3. National Research Council. (1989). *Everybody counts*. Washington DC: National Academy Press, p. 63.
4. National Council of Teachers of Mathematics. (2000). *Principles and standards for school mathematics*. Reston, VA: Author, p. 36.
5. For a discussion of algorithmic thinking, see T. Mingus, & R. Grassl (1998). Algorithmic and recursive thinking: Current beliefs and their implications for the future. In L. Morrow & M. Kenney (Eds.), *The teaching and learning of algorithms in school mathematics* (pp. 32-43). Reston, VA: National Council of Teachers of Mathematics.
6. Polya, G. (1971). *How to solve it: A new aspect of mathematical method* (2nd ed.). Princeton, NJ: Princeton University Press.
7. Usiskin, Z. (1998). Paper-and-pencil algorithms in a calculator-and-computer age. In L. Morrow & M. Kenney (Eds.), *The teaching and learning of algorithms in school mathematics* (pp. 7-20). Reston, VA: National Council of Teachers of Mathematics.
8. For an in-depth discussion of conceptual knowledge and procedural knowledge, see J. Hiebert (Ed.). (1986), *Conceptual and procedural knowledge: The case of mathematics*. Hillsdale, NJ: Lawrence Erlbaum Associates, Publishers.
9. For example, see National Council of Teachers of Mathematics. (2000). *Principles and standards for school mathematics*. Reston, VA: Author, pp. 64-66.
10. For example, see C. Kamii & A. Dominick (1998). The harmful effects of algorithms in grades 1-4. In L. Morrow & M. Kenney (Eds.), *The teaching and learning of algorithms in school mathematics* (pp. 130-140). Reston, VA: National Council of Teachers of Mathematics.
11. Curcio, F. R. & Schwartz, S. L. (1998). There are no algorithms for teaching algorithms. *Teaching Children Mathematics* 5(1), pp. 26-30.
12. Hiebert, J. (2000). What can we expect from research? *Mathematics Teaching in the Middle School* 5(7), p. 415.
13. National Council of Teachers of Mathematics. (2000). *Principles and standards for school mathematics*. Reston, VA: Author, p. 35.

Chapter 2

Diagnosing Misconceptions and Error Patterns in Computation

⌐⌐

I cannot teach students well
if I do not know them well.

Theodore Sizer[1]

Arithmetic is where the answer is right
and everything is nice and you can look
out of the window and see the blue
sky—or the answer is wrong and you
have to start all over and try again and
see how it comes out this time.

Carl Sandburg[2]

As Sizer reminds us, before we can teach our students we need to know them well. Learning is a very personal process.

The student into whose mind Sandburg leads us seems to view arithmetic and possibly all of mathematics as an *either-or* sort of thing. The answer is correct and arithmetic is enjoyable and life is rosy, or the answer is not correct and arithmetic and life are frustrating. We may wonder why this student and others are so answer oriented. Yet, we *do* need to face the question of why *some* students do not seem to be able to get the correct answers they need.

This chapter is designed to help you find out. As you read you will learn why students sometimes learn misconceptions and incorrect procedures. You will discover how to encourage self-assessment, and read about tools you can use for gathering data and making inferences. An extensive discussion of interviews is included. Specific suggestions for creating diagnostic questions and tasks are given as well as principles which should guide diagnosis.

11

As we teach mathematics we need to be *continually* assessing—gathering and using information about student learning. Assessment is one of six Principles for School Mathematics recognized by the National Council of Teachers of Mathematics in *Principles and Standards for School Mathematics.*

Assessment should support the learning of important mathematics and furnish useful information to both teachers and students.[3]

Assessment is the process of gathering information about student learning and the use of that information to plan instruction. Assessment must be aligned with curricular goals; even specific assessment tasks must be planned with these goals in mind. The cyclical process of assessment is pictured in Figure 2.1.

Though we need to be continually assessing, we do *not* need to be continually testing. Rather, we should collect evidences of student learning from varied sources, many of which are described in this chapter. "[E]vidence from a variety of sources is more likely to yield an accurate picture."[4] Some educators assert that we will not know how to teach, or even what specifics to teach, unless we know *how* we will assess it—what evidence of learning we will collect.

The purposes of both assessment and diagnosis are to improve learning performance. The processes are similar: collect evidence in relation to curricular goals, make inferences, and plan instruction. However, the term *assessment* is often used broadly; for example, with reference to a curriculum standard. *Diagnosis,* the term used frequently in this book, typically has a more narrow focus. Evidence collected as a part of a diagnosis usually focuses on a limited number of specific concepts or skills.

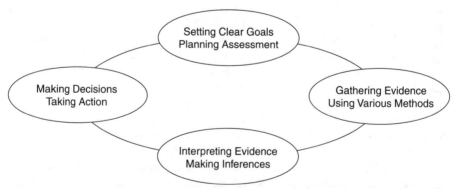

FIGURE 2.1 The classroom assessment cycle. (Source: Reproduced from *Principles and Standards for School Mathematics: Discussion Draft* [Reston, VA: National Council of Teachers of Mathematics, 1998], p. 37, by permission of National Council of Teachers of Mathematics.)

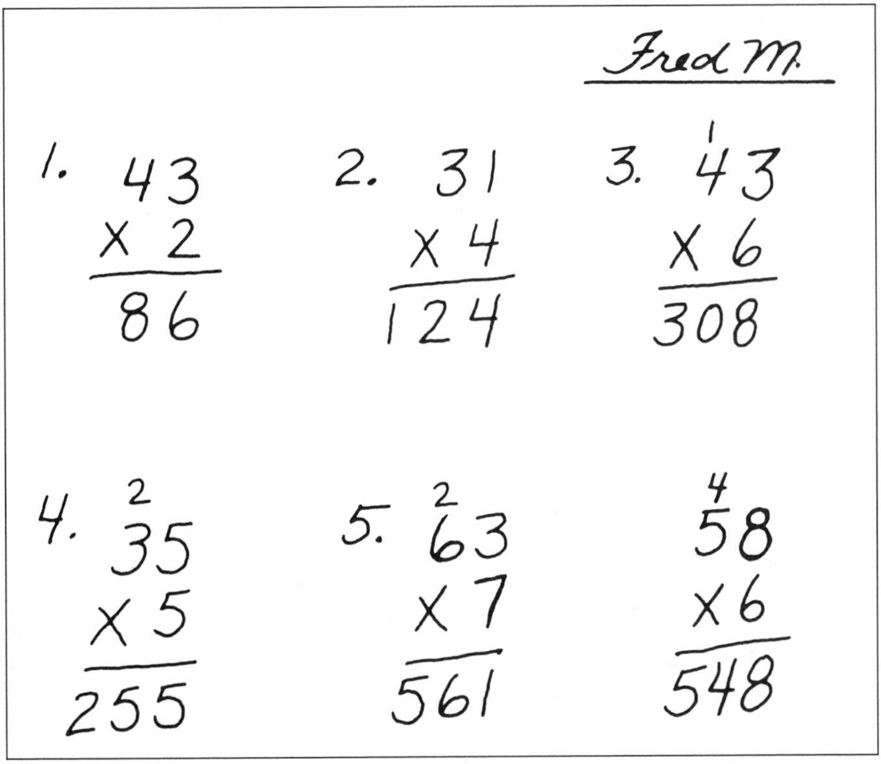

FIGURE 2.2 Sample student paper

Consider Fred's paper (Figure 2.2). If we merely determine how many are correct and how many are incorrect, we will not learn *why* his answers are not correct. Examine Fred's paper and note that when multiplication involves renaming, his answer is often incorrect. Look for a pattern among the incorrect responses; observe that he seems to be adding his "crutch" and then multiplying. This can be verified by studying other examples and briefly interviewing Fred.

Because we observed Fred's error pattern, instruction can be modified as needed. The algorithm may be reviewed as a written record of multiplying "one part at a time" (an application of distributing multiplication over addition), or a modification of the algorithm itself may be suggested so that the "crutch" is recorded with a small half-space digit written below the line. (See Error Pattern M-W-2 in Chapter 5.)

Rather than just scoring papers, we need to examine each student's paper diagnostically—looking for patterns, hypothesizing possible causes, and verifying our ideas. As we learn about each student we will find that a student's paper is sometimes a problem or puzzle to be solved. Researchers have known for a long time that we can learn much by carefully looking for evidence of misconceptions and by observing erroneous procedures.

LEARNING MISCONCEPTIONS AND ERROR PATTERNS

Error patterns reveal misconceptions that have been learned, but how are they learned? The mathematical ideas and procedures (or rules) a student learns may be correct or full of misconceptions, but the *process* of learning those ideas and procedures is basically the same. During experiences with a concept or a process (or a procedure) a student focuses on whatever the experiences appear to have in common, and connects that information to information already known.

Consider the student whose only experiences with the number idea we call *five* involve manila cards with black dots in the familiar domino pattern (Figure 2.3a). That student may draw from those experiences a notion of five that includes many or all of the characteristics his experiences had in common: possibly black on manila paper, round dots, or a specific configuration. One of the author's own students, when presenting to her students the configuration associated with Stern pattern boards (Figure 2.3b) was told, "That's not five. Five doesn't look like that."

More young students will name as a triangle the shape in Figure 2.3c than the shape in Figure 2.3d; yet both are triangles. Again, configuration (or even the orientation of the figure) may be a common characteristic of a child's limited range of experiences with triangles.

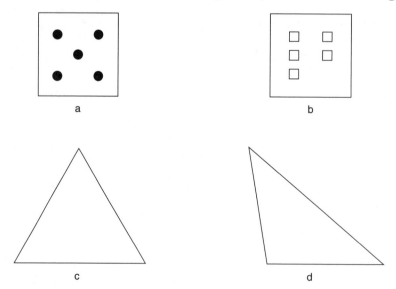

FIGURE 2.3   Pattern boards and triangles

Dr. Geoffrey Matthews, who organized the Nuffield Mathematics Teaching Project in England, told about a child who computed correctly one year but missed half of the problems the next year. As the child learned to compute, he adopted the rule, "Begin on the side by the piano." The next school year the child was in a room with the piano on the other side, and he was understandably confused about where to start computing.

Creature Cards also illustrate this view of concept formation (Figure 2.4). As a student examines a Creature Card he sees a name or label such as Gruffle and is told to decide what a Gruffle is. He looks for common characteristics among a set of Gruffles. Then, experiences with non-Gruffles help him eliminate from consideration those characteristics which happen to be common in the particular set of Gruffles but are not essential to "Gruffleness" (i.e., the definition of a Gruffle would not include such attributes). Finally, the cards provide an opportunity for the student to test out his newly derived definition.

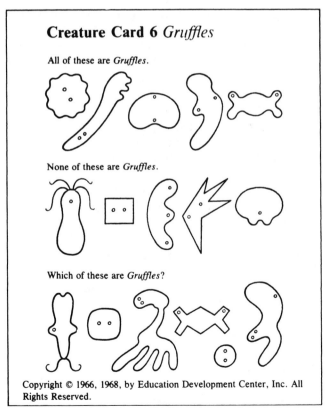

Creature Card 6 *Gruffles*

All of these are *Gruffles*.

None of these are *Gruffles*.

Which of these are *Gruffles*?

FIGURE 2.4 Creature Card. (Source: Reproduced from the Elementary Science Study unit, *Attribute Games and Problems,* by permission of Education Development Center, Inc.)

Students often learn erroneous concepts and processes similarly. They look for commonalties among their initial contacts with an idea or procedure. They form an abstraction with certain common characteristics, and their concept or algorithm is formed. The common attributes may be very specific, such as crossing out a digit, placing a digit in front of another, or finding the difference between two one-digit numbers (regardless of order). Failure to consider enough examples is one of the errors of inductive learning often cited by those who study thinking.

Because our students connect new information with what they already know, it is very important that we assess the preconceptions of our students. Prior knowledge is not always correct knowledge; misconceptions are common. Even when our students correctly observe particular characteristics that examples have in common, they may connect a pattern with a misconception and thereby learn an erroneous procedure.

When multiplication with fractions is introduced students often have difficulty believing that correct answers make sense; throughout their previous experiences with factors and products the product was always at least as great as the smaller factor. (Actually, the product is noticeably greater than either factor in most cases.) In the mind of these students the concept *product* had come to include the idea of a greater number, because this was common throughout most of their experiences with products.

From time to time an erroneous procedure produces a correct answer. When it does, use of the error pattern is reinforced. For example, a student may decide that "rounding whole numbers to the nearest ten" means erasing the units digit and writing a zero. The student is correct about half of the time!

There are many reasons why students are prone to learn patterns of error. It most certainly is not the intentional result of our instruction. Yet all too often individual students do not have all the prerequisite understandings and skills they need when introduced to new ideas and procedures. When this happens they may "grab at straws." A teacher who introduces paper-and-pencil procedures while a particular student still needs to work problems out with concrete aids encourages that student to try to memorize a complex sequence of mechanical acts, thereby prompting the student to adopt simplistic procedures that can be remembered. Because incorrect algorithms do not usually result in correct answers, it would appear that a student receives limited positive reinforcement for continued use of erroneous procedures. But students sometimes hold tenaciously to incorrect procedures, even during instruction that confronts their beliefs directly.

Each incorrect algorithm is an interesting study in itself. In succeeding sections of this book you will have opportunities to identify erroneous computational procedures and consider possible reasons students have adopted them. A discussion of research on errors in computation, especially error patterns, is in Appendix B.

Keep in mind the fact that those who learn erroneous patterns *are* capable of learning. Typically, these students have what we might call a learn*ed* disability, not a learn*ing* disability. The rules that children construct are derived from their search for meaning; a sensible learning process is involved. This is true even for the erroneous rules they invent though such rules may involve a distortion or a poor application.

More than procedural learning is in view here. Students often invent similar rules when introduced to the sign for *equals*. For example, they may decide "The equals sign means 'the answer turns out to be.' "

Overgeneralizing

Many misconceptions and erroneous procedures are generated as students overgeneralize during the learning process.

Most of us are prone to overgeneralize on occasion; we "jump to a conclusion" before we have adequate data at hand. Examples of overgeneralizing abound in many areas of mathematics learning. Several interesting examples were observed by project staff at the University of Maryland during their study of misconceptions among secondary school students.[5] At the University of Pittsburgh, Mack studied the development of students' understanding of fractions during instruction, and she also observed students overgeneralizing.[6]

Consider the following examples of overgeneralizing.

- What is a sum? Sometimes students decide that a sum is the number written on the right side of an equals sign.

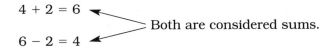

- Consider students who agree that all three of these figures are triangles.

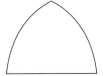 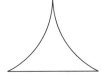 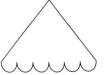

Graeber reports an interesting speculation on this situation.

These students may be reasoning from a definition of triangle position. Extension of this definition to simple closed curves that are not polygons may lead to this error of including such shapes in the set of triangles.[7]

- Sometimes students are exposed to right triangles like these . . .

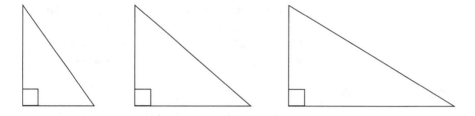

. . . and conclude that a right angle is oriented to the right as well as measuring 90 degrees.

a right angle   . . . therefore . . .   a left angle

- The student who believes that $2y$ means $20 + y$ may be over-generalizing from expressions like $23 = 20 + 3$.
- Other students always use ten for regrouping, even when computing with measurements.

$$
\begin{array}{r}
3 \text{ gal. } 2 \text{ qt.} \\
- 1 \text{ gal. } 3 \text{ qt.}
\end{array}
\quad \longrightarrow \quad
\begin{array}{r}
\overset{2}{\cancel{3}} \text{ gal. } \overset{1}{2} \text{ qt.} \\
- 1 \text{ gal. } 3 \text{ qt.}
\end{array}
$$

- Secondary school students sometimes think of the longest side of a triangle as a hypotenuse. They assume the Pythagorean Theorem applies even when the triangle is not a right triangle.[8]

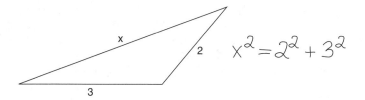

Overspecializing

Other misconceptions and erroneous procedures are generated when a student overspecializes during the learning process. The resulting procedures are restricted inappropriately. For example, a student may decide that in order to add or subtract decimals, there must be the same number of digits on either side of the decimal point. Therefore, the student will write 100.36 + 12.57 as 100.36 + 125.70. Also, students know that in order to add or subtract fractions, the fractions must have like denominators. Sometimes students believe that multiplication and division of fractions require like denominators.[9]

It is quite common for students to restrict their concept of altitude of a triangle to only that which can be contained within the triangle.[10]

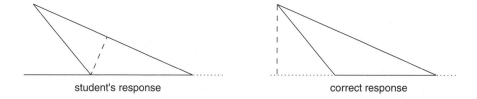

student's response   correct response

As we diagnose students who are experiencing difficulty we need to be alert for both overgeneralization and overspecialization. We need to probe deeply as we examine written work—looking for misconceptions and erroneous procedures that form patterns across examples—and try to find out why specific procedures were learned. Our discoveries will help us provide needed instruction.

ENCOURAGING SELF-ASSESSMENT

We have an important role in the diagnosis of areas where our students need instruction. But each student also has a significant role in diagnosis. Self-assessment may be the most important aspect of the assessment process.

The most effective assessment of all is that of one's own learning. One of the most valuable lifelong skills students can acquire is the ability to look back and reflect on what they have done and what they still need to do. Students who develop a habit of self-assessment will also develop their potential for continued learning.[11]

After our students complete an assignment we may want to hold a debriefing session to help them reflect on what they did. A debriefing can take the form of large or small group discussions, or individual interviews. Questions can be posed that will help our students evaluate their experiences. Although specific questions may help students make judgments about relevant data, we need to include open-ended questions like:

- How do you think you did with this assignment?
- What does someone need to know to be able to do this assignment?
- What was easy for you in this assignment?
- What was difficult for you?

Self-assessment can also be facilitated if each student has a mathematics portfolio. (See "Using Portfolios to Monitor Progress During Instruction" in Chapter 3 for specific suggestions.)

Another way we can help our students acquire the habits of mind needed for self-assessment is to provide experiences with checklists. Students can use checklists as they reflect upon and comment about their own written work. Figure 2.5 is an example of a brief checklist completed after an assignment with paper-and-pencil computation; Figure 2.6 is an example of a longer checklist to be completed by students and turned in with a division assignment when completed.

We can also involve our students in self-assessment by using a questionnaire designed to follow up a particular assignment. Figure 2.7 is an example of a questionnaire for students to use after they have solved a set of nonroutine problems.

Self-assessment is also involved when students score written work with the help of a rubric *that focuses on more than correct answers*. Figure 2.8 is an example of a rubric used with a practice assignment for division by a one-digit number. After students complete the assignment they score it twice: students determine the number of correct answers first, then they determine a rubric score.

Less structured comments like those written in student journals often involve self-assessment. Journals along with selected student

	Name		
	Date		

1. My digits are written in place-value columns.   Y   ?   N
2. Others can read my numerals.   Y   ?   N
3. Sometimes I was "stuck."   Y   ?   N
4. I checked my answers.   Y   ?   N
5. Describe a situation in which this computation could be used.

_____

_____

Comments

FIGURE 2.5 Sample checklist for self-assessment

Turn in this evaluation page with your assignment.

	Name		
	Date		

1. I made sure my digits are written in place-value columns.   Y   ?   N
2. Others will be able to read my numerals and my writing.   Y   ?   N
3. I checked my work to learn which answers are correct.   Y   ?   N
4. Sometimes I don't know how to start or what to do.   Y   ?   N
5. I think I will be able to really use division.   Y   ?   N
6. Sometimes I give up if the problem is hard.   Y   ?   N
7. I like to do division problems.   Y   ?   N
8. I used multiplication to check my work.   Y   ?   N
9. Dividing is often easy for me.   Y   ?   N
10. I like to work alone on problems like these.   Y   ?   N

Comments

FIGURE 2.6 Checklist for self-assessment with a division lesson

written work can be filed in individual assessment portfolios. Include in assessment portfolios any checklists, questionnaires, or rubrics students have completed. Later, have students examine these papers and reflect on what they find. Have they grown in their ability to assess themselves?

Turn in this questionnaire with the assignment.

Name _____

Date _____

1. What mathematics did you use to solve these problems?

2. Did you use drawings or manipulatives to help you solve the problems? If so, describe how you used them.

3. Did you use a calculator? If so, how did you use it?

4. Explain how you solved Problem 3.

5. Did you get "stuck" at any place with Problem 3? If so, tell about it.

6. How do you know your answer to Problem 3 is correct?

7. Are there other correct answers for Problem 3?

Comments

FIGURE 2.7 Questionnaire for self-assessment

Turn this rubic in with the assignment.

Name _____

Date _____

Look at all of the examples in the assignment. Next, read all five paragraphs. Then decide which paragraph you think best describes what you have done. Finally, circle the number of points in front of that paragraph.

1. I did a few examples, but I did not complete all of them.

2. I did all of the examples. Several do not have correct answers. Digits are not always in place value columns.

3. I did all of the examples. One or two do not have correct answers. Digits are written in place value columns.

4. All examples have correct answers. Digits are written in place value columns.

5. All examples are correct, and I can show why they are correct with base ten blocks. I can also write a story problem for examples like these.

FIGURE 2.8 Rubric for division by a one-digit number

INVOLVING PEERS IN ASSESSMENT

Peer assessment occurs when students thoughtfully consider examples of work by other students, keeping specific criteria in mind. Students need to know what criteria are relevant to the situation at hand and the criteria must make sense to them.

There is a very close relationship between peer assessment and self-assessment. When the same criteria are used for both self-assessment and peer assessment, students who assess peers also reflect on their own mathematical knowledge and skills.[12] Students who respond to the work of other students (in reality or simulation) become more aware of their own knowledge and skills. Consider the sample in Figure 2.9.

For those students involved in peer assessment, there is value in the self-assessment that takes place; but there is also great value in students using what they know about mathematics to help others. At the same time, we as teachers learn much about both the student assessors and the peers who they assess.

A checklist can sometimes be used to guide peer assessment, for example the checklist in Figure 2.10. The assessor circles the **Y** (yes), the **?** (I'm not sure), or the **N** (no).

FIGURE 2.9   Sample peer assessment

Here is the way Gary multiplied. What could you tell Gary or show him to help him understand?	$\dfrac{5}{8} \times 3 = \dfrac{15}{24}$

Name of student _____

Date on paper _____

1. Are digits written in place-value columns?   Y   ?   N
2. Can the student explain the procedure used?   Y   ?   N
3. Will the procedure used always produce the correct answer?   Y   ?   N
4. Did the student check the answer?   Y   ?   N
5. Can the student describe a situation in which this computation
   could be used?   Y   ?   N

Comments

Signature of student evaluator _____

FIGURE 2.10   Sample checklist for peer assessment

INTERVIEWING: OBSERVING, RECORDING, AND REFLECTING

Interviews have long been recognized as an effective way to collect information about a student's mathematical concepts and skills, a way to gain both quantitative and qualitative data about an individual.

Consider the following vignette of the first part of an interview. It is October, and Ms. Barnes is interviewing Dexter while other students are working individually and in groups. Dexter was recently assigned to Ms. Barnes' third-grade class. Dexter and Ms. Barnes are seated at a table in a corner of the classroom; Ms. Barnes faces the center of the classroom and Dexter faces her.

The class is learning to add with regrouping. Dexter computed as follows:

A.
$$
\begin{array}{r}
43 \\
+75 \\
\hline
118
\end{array}
$$

B.
$$
\begin{array}{r}
87 \\
+49 \\
\hline
1216
\end{array}
$$

MS. BARNES: I need to find out more about how you add, so we can plan our work together.

(*She shows him his paper and points to example A.*) Tell me, how did you add this example? The sum is correct, but I need to know *how* you added. I'll write the problem and you can add. Think out loud so I can learn how you added.

DEXTER: Three and five is eight.

(*He writes "8" below the line.*) Four tens and seven tens is eleven tens.

(*He writes "11" below the line.*)

MS. BARNES: And what is the sum? What is the total amount?

DEXTER: Eleven tens and 8 ones.

MS. BARNES: (*She encircles the "118" with her finger.*) Can you read this number for me a different way?

DEXTER: One, one, eight . . .?

MS. BARNES: Thank you. That's very helpful.

(*She points to Example B.*) Tell me, how did you add this example? I'll write the problem here, and you can add. Again, think out loud so I can learn how you added.

DEXTER:	Seven and nine is 16.
	(*He writes "16" below the line.*)
	Eight tens and four tens is twelve tens.
	(*He writes "12" below the line.*)
MS. BARNES:	What is the sum? What is the total amount?
DEXTER:	Twelve tens and 16 ones.
MS. BARNES:	(*She encircles the "1216" with her finger.*)
	Can you read this number for me a different way?
DEXTER:	One, two, one, six . . .?
MS. BARNES:	(*She reaches for a set of base ten blocks from a nearby shelf.*)
	Dexter, have you ever worked with blocks like these?
DEXTER:	We had them in our class at my old school.
MS. BARNES:	(*She writes the numeral "1216" on a separate sheet of paper, then holds up a unit block.*)
	This is one.
	(*She points to the numeral.*)
	I want you to show me this much with the blocks.
DEXTER:	(*He counts out 12 longs or tens blocks, and 16 unit blocks.*)
MS. BARNES:	And how much is that altogether?
DEXTER:	Twelve tens and 16 ones.
MS. BARNES:	Could you show me that much using fewer pieces of wood?
DEXTER:	(*He studies awhile, but is not sure how to proceed.*)

Various forms of assessment incorporated into the everyday routines of a classroom allow busy teachers to monitor individual growth and plan needed activities. Interviews are worth the time they take because they enable teachers to:

- Gain insights into a student's conceptual understanding and reasoning,
- Identify misconceptions and error patterns,
- Discover attitudes toward mathematics, and
- Assess a student's ability to communicate mathematical ideas.[13]

An interview is not just "oral testing" to determine whether a student can do a task. If we are going to interview a student, we need to think like an assessor and ask ourselves questions like these listed by Wiggins and McTighe:

- What would be sufficient and revealing evidence of understanding?
- How will I be able to distinguish between those who really understand and those who don't (though they may seem to)?
- What misunderstandings are likely? How will I check for these?[14]

An interview is not a time for expressing our opinions or asking questions prompted by mere curiosity. Rather, it is a time to observe the student carefully and a time to *listen*. We need to avoid giving clues or asking leading questions. It has been said that we are all born with two ears and one mouth, and we probably should use them in that proportion. This applies quite specifically to us as teachers, because we sometimes want to talk and explain when we should listen.

The pace of the interview should be adapted so the student will respond comfortably.

Getting at a Student's Thinking

Interviews can vary widely in regard to the way we ask a student to respond, but generally we want to encourage students to respond with as much detail as possible. When we ask a student to choose among alternatives that we present, we can ask *why* the particular choice was made.

If we are to get at a student's thinking we need to have the student comment on his or her own thought process. This can be accomplished through either introspection or retrospection.

When eliciting *introspection* ask the student to comment on thoughts as the task is being done; have the student "think out loud" while doing the task. For example, ask "What do you say to yourself as you do this? Say it out loud so I can understand, too." But when using introspection the very process of commenting aloud can influence the thinking a student does.

On the other hand, when eliciting *retrospection* do not ask the student to comment on thoughts until after the task is completed. Then have the student explain the problem situation in his or her own words; ask how the task was done, and why it was completed the way it was. Try to determine the reasoning used. But when using retrospection remember that the student may forget wrong turns that were taken.

It is probably best to elicit introspection part of the time and retrospection part of the time.

Following is a transcript of part of an interview I had with a fourth grader. We were discussing what she had written:

$$\frac{1}{3} = \frac{4}{12}$$

$$+ \qquad \qquad \frac{7}{12}$$

$$\frac{1}{4} = \frac{3}{12}$$

TEACHER: What do the equal signs tell us?
STUDENT: They tell us . . . that you just do the answer.
TEACHER: Which is more, one third or four twelfths?
STUDENT: (pause) one third? . . . no

This student knows a procedure but her understanding of the concept *equals* is inadequate. The interview may even help her evaluate her own thinking.

Teachers and researchers have studied metacognition with interest, that is, what a student knows about her own cognitive performance and her ability to regulate that performance. Many mathematics educators believe that what a student knows about herself as a learner and doer of mathematics—and how she regulates her own thinking and doing while working through problems—can affect her performance significantly.

Many of the questions we ask while interviewing a student will help the student become more aware of her own cognitive processes. For example:

- How did you get that answer?
- If you had to teach your brother to do this, how would you do it? What would you say to him?
- If someone said that your answer is not correct, how would you explain that it *is* correct? Could you explain it another way?
- Can you make a drawing to show that your answer is correct?

Garofalo lists other questions that can help students become more aware of their cognitive processes. His questions include:

- What kinds of errors do you usually make? Why do you think you make these errors? What can you do about them?
- What do you do when you see an unfamiliar problem? Why?
- What kinds of problems are you best at? Why?
- What kinds of problems are you worst at? Why? What can you do to get better at these?[15]

In addition to interview questions, we can use written responses (such as journal entries) to increase awareness of cognitive processes.

> By requiring students to examine the processes carefully that they are going through and to verbalize them on paper, the teacher (or other students) can follow the students' algorithms and find the hidden bugs in their thought processes.[16]

Whenever we try to get at a student's thinking, we should try to focus not only on what the student is thinking but also on what the student understands about his or her own knowledge. Bright comments about this perspective.

> I now think about diagnosis as helping learners understand both the power and the limits of their knowledge so that they will know how they need to adjust their knowledge base to fit the problems they have to solve. In this view, learners assume substantial responsibility for the quality of learning . . . teachers set tasks and ask questions that have a high potential to reveal the power and limits of students' knowledge. Knowing what tasks and questions to pose requires a deep understanding of students' thinking.[17]

When we learn how students are thinking, we must remember to help students understand their own thinking.

Observing Student Behavior

As we interview our students we observe their behaviors. Here the term *observe* refers not only to seeing, but also to listening attentively. Observing a student is more complex than it sounds because students often develop defense mechanisms to cover their confusion, and to make us believe they understand even when they do not. Observations may be quite informal, or they may be more structured.

Informal Observations.   Informal observations take place wherever we have opportunities to observe students. These observations can be a source of information whether the student is engaged in a classroom lesson, participating in a cooperative group, working at a learning center, or playing on the playground.

Our students bring informal mathematical knowledge to school settings. Note how your students get the mathematical information they need as you watch them play games, plan bulletin boards, or do any other activities. Listen to their conversations, and pose a diagnostic question from time to time.

Structured Observations.   Interviews that involve more structured observations take place within contexts as varied as clinical settings and one-on-one interaction between a student and a classroom teacher or aide.

The *structure* in a structured observation comes from a script for the interviewer. The actual words used in the interview may or may not vary from the script, depending upon the purpose of the interview. (Research studies are more apt to require strict adherence to a planned script.) Even when we use a script of some kind, we must remember that we are involved in structured *observation*. Keep eyes and ears open as the student responds, and make appropriate records!

Here is an example of a simple script; it was used to diagnose a student who is experiencing difficulty solving verbal problems.

- Read me the problem, please.
- What is the question asking you to do?
- How are you going to find the answer?
- Do the work to get the answer and tell me about your thinking as you work.
- Write down the answer to the question.[18]

Recording Student Behavior

A record of responses needs to be made during an interview. This can be done by writing notes and/or by audio or video recording. (Do not rely on your memory to make a record at a later time.) Even when a recording is made, it may be wise to supplement the recording with written notations that describe only those things that will *not* appear on tape. We may also want to record our judgments about the student's level of understanding.

Written responses can take different forms, but regardless of the form, they should end up in some kind of student assessment folder so we can look for patterns across different kinds of responses.

Notes can be written on three-by-five-inch cards. Cards such as the one shown in Figure 2.11 are useful for making records of brief interviews during instruction. Or, we can keep an observation sheet for each student, similar to Figure 2.12. An advantage of an observation sheet is that it gives us a single record over time, a record we can easily share with parents. A disadvantage is that a particular student's sheet is not likely to be readily available when we want it; we may have to make a quick note and later transfer it to the observation sheet.

When conducting a more structured interview, we may want to write notes in a space provided at the side of our planned question. Our script can be on a sheet of paper or on a set of cards. Figure 2.13 shows what one card might look like.

We need to plan ahead so we will be able to make records of pertinent observations. Forms such as the examples in Figures 2.11–2.13 can be adapted to fit our own situations.

| Student _____ Date _____ | | |
Observation/Interview		
Activity	**Observed Behavior**	**Suggestion for Instruction**

FIGURE 2.11   A simple observation form for general use

OBSERVATION SHEET
Name _____

Date	**Activity**	**Observed Behavior**	**Program Suggestions**

FIGURE 2.12   An observation sheet for an individual. (Source: Adapted from J. K. Stenmark (Ed.). (1991) *Mathematics assessment: Myths, models, good questions, and practical suggestions* (p. 33). [Reston, VA: National Council of Teachers of Mathematics].)

QUESTION/TASK	OBSERVED BEHAVIOR
Show: Numeral "243" Set of base ten blocks **Ask:** How would you show this number using as *few* blocks as possible?	

FIGURE 2.13   Card for question and record of observation

Watching Language: Ours and Theirs

Usually, written and oral language in mathematics is grammatically simple, but sometimes it is more complex linguistically. Even with young children, an expression as simple as 2 + 3 is interpreted in varied ways.

- two and three
- two plus three
- two and three more
- three more than two

As adults we know that these expressions are equivalent, but young students are confused by such a diversity of interpretations.

What we say is sometimes complex linguistically because we tend to use pre- and post-modifiers. Needlessly complex expressions abound, and include sentences like:

- Find the pair of numbers whose product is greater than 100.
- The value of this digit's place is one tenth of the value of what place?

It is also true that we verbally interpret the question asked by an open number sentence in different ways. For example, $N - 28 = 52$ might be expressed as "28 less than what number is 52?" or as "What number less 28 is 52?" Sometimes our students do not know what we mean because of the way we say it.

How might the student say it? We may be able to gain an insight into a student's use of language by asking the student to read or interpret an expression with the same structure, but with single-digit numbers. For example, before asking the question posed by $N - 28 = 52$ show $N - 3 = 5$ and ask, "What question does this ask?"

Probing for Key Understandings

When we need to learn what a particular student understands about *specific* ideas, we can solicit evidence of understanding by asking a question or presenting a carefully designed task for the student to do; then observe the student's response.

Likely, we will need to present follow-up questions or related tasks before we can make appropriate inferences regarding what the student understands. Think how the particulars in the task could be changed a bit to create a related task.

Rather than always focusing on computation skills per se, we frequently need to focus on concepts related to number sense; for example, on understanding the operations of arithmetic—concepts that enable students to know which operation to use when solving problems.

During such interviews, how might we get at a student's understanding of each of the following stated key ideas? What evidence of understanding might we elicit? What could we say or do? Possibilities are illustrated for each statement: a question that could be asked or a task that could be presented follows the statement. (If you try these with your students, you may have to adapt them to the appropriate level.)

- A digit's value in a numeral is determined by the place where it is written.

> With base ten blocks at hand, show the numeral "243" and say: "Can you show this much with the blocks? Try it." Then, "How do you know which blocks to use for the two?"

- The values of places within a numeral are powers of ten in sequence.

> Show a numeral for a whole number (as great as appropriate) and say, "Start at this end, and tell me the values of each place within the numeral." Then, "Can you do it if you start at the other end? Try it." Then, "Is there some kind of pattern? Can you tell me about it?"

- The value of a numeral for a whole number is the sum of all the products (face value × place value) for each digit.

> Lay out a collection of base ten blocks and show the nu-
> meral "2453" saying, "Show me this much with the base ten
> blocks." Then repeat the procedure with a place value chart
> or an abacus. Next say, "How do you know how much the
> numeral shows?" After the student responds, you may want
> to ask, "As you decide what the number is, do you add? . . .
> or subtract? . . . or multiply? . . . or divide? Think about it."

- Equals means "the same as."

> Show the equation $25 + 12 =$ ▢ and ask, "Can you tell me
> the sum?" Then point to the equals sign and ask, "What does
> this mean?" (If the student responds "equals" ask "What
> does that mean?") Then present the equation ▢ $= 13 + 22$
> and ask, "Can you tell me the sum?" Again, point to the
> equals sign and ask, "What does this mean?"

The student who thinks equals means "results in" rather than "is the
same as" may respond to the second equation: "You can't do that."

- Addition tells the sum if you know both addends.

> Show the equation ▢ $- 3,278 = 5,190$ and ask, "How
> would you find the missing number? Then ask, "Why would
> you do that?"

- Division tells the missing factor if you know the product and
  only one factor.

> Show the equation ▢ $\times 624 = 1,872$ and ask, "How would
> you find the missing number?" Then ask, "Why would you
> do that?"

- A fraction in which the numerator and denominator name the
  same number is a name for one.

> Show a number line for whole numbers 0–100, then also
> show the numeral $\frac{3}{3}$. Point to the fraction and say, "Can you
> point to where this amount is on the number line?" Then,
> "Can you write other fractions for one?"

Designing Questions and Tasks

When we present a question or a task to a student during an interview (or at any other time for that matter) we actually provide a stimulus situation to which the student responds. Stimulus situations can be presented in varied modes.

Mode	Examples
Verbal	Words, oral and written
Written symbols	Numerals
Two-dimensional representations	Paper-and-pencil diagrams, photographs
Three-dimensional representations	Base ten blocks, math balance, place value chart

Each stimulus calls for a response; responses for a given stimulus can be similarly varied among modes. We increase our confidence in what we learn about a student when we use a variety of questions and tasks to elicit evidences of understanding.

Make sure directions are included—directions that clearly indicate what is expected. Tasks should engage students and elicit their best performances.

Consider the following techniques: they may help us obtain information we will get no other way.

1. Say, "This time I'll hold the pencil and you tell me what to do."
2. Have students describe to other students how they solved a problem, or have them write their descriptions on paper.
3. Provide a slightly different context, and ask students to use the idea.
4. Ask students to rate mathematical examples on a scale of 1–4. For example, ask students to "Show how you see each example as multiplication."

	It Is Multiplication			It Is Not Multiplication
A. 5×3	1	2	3	4
B. $(-5)(-3)$	1	2	3	4
C. $\sqrt{5}\pi$	1	2	3	4

Discuss responses with the student. Those who interpret multiplication only as repeated addition usually consider example A to be more truly an example of multiplication than B or C.

5. Sometimes we can have a student explain a graphic organizer she has made: a number line, a cognitive map, a flow chart, etc.

6. We may want to ask the student to tell how he would explain the idea or procedure to a younger sibling, or have him make a poster that explains what he did.

7. At different times it may be helpful to say: "Your answer is different than mine. I could be wrong and you could be correct. Show me that yours is correct." Or "Can you show me another way?"

8. We can often get useful information about what a student understands by asking questions like:

How do you know that $4/9 \times 60$ is < 30?
How do you know that $1/4 > 1/5$?

As we design our questions and tasks, it is helpful to remember the following:

- We may need to diagnose a student's ability to estimate; instruction may well need to focus on this important skill and the concepts involved.
- Realistic contexts in assessment as well as instruction can help to engage and motivate students.[19]
- Students with learning disabilities often communicate information that is incorrect, yet it is what they actually see.

USING GRAPHIC ORGANIZERS FOR DIAGNOSIS

Diagnoses regarding students' areas of strength and needed instruction should be based on information about student performance. These all provide useful data for making such diagnoses: checklists, questionnaires, and journal entries used for self-assessment; written assignments; project results; interviews; and other items in an assessment portfolio.

Our assessment tasks should be varied in format so that students with different intelligences and learning styles can demonstrate what they understand and are able to do. A graphic organizer often provides a useful format for an assessment task; it can focus on relationships while requiring fewer verbal skills. Also, tasks based on graphic organizers can usually be administered to a group of children at one time.

Graphic organizers that have been used during instruction are especially useful for diagnosis. When numeration has been related to number lines, for example, a number line task can be used to help determine what the student understands about numeration (see Figure 2.14). Figure 2.15 is another assessment item focusing on numeration concepts, but it is based on a cognitive map.

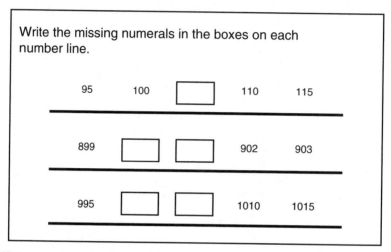

FIGURE 2.14   A number line used for assessing numeration concepts

FIGURE 2.15   A teacher-made item using a concept map

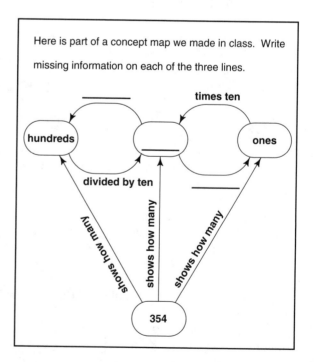

If our students have had experiences interpreting flow charts, then we can construct performance items from flow charts they used or from similar flow charts. Figures 2.16 and 2.17 are examples of items based on flow charts.

We may also want to have students make concept maps to communicate what they know about mathematics. A concept is written on paper, then relationships are shown with lines. Linking words (usually verbs) can also be added. It is important that students put *their* thoughts on paper. Figure 2.18 points to a fourth-grade boy's *very* limited understanding of "subtraction." And Figure 2.19 shows how another fourth grader responded to "fractions." She associated fractions with drawings, which she labeled incorrectly.

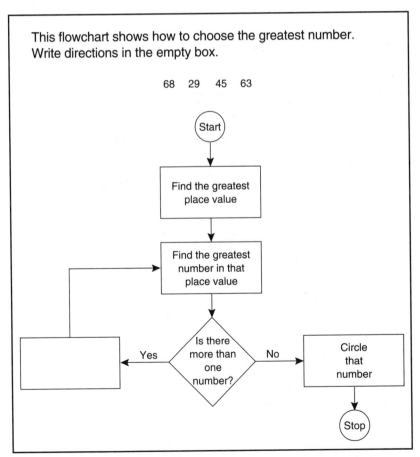

FIGURE 2.16   A teacher-made item using a flowchart

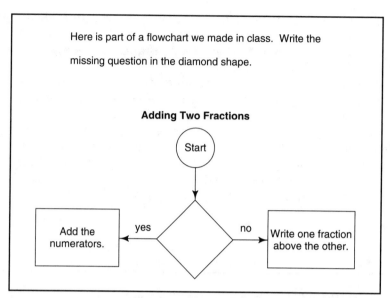

Here is part of a flowchart we made in class. Write the missing question in the diamond shape.

Adding Two Fractions

Start

yes ← | no →

Add the numerators.

Write one fraction above the other.

FIGURE 2.17 A teacher-made item focusing on procedural knowledge for adding fractions

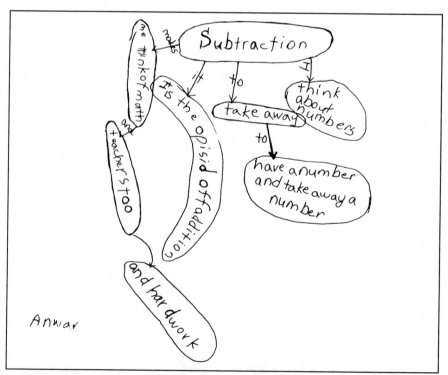

FIGURE 2.18 Cognitive map for subtraction by a fourth-grade boy

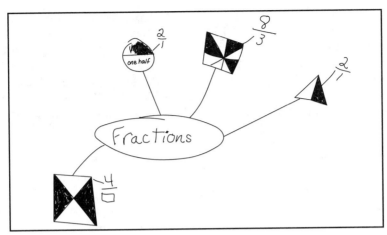

FIGURE 2.19   Cognitive map for fractions by a fourth-grade girl

USING TESTS AND COMPUTERS FOR DIAGNOSIS

Although effective assessment is integrated with teaching, there are times when a more focused and complete look at students' strengths is helpful. For example, we may administer a diagnostic test when we begin working with a new class of students, when a new student is assigned to us, or when a student is experiencing difficulty.

Any diagnostic test we use should be curriculum-based. It is within the *specific* areas of mathematics that constitute our curriculum that we need to learn about a student's strengths. We may then plan instruction that will build on those strengths.

As we diagnose what students understand about mathematics and their skills in problem solving and computation, part of what we learn comes from written work. Even when calculators are used in assessment, arithmetic computation is often tested on the *non*-calculator portion of an assessment procedure. Student papers shown in later chapters in this book illustrate some of what we can learn by examining paper-and-pencil assignments very carefully.

When appropriate, diagnostic data gathering may include a test—a sequence of performance tasks—to be completed by individuals. Whether administered individually or to a group of students, a test can often help us learn about each individual's strengths within selected areas of mathematics.

Standardized *achievement* tests have limited value for diagnostic purposes. They can help identify broad areas of strength and weakness and, thereby, serve as a springboard to further assessment. For example, they might show a student performing at grade level in one operation but not in another. However, they usually sample such a broad range of content that we are not likely to learn what we need to know about more specific concept and skill categories. According to Kamii and Lewis, achievement tests emphasize lower-order thinking and can result in misleading information—at least in the lower grades.[20]

Commercial *diagnostic* tests are available. Examples include *Key-Math-R*[21] along with *KeyMath Teach and Practice*[22], and the *Stanford Diagnostic Mathematics Test, Fourth Edition*[23]. *KeyMath-R* includes thirteen untimed subtests packaged in an attractive format for administration to individual students in kindergarten through grade nine. *KeyMath Teach and Practice* is for both diagnosis and instruction, and can be used in a classroom setting—it reflects NCTM curriculum standards more completely than the *KeyMath-R*. *The Stanford Diagnostic Mathematics Test* is a standardized paper-and-pencil diagnostic test that comes in both multiple choice and free response formats. Different forms of the test are available for various grade levels. These assessment instruments are all designed to help us plan appropriate intervention strategies for low achievers.

Computers are powerful tools. Many teachers hope computers will be able to help them diagnose the strengths of their students, thereby assisting them as they plan instruction. But software has not greatly advanced beyond a set of paper-and-pencil tests. As we look to computer programs for help with diagnosis, we need to make sure each program is more satisfactory for our purposes than a paper-and-pencil test—including brief, focused tests we could design ourselves.

It is possible to enter a student's written computational work into a computer and then analyze it; but when this is done other variables such as keyboarding ability are introduced.

STAR Math[24] is a recent attempt to provide computer-assisted norm-referenced tests that a classroom teacher can use. Branching technology is used so that each student can be tested as quickly as possible. The test focuses more on appropriate levels of instruction for each student and preparing useful reports, than on diagnosis of very specific knowledge and skills.

As we interpret diagnostic test performances, especially in the area of computation, we must try to distinguish between a student's lack of conceptual understanding and any errors in knowing the correct procedure to follow. For example, among a group of students learning to add with renaming, one student may understand that a two-digit number consists of tens and ones, but he records the two-digit sum at the bottom in the one's column. For that student, procedural instruction appears to be needed. On the other hand, another student may write "1" at the top of the tens column (correct procedure) but not actually understand that the sum for the one's column is so many tens and ones.

Most often we do not have time to interview *each* student to determine their knowledge and skill related to a particular concept or procedure; so, from time to time, we probably need to prepare our own assessment items for a specific concept or skill category. For instance, we may need a short test to administer to those students who have experienced some difficulty subtracting when regrouping is involved.

The error patterns presented in Chapter 4 suggest distractors we can use when constructing diagnostic test items for subtraction of whole numbers. Distractors drawn from common error patterns may give us clues to students' thought processes. The following multiple-choice item was built from error patterns: each distractor is an answer a student might choose if she has learned an erroneous procedure.

$$
\begin{array}{ll}
& \text{The answer is:} \\
4372 & \text{a. } 2526 \\
-2858 & \text{b. } 1514 \\
\hline
& \text{c. \ \ } 524 \\
& \text{d. } 2524
\end{array}
$$

GUIDING DIAGNOSIS IN COMPUTATION

A student's work must not only be scored, it must be analyzed if it is to provide useful information. Whenever someone else marks examples correct or incorrect (students or an aide) we can spend more of our time analyzing student work and planning needed instruction.

Observe what a particular student does, and also what the student does not do; note computation with a correct answer and also computation that has an incorrect answer; and look for those procedures that might be called mature and those that appear less mature. Distinguish between situations in which the student uses an incorrect procedure and situations in which he does not know how to proceed at all.

Following are principles to keep in mind as we diagnose the work of students who are having difficulty with computation.

1. *Be accepting.* Diagnosis is a highly personal process. Before a student will cooperate with us in a manner that may lead to lessening of problems with computation, he must perceive that we are interested in and respect him as a person, that we are genuinely interested in helping him, and that we are quite willing to accept a response—even when that response is not correct. We must exhibit something of an attitude of a good physician toward his patient. As Tournier, a Swiss physician and author noted many years ago, "What antagonizes a patient is not the truth, but the tone of scorn, pity, criticism, or reproof which so often colors the statement of the truth by those around him."[25]

2. *Focus on collecting data.* It is true that assessment is a continuous process; even during instruction we need to keep
alert for evidence that a student does not understand or has
learned an error pattern. Even so, there are times when we
need to make a focused diagnosis; and at those times we must
differentiate between the role of collecting data and the role of
teaching—we need to collect data, but not instruct. Diagnosing involves gathering as much useful data as possible and
making judgments on the basis of data collected; in general,
the more data, the more adequate the judgments which follow. A student is apt to provide many samples of incorrect and
immature procedures if he sees that we are merely collecting
information that will be used to help him overcome his difficulties. However, if we point out errors, label responses as
"wrong," and offer instruction while collecting data, he is far
less likely to expose his own inadequate performance. Many
teachers tend to offer help as soon as they see incorrect or immature performance. When those teachers begin to distinguish between collecting data and instruction, they are often
delighted with the way students begin to open up and lay bare
their thinking.

3. *Be thorough.* A single diagnosis is rarely thorough enough to
provide direction for ongoing instruction. If we are alert during instruction following a diagnosis we may pick up cues that
suggest additional diagnostic activities.

4. *Examine specific understandings and skills.* More formal assessments, published tests or computer-generated tests may
help to identify broad areas of strength and weakness. Let
them serve as springboards for further assessment in which
more specific concepts and skill performances are examined—often through an interview.

5. *Look for patterns.* Data should be evaluated in terms of patterns, not isolated events. A decision about corrective instruction can hardly be based upon collected bits of unrelated
information. As we look for patterns we look for elements
common to several examples of a student's work—a kind of
problem-solving activity. We try to find repeated applications
of erroneous definitions and consistent use of incorrect or immature procedures. The importance of looking for patterns
can hardly be overstressed. Many erroneous procedures are
practiced by students, while teachers and parents assume
they are merely careless or "don't know their facts."

6. *Discuss progress with parents.* Be sure to help parents understand the full scope of the mathematics curriculum and
what their child is learning and will be learning. In regard to

areas of difficulty, be sure to discuss the student's progress. Our conversations with parents often give us additional clues that help us plan instruction.

REFLECTING ON DIAGNOSIS OF MISCONCEPTIONS AND ERROR PATTERNS

As we teach mathematics we need to be continually gathering and using information about student learning. This is no less true when we teach concepts and skills related to computation. As we examine students' papers diagnostically we look for patterns, hypothesize possible causes, and verify our ideas.

Checklists, rubrics, and questionnaires can sometimes facilitate self-assessment, which is to be encouraged; and peers can be involved in the assessment process. Published tests may help identify areas of strength and weakness, but interviews are likely to be needed from time to time to get at students' thinking and probe for specific understandings and skills. We may have to design performance tasks, possibly using manipulatives or graphic organizers, to examine specific concepts.

Serious students of diagnosis will want to examine many of the references listed at the end of this book. Diagnosis of misconceptions and error patterns in computation is a continuing process; it interacts with instruction in computation—which is the focus of the next chapter.

REFERENCES

1. Sizer, T. R. (1999). No two are quite alike. *Educational Leadership 57*(1), 6–11.
2. Excerpt from "Arithmetic" in *The Complete Poems of Carl Sandburg*, copyright © 1970, 1969 by Lilian Steichen Sandburg, Trustee, reprinted by permission of Harcourt, Inc.
3. National Council of Teachers of Mathematics. (2000). *Principles and standards for school mathematics*. Reston, VA: The Council, pp. 22–24.
4. National Council of Teachers of Mathematics. (2000). *Principles and standards for school mathematics*. Reston, VA: The Council, p. 24.
5. See A. O. Graeber (1992). *Methods and materials for preservice teacher education in diagnostic and prescriptive teaching of secondary mathematics: Project final report*. (NSF funded grant). College Park, MD: University of Maryland, pp. 4–49.
6. Mack, N. K. (1995). Confounding whole-number and fraction concepts when building on informal knowledge. *Journal for Research in Mathematics Education 26*(5), 422–441.
7. A. O. Graeber, op. Cit., 4–5.
8. Ibid., 4–12.
9. Ibid., 4–35.
10. Ibid., 4–31.

11. Stenmark, J. K. (Ed.). (1991). *Mathematics assessment: Myths, models, good questions, and practical suggestions.* Reston, VA: National Council of Teachers of Mathematics, p. 6.
12. Moon, J. & Schulman, L. (1995). *Finding the connections: Linking assessment, instruction, and curriculum in elementary mathematics.* Portsmouth, NH: Heinemann, p. 115.
13. Adapted from J. Moon & L. Schulman (1995). *Finding the connections: Linking assessment, instruction, and curriculum in elementary mathematics.* Portsmouth, NH: Heinemann, p. 77.
14. Wiggins, G. & McTighe, J. (1998). *Understanding by design.* Alexandria, VA: Association for Supervision and Curriculum Development, p. 68.
15. Garofalo, J. (1987). Metacognition and school mathematics. *The Arithmetic Teacher 34*(9), pp. 22–23.
16. Mingus, T. & Grassl, R. (1998). Algorithmic and recursive thinking: Current beliefs and their implications for the future. In L. Morrow & M. Kenney (Eds.), *The teaching and learning of algorithms in school mathematics* (p. 38). Reston, VA: National Council of Teachers of Mathematics.
17. Bright, G. 1995, October). Helping teachers understand children's thinking. *RCDPM Newsletter 20*(2), p. 2.
18. Clarke, D. (1991). Assessment alternatives in mathematics. In J. K. Stenmark (Ed.). *Mathematics assessment: Myths, models, good questions, and practical suggestions.* (p. 30). Reston, VA: National Council of Teachers of Mathematics.
19. C. Santel-Parke & J. Cai (1997). Does the task truly measure what was intended? *Mathematics Teaching in the Middle School 3*(1), 74–82.
20. C. Kamii & B. A. Lewis (1991). Achievement tests in primary mathematics: Perpetuating lower-order thinking. *The Arithmetic Teacher 38*(9), 4–9.
21. American Guidance Service (1988).
22. American Guidance Service (1992).
23. Harcourt Brace & Company (1994 & 1995).
24. Advantage Learning Systems, Inc. (1999).
25. Tournier, P. (1965). *The healing of persons.* (p. 243). New York: Harper and Row.

Chapter 3

Providing Needed Instruction in Computation

⌐⌐

We have learned that when Fred multiplies whole numbers, he usually adds the "crutch" before multiplying. Now we need to plan instruction that will help Fred.

This chapter is designed to help us provide effective instruction in computation. We are urged to make sure our students understand numerals before we teach them to compute. Different methods of computation are stressed, as is the importance of using manipulatives appropriately. Varied instructional activities are encouraged: talking and writing math, graphic organizers, calculators, alternative algorithms, and cooperative groups. Guidelines for instruction are included; and later, in Chapters 4–12, specific suggestions are listed for particular error patterns.

The previous chapter focused on diagnosis because it is important to collect varied forms of data and make thoughtful inferences about student learning. But diagnosis must serve instruction. We need "diagnostic teaching" in which diagnosis is *continuous* throughout instruction. As Rowan asserts, "Diagnosing instructional needs is an integral part of the instructional process . . ."[1] We can interweave instruction and diagnosis as we teach computational procedures—always alert to what each student is actually doing and eager to probe deeper. We can be willing to change our plans as soon as what we see or hear suggests that an alternative would be more fruitful in the long run. Diagnostic teaching is, first of all, an attitude of caring very much about each student's learning.

Diagnostic teaching is cyclical. After an initial diagnosis we plan and conduct a lesson, but what we see and hear during the lesson prompts us to modify our previous judgments and seek more information before planning the next lesson. Sometimes we move through a cycle several times in the course of a single lesson. At other times, one cycle occurs over a span of several lessons.

The instruction we plan should elicit thinking. Our students will learn various forms of computation and also concepts and principles that underlie different forms of computation; and as they learn, they will observe patterns and construct knowledge—but more is needed. If our students are to understand and actually use what they are learning, they must *reflect* on what they observe, and connect it with other mathematical ideas they already know. We must help students not only learn concepts, principles and procedures, but also help students *understand how they are related.*

Furthermore, we inevitably model a disposition toward mathematics and learning mathematics as we teach. We need to demonstrate an approach to mathematical situations and to learning mathematics that is confident, flexible, curious, and inventive.

DEVELOPING NUMBER SENSE

When students develop a good foundation, including required number concepts and principles, they are ready to learn about operations and computation. What we sometimes call *number sense* is the most basic component of that foundation.

> **During the early years teachers must help students strengthen their sense of number, moving from the initial development of basic counting techniques to more sophisticated understandings of the size of numbers, number relationships, patterns, operations, and place value.**[2]

The following NCTM expectations for pre-K through second grade suggest what is meant by number sense:

- count with understanding and recognize "how many" in sets of objects;
- use multiple models to develop initial understandings of place value and the base-ten number system;
- develop understanding of the relative position and magnitude of whole numbers and of ordinal and cardinal numbers and their connections;
- develop a sense of whole numbers and represent and use them in flexible ways, including relating, composing, and decomposing numbers;
- connect number words and numerals to the quantities they represent, using various physical models and representations;

- understand and represent commonly used fractions, such as $\frac{1}{4}$, $\frac{1}{3}$, and $\frac{1}{2}$.[3]

These expectations suggest activities for developing number sense in the early grades, and thereby providing a good foundation for teaching computation.

UNDERSTANDING CONCEPTS AND PRINCIPLES

Some students have difficulty learning to compute because they do not adequately understand the concepts and principles that underlie algorithms. Their understanding of multidigit numerals and what the operations mean does not provide the foundation needed to learn procedures that make sense to them. Similarly, when they are introduced to algorithms with fractions their understanding of fractions and what the operations mean is not adequate for them to make sense of the procedures. Very often, computation procedures that make no sense to a student are not remembered accurately—nor are they used appropriately.

Learning specific algorithms involves procedural learning, and Chapter 1 emphasized that procedural learning should be tied to conceptual learning. During developmental instruction we need to encourage our students to think about *why* they are doing what they are doing as they compute; we need ". . .to require reasoning that justifies procedures rather than statements of the procedures themselves."[4] Students need to *reflect* on what they are doing.

In our students' minds, symbols need to be connected not only to words but also to concepts and to principles. The systems we use for creating numerals for whole and rational numbers involve many concepts, some of which are not easy for young children to understand. Equality is an important idea, and we tend to assume our students understand more than they do when they say "equals." Mathematical principles are applied when our students compute. These are principles that need to be understood intuitively—though students do not need to be able to express them with precise language in order to compute.

Numeration

Place value is the key to teaching computation with our base-ten numerals,[5] but understanding Hindu-Arabic numerals for whole numbers is *not* just identifying place values. The concept of values assigned to places is important, but it is only part of what students need to know if they are to understand multidigit numerals and learn computational procedures readily.

Consider this principle: "A multidigit numeral names a number which is the sum of the products of each digit's face value and place value."[6] [For example: $398 = (3 \times 100) + (9 \times 10) + (8 \times 1)$.] The terms used in this statement alert us to different ideas that are incorporated within multidigit numerals. To understand multidigit numerals a student must first have some understanding of the operations of addition and multiplication, and be able to distinguish between a digit and the complete numeral.

Understanding a digit's face value involves the cardinality of the numbers zero through nine. Place value itself involves assignment of a value to each position within a multidigit numeral; that is, each place within the numeral is assigned a power of ten. We, therefore, identify and name the tens place and the thousands place. This rather specific association of value with place is independent of whatever digit may happen to occupy the position within a given numeral.

Often students having difficulty with computation can identify and name place values, but they cannot get the next step. They have not learned to combine the concepts of face value and place value. It is the *product* of a digit's face value and its place value, sometimes called "total value of the digit" or "product value," which must be used. The *sum* of such products is the value of the numeral. In renaming a number (as we often do when computing), these products of face value and place value must continually be considered; and while considering these things, our students also need to think about the numeral as a whole.

Children do not quickly develop the conceptual structures associated with our place-value system for writing numbers; it takes a long time.[7] Jones and others identified four key constructs that "appear to be central to the development of multidigit number sense—counting, grouping, partitioning, and ordering numbers."[8]

When we teach our students about numerals, we should introduce numerals as a written record of observations made while looking at or manipulating objects. For multidigit numerals for whole numbers, these observations frequently follow manipulation of materials according to accepted rules in order to obtain the fewest pieces of wood (or the like). We may need to trade ten objects for one object that is equivalent to the ten if we can, or we may be required to exchange chips in a trading game. Thereby, representations for the standard or simplest numerical name for a number are obtained.

When students associate a numeral with concrete aids it is important that they have opportunities to "go both ways." On the one hand, students may be given materials to sort, regroup, trade, and so on, and then record the numeral that shows how much is observed. But they also need to be given a multidigit numeral to interpret by selecting or constructing materials that show how much the numeral represents. If our students are able to go from objects to symbol and also from symbol to objects, they are coming to understand what multidigit numerals mean.

Initially, we should have our students work with concrete aids that make it possible to compare the value of a collection of objects with the equivalent value of a *single* object (e.g., bundled sticks or base blocks). Later, they can use aids in which many objects are traded for a single object—an object that is identical except for its placement (e.g., sticks in place-value cans or trading activities with chips of one color on a place-value mat). These aids are helpful because they more accurately picture the way digits are used within multidigit numerals.

In our base-ten numeration system, the value represented by each digit involves a relationship with the unit. This is true not only for numerals for whole numbers that state the number of units, but also for decimals which must be interpreted as part of a unit. We must help our students *focus on the unit.*

Decimals are numerals for rational numbers—but so are fractions and percents. If our students are to use all of these numerals effectively in computation, they need much experience with the varied meanings associated with the numerals (e.g., part of a whole; indicated division) and they need to be able to compare different kinds of numerals for rational numbers.

Equals

When two different symbolic expressions actually name the same number, we express that relationship with the word (or symbol) *equals.* Therefore, we say that $20 + 4 = 24$ and $8 + 7 = 9 + 6$ and $21 = 15 + 6$. Both $20 + 4$ and 24 are names for the number we call *twenty-four.* There is only one such number (it is one point on the number line) but it can be named many different ways—with different numeration systems, and with mathematical expressions involving various operations. Both symbolic expressions name *the same* number. Students are often taught to say "equals means *is the same as;*" but too often it is a rote response—they do not actually apply such an understanding.

The basic relational concept we call "equals" is difficult for many young students. Early instruction too often encourages students to conceive of equals as a step in a procedure. To them it actually means *results in;* therefore $2 + 4 = 6$ becomes "two and (plus) four results in six." Or it is understood to follow a question where it means "do it now," with the answer given next. The relational concept equals is not learned in actuality; instead, students understand equals to be an operator. It is not surprising that the author finds that when presented

with an equation like $\square$=7+8, many young students merely respond,
"You can't do that." Or given an equation like $3 + 2 = 4 + 1$ they respond, "You can only have one number after equals."

It is extremely important that students come to an accurate understanding of equality if they are to enjoy success with arithmetic
and with all of mathematics. Many mathematics educators view the
understanding of equality as a foundation for algebra.[9]

Other Concepts and Principles

Other concepts and principles are incorporated within computational
procedures, and our students need to investigate them while studying algorithms. For example, students can reflect on the following
compensation principles.

- When adding two numbers, if the same number is added to one
  number and subtracted from the other number the sum of the
  two numbers stays the same. ($398 + 552 = 400 + 550 = 950$)
- When subtracting one number from another number, if the same
  number is added to both numbers (or subtracted from both) the
  difference remains the same. ($552 - 398 = 554 - 400 = 154$)

Students can investigate other concepts and principles too, and apply
them to computational procedures. Many of these are properties of
operations.

- When we add or subtract zero, the result is the number we
  started with. ($1,000,000 - 0 = 1,000,000$)
- A number minus that same number equals zero. ($367 - 367 = 0$)
- We can multiply in parts. We can distribute multiplication over
  addition
  $4 \times \mathbf{65} = 4 \times (\mathbf{60 + 5}) = (4 \times 60) + (4 \times 5) = 240 + 20 = 260$
  and we can distribute multiplication over subtraction.
  $4 \times \mathbf{58} = 4 \times (\mathbf{60 - 2}) = (4 \times 60) - (4 \times 2) = 240 - 8 = 232$

Clearly, many of these concepts and principles apply not only to
paper-and-pencil computation, but they can help our students estimate and compute mentally.

UNDERSTANDING OPERATIONS

Algorithms will be of little value to students if they do not know *when*
to use particular operations to solve problems. Our students must
understand the meanings of operations if they are to know which
computational procedure to use.

In *Principles and Standards for School Mathematics,* NCTM emphasizes the need for students to understand what the operations mean and how they relate to each other.[10] During the early grades, students encounter subtraction interpreted as "take away" and as "comparison;" they also encounter what are called "missing addend" situations in which the problem situation may be recorded with a plus sign, but subtraction is used to solve the problem (e.g., $24 + \square = 53$). They may also encounter what might be called "missing sum" situations in which the problem situation is recorded with a minus sign, but addition is used to solve the problem (e.g., $\square - 37 = 28$). Later, students encounter comparable situations involving multiplication and division.

Meanings for the different operations are often described in terms of structures characteristic of problem situations for particular operations; and these structures can be investigated. While studying addition and subtraction situations, students can explore relationships between the numbers for parts and the total amount. Later, when they study multiplication and division situations, they can investigate relationships between the numbers that tell about equivalent parts and the total amount. The structures they learn for each operation are useful, whether problem situations involve whole numbers or rational numbers. One way of summarizing these structures follows:

- *Addition* tells the total amount (sum) whenever you know the amounts for the two parts (addends).
- *Subtraction* tells the amount in one part (addend) whenever you know the total amount (sum) and the amount in the other part (addend).
- *Multiplication* tells the total amount (product) whenever you know the amount for both numbers about equivalent parts (factors).
- *Division* tells the amount for one number about equivalent parts (factor) whenever you know the total amount (product) and the other number about equivalent parts (factor).[11]

These understandings are very useful when there are equations or problems to solve. Students can reflect on these ideas even as they encounter the number combinations of arithmetic.

Error patterns are sometimes learned by students who lack adequate understanding of what the operations mean and how they are related. Consider the papers that follow. Can you decide how these students determined the unknown in each case?

These students would find it helpful to apply the understandings listed above.

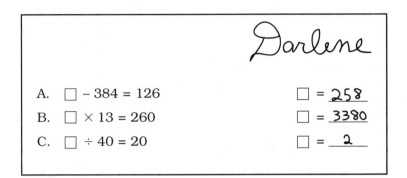

Darlene

A. $\square - 384 = 126$ $\square = \underline{258}$

B. $\square \times 13 = 260$ $\square = \underline{3380}$

C. $\square \div 40 = 20$ $\square = \underline{2}$

Ronnie

1. $65 \div 13 = \square$ $\square = \underline{5}$

2. $\square \div 12 = 36$ $\square = \underline{432}$

3. $17 \times \square = 68$ $\square = \underline{4}$

4. $60 \div \square = 30$ $\square = \underline{1800}$

5. $24 \times 8 = \square$ $\square = \underline{192}$

6. $90 \div \square = 15$ $\square = \underline{1350}$

ATTAINING COMPUTATIONAL FLUENCY

Admittedly, before we teach our students how to find sums, differences, products, or missing factors, we must teach when such numbers are needed. Students must understand the meanings of the operations in order to know which button to push on the calculator or which algorithm to use; that is, whether to add, subtract, multiply, or divide.

When a student *does* need to compute, there are actually four different ways to obtain the number: estimation, mental computation, paper-and-pencil algorithm, and calculator (or computer). As adults we compute in all these ways; we use the method appropriate to the situation. Our students, if they are to be fluent in computation, also need to be able to compute in each of these ways; and they need practice in choosing the appropriate method for particular situations. They need to practice choosing the appropriate form of computation to use while solving varied problems in unfamiliar situations—in-

CONTEXT: Problem Solving

1. Understand the problem

2. Devise a plan
   This often involves understanding the meanings of the different operations on numbers.

3. Carry out the plan
   This often involves choosing the appropriate method of computation.

METHODS OF COMPUTATION

Approximation   Exact Computation

• Estimation   • Mental computation
                             • Paper-and-pencil algorithm
                             • Calculator or computer

4. Look back

FIGURE 3.1 Methods of computation chosen within a problem-solving context. (Source: Adapted from George Polya, *How to Solve It*, 2d. ed. [Princeton, NJ: Princeton University Press, 1973], xvi–xvii.)

cluding real-world contexts. Figure 3.1 illustrates how methods of computation fit within a problem-solving context.

When should each method of computation be used? This is a judgement that must be made in context, but the guidelines in Figure 3.2 may be helpful.

In *Principles and Standards for School Mathematics* NCTM stresses the need for students at all levels of instruction to be able to use computational tools and strategies fluently and estimate appropriately. The term "computational fluency" reflects the ability to efficiently use different forms of computation as appropriate.[12]

When computation procedures are taught, a balance between conceptual and procedural learning is needed. If instruction focuses exclusively on following procedures and rote memorization, students' habits of mind are likely to become less curious and creative in their approach to solving problems; if students memorize procedures by rote, they are less likely to remember them. When students ". . . have memorized procedures and practiced them a lot, it is difficult for them to go back and understand them later."[13] Students need instruction that is balanced—instruction that involves both conceptual and procedural learning.

But that balance *does* include practice. Students need to practice reliable algorithms and develop computational fluency if they are to become good problem solvers. As much as possible, our instruction in computation should be within real-world problem-centered contexts,

---

Guidelines for Selecting the Method of Computation

Use

- *Estimation* when an approximate answer is sufficient, for example when the question is: About how many?
- *Mental computation* when a exact answer is needed, and it can be readily computed mentally by using known facts and principles: for example, basic facts, multiplying by powers of ten, and distributivity, as in problems like
$$7 \times 604 \quad \text{or} \quad 6 \times 98$$
- *Calculator or computer* when an exact answer is needed, a calculator or computer is readily available, and computation would be quicker than using other methods, as in $508,032 \div 896$
- *Paper-and-pencil* when an exact answer is needed and other methods are not appropriate or available.

FIGURE 3.2   Guidelines for selecting the method of computation

with isolated drills or games as supplemental instruction when required to enhance specific skills. Keep the focus on problem solving.

TEACHING MENTAL COMPUTATION

Students and adults use mental computation during daily living more often than they use written computation. Truly, mental computation is an important skill for students to learn. It is also a "natural stepping-stone to developing written computation and computational estimation."[14]

Mental computation is concerned with exact answers, but there is no set procedure for computing a particular operation such as addition. Instead, strategies involving known concepts and principles are applied thoughtfully, flexibly, and creatively within particular situations. For example, to mentally compute the sum 98 + 99 an individual may choose to apply knowledge that 98 is also 100 – 2 and 99 is 100 – 1, and reason that their sum is 200 – 3 or 197. (This is actually easier than doing the paper-and-pencil procedure "in your head.") As our students come to understand an operation like addition and how a number can be renamed as a difference, they should be given opportunities to apply this knowledge by computing mentally.

Mental computation strategies can often be learned and practiced as warm-ups before math lessons. We should not wait until after we teach paper-and-pencil algorithms. Mochón and Román conclude from their research that it is ". . . wise to develop strategies of mental computation before or simultaneously with introduction of the formal algorithms."[15]

Instruction in mental computation often applies principles of numeration like place value, and properties of operations like commutativity, associativity, and distributivity. Many specific strategies can be taught to facilitate mental computation. Examples include the following.

- Find pairs of numbers that add to one or to 10 or to 100. For example, think of $45 + 76 + 55$ as $45 + 55 + 76$, then $100 + 76$ is 176.
- Find a more useful name for a number. For example, **28** + 56 is the same as (**30 − 2**) + 56, which is $86 - 2$ or 84.
- Do the operation "in parts." Distributivity can often be used. For example, 4×7 is the same as $4 \times$ (**5 + 2**), and $20 + 8$ is 28 (a partitioned array will help).
- Use numbers that are multiples of 10 and 100 and 1000. For example, $4 \times$ **298** is the same as $4 \times$ **300 − 2,** and $1200 - 8$ is 1192.

Instruction in mental computation can help many of our students develop a flexible approach to computation. They will be less likely to limit a needed computation to a particular procedure.

TEACHING STUDENTS TO ESTIMATE

Our students need to learn to estimate not only to solve problems which do not require an exact number, but also to make sure results are reasonable when performing exact computations. A proper emphasis on estimation will eliminate much of the need for future corrective instruction.

Instruction in estimation must begin early and occur often. Students who estimate well are thoroughly grounded conceptually. But any student who thinks that 27 is closer to 20 than 30 will have difficulty estimating, as will the student who does not understand that $\frac{7}{8}$ is almost 1. Students need a robust number sense in which numeration concepts are understood and applied, and number combinations are easily used as are compensation principles and other relational understandings.

Attitudes toward estimation are also important. Typically, students believe "there is only one correct answer;" but when estimating there are only reasonable answers—and some answers are more reasonable than other answers. Our students must learn to recognize when an estimate is all that is needed, and they must feel free to use terms like *almost, a bit more than, about, a little less than,* and *in the ballpark.*

The ability to estimate incorporates varied mental computation skills, any one of which may require instruction. Included among such skills for whole numbers are:

- Adding a little bit more than one number to a little bit more than another; adding a little bit less than one number to a little bit less than another; and, in general, adding, subtracting, and so on, with a little bit more than or a little bit less than.
- Rounding a whole number to the nearest ten, hundred, and so on.
- Multiplying by ten, and by powers of ten—in one step.
- Multiplying two numbers, each of which is a multiple of a power of ten (e.g., 20 × 300). This should be done as one step, without the use of a written algorithm.

With fractions and decimals less than one, estimation often involves using benchmarks; determining if a particular number is closer to zero, one-half, or one.

When possible we should teach estimation informally in the context of problem solving. Here are a couple of examples:

- Problems involving the total cost of items purchased are reasonable to estimate because the buyer needs to know how much money to have at hand for the cashier.
- The purchase of a discounted item also requires an estimate of actual cost and the amount of money needed for the cashier.

Several estimation strategies can be taught with the hope that students will use them flexibly as appropriate. Strategies listed by Reys can be explained and illustrated as follows.[16]

- *Front-end strategy* in which numbers are rounded to greater place values and then the operation is performed. For example, for the sum 678 + 724 think 700 + 700, and the estimate is about 1400.
- *Clustering strategy* when the numbers are close in value and an "average" is obvious. For example, the average of 24,135 and 23,687 and 25,798 is about 24,000.
- *Rounding strategies* such as using upper and lower bounds for multiplication. For example, the product for 63 × 89 is between 60 × 80 and 70 × 90; it is between 4800 and 6300, possibly near 5500.
- *Compatible numbers strategy* in which alternative numbers are selected because they can be computed mentally. Con-

sider the example $6128 \div 9$. Think $6300 \div 9$ and the estimate is almost 700.

- *Special numbers strategy* in which it is noted that given numbers are about as much as a benchmark number (0, 0.5, 1, 10, 100, and so on). Consider the example $\frac{7}{8} + \frac{8}{9}$. Think $1 + 1$ and the estimate is a little less than 2.

One way to provide practice with estimation is to present students with a problem and several possible answers. Students can then use estimation to choose the answer that is most reasonable. Here is a problem with possible answers:

A \$1,495 large-screen television set has been discounted 20%. Which cost is most reasonable?

$1,000 $1,100 $1,200 $1,300 $1,400

In general, our students will become more and more able to determine when an answer is reasonable as they gain the habit of asking if the answer makes sense, and as they develop a more robust number sense. Students who habitually consider the reasonableness of their answers are not likely to adopt incorrect computational procedures.

TEACHING STUDENTS TO USE CALCULATORS

When solving a problem, sometimes the sensible choice for computation is a calculator. Occasionally students think that using a calculator is cheating, so we need to make sure our students occasionally experience and think about a calculator as a viable choice for computation.

Of course there are times during instruction when calculators should be set aside—when mental computation or estimation is the focus, for example. Usually, when students are being encouraged to invent paper-and-pencil procedures or when they are studying particular conventional algorithms, calculators are not used.

Often, students who are free to use calculators can solve a more extensive range of problems, and they can approach these problems earlier. For example, they can use real-world problems based on situations reported in the local newspaper—even when they have not developed paper-and-pencil procedures for the required computations.

There is not yet a consensus among mathematics educators about how calculators are to be used at every level of instruction.[17] Research does suggest that "calculators should be an integral part of mathematics instruction including the development of concepts and computational skills."[18]

As we teach our students how to use calculators, we must be careful not to focus exclusively on answers. Rather, we must focus on the thinking processes of students and their application of concepts and mathematical principles. Reasoning through a two-step problem, for example, requires much more than entering numbers in a calculator.[19]

We must help our students understand what a calculator can do and how to use it, then give them opportunities to use calculators *throughout* the mathematics program. Used appropriately, calculators can even help students develop number sense and mental computation skills and understand numeration concepts and the meanings of operations. When our students use calculators, we should talk with them from time to time and have them explain what they are doing and why specific choices are made.

A calculator is not simply an alternative to paper-and-pencil procedures; it can help our students *learn* those procedures. For example, a calculator can be used to focus attention on one step within an algorithm. Calculators can also be used to practice estimating quotients. Consider the following game.

- Provide several examples similar to $83{,}562 \div 36$ or $17{,}841 \div 892$; then have students agree together on one example.
- Each person estimates the answer to that example and writes it.
- One student determines the exact answer with a calculator.
- Players score one point if they have the correct number of digits in their estimate; and they score two points if they have the correct number of digits and also the first digit is correct.[20]

Of course a calculator can be used to reinforce underlying concepts and procedures—especially numeration concepts. For example, students can practice naming what some call the "product value of a digit" (face value $\times$ place value). Consider these instructions for a game.

Everyone enter "1111" in your calculator.

I have a set of cards; each has one of the digits 2–9 on it.

When I draw a card, use addition or subtraction to change a one on your calculator to the number shown on the card. *You* decide which one to change.

Then I will draw another card and you can change another of your ones.

After four cards are drawn and you have changed all four ones, we will see who shows the greatest number on their calculator.

Basic multiplication products can be generated by using the repeat function of calculators.

$$6 \times 7 = ? \text{ Think of } 6 \times 7 \text{ as } 6 \text{ sevens.}$$

Key $\boxed{7}$ $\boxed{+}$ $\boxed{7}$ $\boxed{=}$ $\boxed{=}$ $\boxed{=}$ $\boxed{=}$ $\boxed{=}$
counting 2, 3, 4, 5, 6,

We can even use calculators to provide immediate feedback when students practice recalling number combinations.

Yes, a calculator has many uses—but its limitations must also be demonstrated. For example, it takes more time to multiply by a power of ten on a calculator than to perform the multiplication mentally.

TEACHING PAPER-AND-PENCIL PROCEDURES

Conventional paper-and-pencil algorithms involve more than procedural knowledge; they entail conceptual knowledge as well. Many of the instructional activities described in this book are included because of the need for conceptual understanding. Students are not merely mechanical processors, they must be involved conceptually when learning and using paper-and-pencil procedures.

Even so, it must be recognized that as a student uses a specific paper-and-pencil algorithm over time, the procedure becomes more automatic. Students gradually use less conceptual knowledge and more procedural knowledge while doing the procedure, a process researchers sometimes call "proceduralization."

We must be careful not to introduce a paper-and-pencil procedure too early; we need to be *especially* careful not to use direct instruction about steps in a procedure too soon. Frequently, we can introduce an algorithm with a verbal problem, and challenge our students to use what they already know to work out a solution—even if their prior knowledge is quite informal. When we let students use their own informal techniques initially, we will find that some students know more than we thought! Others will creatively use what they already know and the manipulatives we make available. By beginning this way we will help students relate the algorithm we are teaching to their prior knowledge. We may even want to have a group of students investigate different ways of finding a sum, a product, and so on. Students should stay with the investigation long enough for several alternatives to be developed and shared; they could even write about their experiences.

Students who are permitted to work out solutions using informal knowledge before they are taught a specific computational procedure sometimes develop "invented" paper-and-pencil procedures. Place a high value on all invented procedures and the creativity involved; say something like, "That's great! Why does it work? Will your procedure give you the correct number every time? How can you find out?" Invented algorithms are often evidence of conceptual understanding. Invented computational procedures are not always efficient, but they are correct procedures if they always produce the number needed.

Instruction in Grades 1–2

Mathematics educators agree that in Grades 1–2 they want students to understand numbers and how numbers are related to one another. They want students to be able to represent quantities and to understand addition and subtraction and how those operations are related to one another. Fluency with addition and subtraction number combinations is also a goal.[21] There is less agreement on the place of computational procedures in the mathematics curriculum for Grades 1–2.

Should the emphasis be on students inventing procedures or on students learning conventional algorithms? In *Principles and Standards for School Mathematics,* NCTM includes the following statements in its discussion of standards for number and operations for Pre-K–2 (emphases added):

- Students learn basic number combinations and **develop strategies for computing that make sense to them** when they solve problems with interesting and challenging contexts.
- Through class discussions, they can compare the ease of use and ease of explanation of various strategies. In some cases, their strategies for computing will be close to conventional algorithms; in other cases, they will be quite different.
- [W]hen students compute with **strategies they invent or choose because they are meaningful,** their learning tends to be robust—they are able to remember and apply their knowledge.
- Students can learn to compute accurately and efficiently through regular **experience with meaningful procedures.** They benefit from instruction that **blends procedural fluency and conceptual understanding** . . . . This is true for all students, including those with special educational needs.[22]

Clearly, NCTM recommends that we focus on meaningful learning. In the earliest grades this can involve both invented procedures and conventional algorithms, but *the stress should be on thinking and on procedures that make sense to students.*

Student invention of algorithms can result in a greater focus on understanding. It can help students learn about multidigit numerals and the meanings of addition and subtraction; it can also help students increase their number sense. "Invented procedures promote the idea of mathematics as a meaningful activity."[23]

When our students invent procedures and record them, we can ask questions that point toward more efficient refinements in the procedures students are developing. Invented algorithms can often be further developed into conventional algorithms, but some question the need to do this if the invented algorithm is correct and a reasonably efficient procedure. It is probably true that in grades 1–2 we should encourage students to invent procedures, but also be open to helping them learn about conventional algorithms as warranted. Curcio and Schwartz argue for a balance.[24]

Some would delay teaching conventional procedures. In their proposed sequence for teaching computation Reys and Reys suggest that conventional algorithms for addition and subtraction of whole numbers be delayed until Grade 3, and taught then only if students have not already developed ways of computing that are efficient.[25]

Whenever they are taught, conventional algorithms should be yet another context for investigating mathematics that makes sense. Conventional procedures can be taught so students understand the algorithms. When this is done, instruction typically involves the use of manipulatives.

The Role of Manipulatives

Instruction should not be a demonstration of "how to do it" accompanied by a verbal explanation. Such attempts are inadequate for most students, especially young children. They do not result in conceptual learning, and very often they do not even result in procedural learning.

Visual, tactile, and kinesthetic experiences provided through manipulatives can help our students better understand the numbers involved, their numerals, and the operation itself. When manipulatives are used—whether with an invented procedure or a more conventional algorithm—then the steps in the procedure are apt to make sense. Our students are more likely to gain confidence they can learn and do mathematics.

As our students use manipulatives to find needed sums, differences, products, and quotients, we must make it clear that we value their solution attempts. We can challenge students to provide evidence that what they are doing always works. Then, if we choose to guide them toward a paper-and-pencil procedure, we simply encourage them to record what they are doing. Ideally, their manipulations can be recorded on paper "step-by-step."

Gamelike activities using a pattern board are sometimes used as a bridge between students informally working out solutions with

manipulatives, and more direct instruction in conventional algorithms. Such activities for addition, subtraction, and division of
whole numbers are described in Appendix C. The pattern board
serves as an organizing center; and a step-by-step record of what is
done on the board turns out to be a conventional algorithm that can
be seen as a mathematical representation of what was observed. The
paper-and-pencil computation procedure makes sense to students
because they have observed relationships and patterns; they have a
visual referent for the algorithm itself.

Developmental Instruction

Developmental instruction in conventional computational procedures
must be distinguished from corrective instruction, which is discussed
briefly in the section that follows. The term *developmental instruction,*
as used here, is the initial sequence of instructional activities over time
that enables students to understand, execute, and gain skill in using
particular algorithms. *Corrective instruction* follows developmental instruction whenever a student has not learned a correct procedure; for
example, a student may have learned an error pattern during initial
instruction. Careful developmental instruction seeks to help students
learn algorithms *without* learning error patterns.

Before we teach our students to compute on paper, we must
make sure they are able to represent quantities with appropriate notation. Also, they need to be able to make suitable exchanges with manipulatives; when working with whole numbers, chip-trading activities can help our students develop these abilities.

As we introduce a particular algorithm and continue to provide
instruction, we must engage our students in *thinking*—not in mind-
less copying and repetition. While our students are first learning a
computational procedure they need to be making mental connections
and building the procedure in their own heads.

We can begin by having our students use manipulatives to find
solutions to problems; base-ten blocks are frequently used for addition and subtraction of whole numbers, and fraction parts are often
used for addition and subtraction with fractions. Our students need
to use manipulatives initially to solve problems—whether invented
procedures are stressed, gamelike activities are incorporated, or the
instruction has a conventional algorithm as its goal. It is important
that students begin with manipulatives, *then reflect on what they have
done* with the materials.

Eventually, a step-by-step record of manipulations and thinking
is written with numerals. If our goal is to teach a conventional algorithm, we must keep that procedure in mind as we guide the recording; the written record of manipulations can become the algorithm it-

self. When our students are comfortable with this process, they will be able to visualize the manipulatives (but not actually handle them) as they write. In some cases, if students are to develop a more efficient conventional algorithm, they will need to shorten the written record. We may want to say, "Mathematicians like to write fewer symbols whenever they can."

Instruction will be meaningful if it is done within a problem-solving context and the algorithm is developed as a step-by-step record of observations. The computational procedure will make sense to our students because it is a record of what they have actually done. Typical elementary school students move very gradually from making sense through manipulatives to making sense through mathematical reasoning. Any student experiencing difficulty while attempting to learn a computational procedure may need to work more directly with manipulatives for awhile.

Admittedly, there are algorithms that cannot be developed as a record of observations—especially in the middle grades. Sometimes these procedures can be introduced as a short cut. For example, the conventional algorithm for dividing fractions can be developed by reasoning through a rather elaborate but meaningful procedure involving complex fractions, applying the multiplicative identity and the like, then observing a pattern. The obvious implication of the observed pattern is that most of the steps can be eliminated; merely invert the divisor and multiply.

Teachers and curriculum designers are faced with the question, "When should different stages for an algorithm be introduced?" Traditionally, a rather rigid logical sequence was followed in textbooks; for example, addition of whole numbers with no regrouping was taught well before addition with regrouping. But when we teach computation in the context of solving problems, the problems of interest do not always occur within that traditional sequence. This should not

---

Carry? Borrow? Regroup? Rename?

Which term is appropriate when adding or subtracting whole numbers? Obviously, "carry" and "borrow" are misleading mathematically, though the terms are often used. **They may promote mechanical manipulation of symbols instead of a procedure that makes sense to students.**

The term "regroup" is appropriate when manipulatives for a quantity are grouped differently. The term "rename" is mathematically correct; the quantity is actually given a different name. For example, when computing 273 − 186, 2 hundreds + **7 tens + 3 ones** is renamed as 2 hundreds + **6 tens + 13 ones.**

Other terms that may cause students to focus only on a procedure are "reduce," "cancel," and "invert." Make sure students understand the concepts involved.

deter us and our students from exploring solutions for interesting problems that will lead to more generalized written procedures. Usnick found that initial teaching of the generalized procedure for adding whole numbers (regrouping included) led to comparable achievement and effective retention.[26]

When using manipulatives to teach a conventional algorithm, the critical step is progressing from manipulatives to written symbols. This is why a *step-by-step* record is helpful. The resulting record or algorithm must make sense to our students if they are going to do more than push symbols around on paper.

We must be sure our students' paper-and-pencil procedures are correct before we encourage them to make the procedures automatic. When algorithms *are* correct, a certain amount of practice is required for the procedures to be remembered and used effectively; but practice with paper-and-pencil procedures needs to be planned carefully—as does practice for all methods of computation. NCTM notes in *Principles and Standards for School Mathematics*:

> **Practice needs to be motivating and systematic if students are to develop computational fluency, whether mentally, with manipulatives materials, or with paper and pencil. Practice can be conducted in the context of other activities, including games that require computation as part of score keeping, questions that emerge from children's literature, situations in the classroom, or focused activities that are part of another mathematical investigation. Practice should be purposeful and should focus on developing thinking strategies and a knowledge of number relationships . . .[27]**

Continuing diagnosis is very important. When we say "Tell me something about this," we help our students develop the ability to communicate mathematical ideas—even as they give us diagnostic information. We must keep our diagnostic eyes open throughout instruction.

Do not overly test students—especially at-risk students. Although diagnosis should continue throughout instruction, we should never limit instruction to assessment activities. (Sometimes teachers fall into that trap.) The activities we plan should focus on helping students *learn*.

Our written and oral responses to students' written work in mathematics affect students—either positively or negatively. It is best to give an immediate *personal* response to what the student is doing rather than a list of things to be done next time.

"I have no trouble reading your numerals."
"Very interesting! How did you get your answer?"
"Did you think about your answer? Does it make sense?"

Sometimes, when teaching a specific algorithm, it is helpful to have a group of students analyze a completed example. It is important to emphasize thinking as students observe, describe, and hypothesize what was done. Students should discuss why it resulted in the correct number, and try the procedure with different numbers. We may also want to ask some students to analyze incorrect computations, suggesting that they find and explain the errors.

Many of our students will make mistakes while learning to compute. Even so, mistakes can be an important, positive part of the initial learning process. Interestingly, teachers respond differently to errors in different cultures.

> We have been struck by the different reactions of Asian and American teachers to children's errors. For Americans, errors tend to be interpreted as an indication of failure in learning the lesson. For Chinese and Japanese, they are an index of what still needs to be learned. These divergent interpretations result in very different reactions to the display of errors—embarrassment on the part of American children, calm acceptance by Asian children. They also result in differences in the manner in which teachers utilize errors as effective means of instruction.[28]

Our attitudes toward errors are important. We should view them as opportunities for learning!

We must monitor our own expectations of students, making sure we do not assume particular individuals cannot learn. Even so, we do need to be alert to any perceptual difficulties a student may have. In order to respond to instruction, students need to be able to observe and also envision the physical properties of digits: vertical versus horizontal elongation, straightness versus curvature, and degree of closure. And our students need to be able to perceive attributes of multidigit numerals—properties such as position of a digit to the left or right of another digit. Poor spatial ability may affect an individual's capacity to respond to instruction emphasizing place value concepts.

Other students may find it difficult to respond to instruction because of language patterns. The syntax of English language expressions is often different from the structure of mathematical statements, and we complicate the situation by using different but equivalent language expressions for the same concept. For example, *twelve minus four* and *four from twelve* express the same mathematical concept.

Teaching conventional computational procedures requires thorough developmental instruction; each student moves through a carefully planned sequence of learning activities. The amount of time needed for each type of activity will vary from student to student; and for any individual the pace will likely vary from day to day. If we are to lessen the likelihood that students learn patterns of error, we will have to resist the temptation to cover the text or the curriculum guide by completing two pages a day or a similar plan. Careful attention will have to be given to ideas and skills needed by each student in order to learn the concept or algorithm under study.

We can teach in a way that makes the adoption of erroneous procedures unlikely!

Corrective Instruction

Corrective instruction may be necessary whenever one of our students has not been able to learn a computational procedure that produces correct answers in an efficient way. Corrective instruction must be built on a careful diagnosis of what the student has and has not learned, and what the student can and cannot do.

The student may have acquired a simple misconception that can be corrected with focused instruction. Sometimes the student is not adequately grounded in the concepts and principles needed to understand the algorithm, then corrective instruction must begin by teaching foundational concepts and principles rather than the computational procedure itself.

Students need feedback that not only tells them which examples are correct, but also assists in obtaining correct answers. Corrective feedback can take many forms. It can be presented orally along with personal comments to the student which express confidence in his ability to learn, or it can be written on the student's paper. All too frequently teacher feedback does not include *corrective* feedback; papers are merely scored and students are asked to rework the examples. When appropriate, we need to write notes providing personal, corrective assistance on papers.

ACQUIRING SPECIALIZED VOCABULARY

Concepts and principles are named with words and expressed with words and symbols. And it is possible that many of our students will stumble over the specialized vocabulary associated with mathematics. A term may not be associated with the appropriate concept, or a concept understood may not be given the appropriate name. From time to time, something akin to the overgeneralizing and overspecializing illustrated in the previous chapter is likely to happen as our students learn concepts and procedures. The result is muddled communication and confused thinking.

For younger students, a general teaching strategy is to introduce words and symbols as a way of describing and recording what students have already observed and know informally.[29] They use words informally; their math ideas are not expressed in final form initially—but that is also true of professional mathematicians. Student use of informal, everyday language "provides a base on which to build a connection to formal mathematical language."[30] If we begin with students' very informal language—often the way students describe situations—we may be able to introduce more precise terminology in apposition to the informal language, gradually dropping the informal language.

For example, the term "addend" can be developed while students are examining sets separated into two subsets. The number of items in each subset and the total number of items are recorded. At first the number of items in each subset is informally called the "number for the part." Later, something like "the number for this part, *or addend,* is five," is appropriate. Eventually this leads to expressions like, "What is the other addend?" Often older students can simply be told that "We call the number for a part (or subset) an addend."

But we should not be in a hurry for our students to use more precise mathematical terms. Steele cautions that "we should not move students too quickly toward new mathematical language without giving them the opportunity to explore, investigate, describe, and explain ideas."[31]

When they are learning specialized vocabulary, our students need to make connections with concepts and terms they already know. It is often helpful for them to connect with root meanings and with related words. For example, the root of *factor* and the related word *factory* point to a factor doing something (multiplying).[32] Also, a concept web or a simple diagram may help those who are visually oriented. Figure 3.3 shows how the relationship between factors and multiples can be illustrated.

Sometimes we can make specialized vocabulary clearer if we employ one of the key concepts of school mathematics, the idea that a number has many names. For instance, the term "factorization" is sometimes confusing. Factorizations are particularly useful names for numbers, especially factorizations that consist solely of prime numbers; they are called "prime factorizations." Changing a fraction to an equivalent fraction involves another use of the idea that a number has many names. This process involves finding a different name for the same number, a name that is more useful for the purposes at hand.

When our students acquire and use specialized vocabulary, we must support classroom talk about mathematics that moves away from very specific contexts toward applications of mathematical ideas in varied contexts.[33]

FIGURE 3.3   Diagram
for factors and multiples

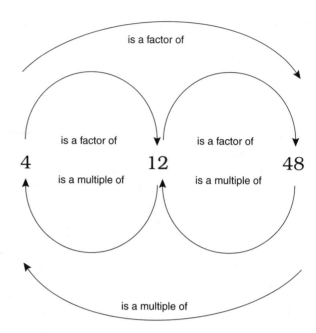

Using Models and Concrete Materials

The experiences we plan for our students help form their dispositions toward mathematics. Our use of concrete materials, frequently called manipulatives, can contribute to a positive disposition—if those experiences include exploration, problem solving, accurate modeling of the mathematics involved, and reflection by each student.

If a teacher believes that getting correct answers is all that is really important, students will believe that it is all right to push digits around whether it makes any sense or not; they also will push manipulatives around without thinking and relating them to a meaningful recording procedure. From his analysis of the use of concrete materials in elementary mathematics, Thompson stresses that students "must first be committed to making sense of their activities and be committed to expressing their sense in meaningful ways."[34] Our classroom talk must focus on thinking, even while students use concrete materials; we must create the expectation throughout all of our mathematics instruction that we want to make sense of the procedures we use and whatever we write down.

In general, well-chosen manipulatives can provide a natural working environment for our students as they learn concepts and procedures. This is especially true for whole numbers, which are very much a part of each student's environment. With fractions, students have less direct experience and they are more apt to rely on rote procedures, so we need to take special care when selecting materials. Materials that we can use to create more natural environments include chip-trading activities for whole numbers and fraction bars for fractions. Extensive modeling with materials like these during the early phases of instruction usually helps students develop meanings they can apply flexibly.

We must make sure that whatever manipulatives we select or design are accurate mathematically. Fraction representations, for example, are sometimes inaccurate; although it is often wise to let students construct the models used, we need to make sure fractional parts are equal in area. Base-ten blocks are sometimes mysterious to students, especially the thousands block because they see only six hundreds on the sides. Although base-ten blocks are accurate mathematically, we need to make sure students understand the mathematics accurately.

Students look for commonalties among their contacts with an idea or an algorithm, and as they come to understand they pull out common characteristics among their experiences and form an abstraction. Therefore, our students need experiences in which all perceptual stimuli are varied except those that are essential to the mathematical idea or algorithm. A cardboard place-value chart may be of great value, but it should not be the only concrete aid we use for numeration activities; other models can be used also, possibly devices made with juice cans or wooden boxes.

We should help our students learn general concepts and procedures rather than ideas or processes specific to a particular model or example. For instance, students need to learn that "ten ones is the same amount as one ten," rather than "take ten yellows to the bank then put one blue in the next place." Similarly, if we do not focus on the general procedure, in the specific subtraction number sentence $42 - 17 = 25$ a student may conclude that the five units in the answer is simply the result of finding the difference between the two and the seven. Models and examples should be varied so irrelevant characteristics are not observed as common attributes.

As our students use manipulatives to model concepts, we should involve our students in experiences which "go both ways" whenever this is possible. This is especially important for numeration concepts. Have students manipulate models and record what they observe with symbols, but also let them begin with symbols and interpret the symbols by modeling the concept. For example, provide a collection of base-ten blocks, and point to a unit block and explain, "This block is one;" then give a student a numeral card such as 1,324 and have the student show that amount with the blocks. In contrast, assemble a collection of base-ten blocks: five hundreds blocks, two unit blocks, one thousands block, and three tens blocks. Ask the student to write a numeral for the amount shown with the blocks.

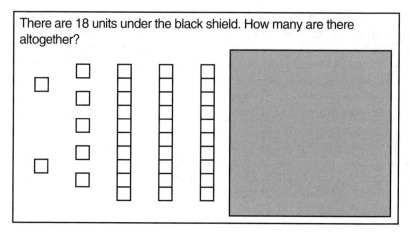

FIGURE 3.4   Sample diagnostic item

While our students are working with manipulatives, there are many opportunities for us to intervene with diagnostic questions. For example, when a student is using base-ten blocks for adding and subtracting two-digit numbers we might find it useful to do what Figure 3.4 suggests.

For students who adopt error patterns, it is often wise to redevelop computational procedures as careful step-by-step records of observations while using manipulatives. Hopefully, this will help the student who has been pushing symbols around in a rote manner to make sense of his record. For most algorithms for whole numbers it is possible to manipulate concrete aids and record the actions step-by-step, so that the resulting record is a desired computational procedure. For algorithms with fractions, especially unlike fractions, it is not always possible to demonstrate each step in the computational procedure with concrete aids; the procedure may need to be developed by reasoning with mathematical ideas. Then manipulatives can sometimes be used to verify the result.

Sometimes manipulatives can be arranged in relation to one another just as digits are placed in relation to one another when computing on paper. This is true for some of the gamelike activities described in Appendix C, and for the way sticks (singles and bundles), base-ten blocks, and place-value charts are often used.

UNDERSTANDING AND RECALLING BASIC NUMBER COMBINATIONS

Ultimately our students need to understand the basic number combinations of arithmetic and be able to recall them. Initially they need to understand the operations, but they eventually need to be able to re-call number combinations without resorting to inefficient procedures.

> . . . students should know the "basic number facts" because such knowledge is essential for mental computation, estimation, per-formance of computational procedures, and problem solving.[35]

The basic number combinations, or basic facts of arithmetic, are the simple equations we use when we compute. They involve two one-digit addends if they are addition or subtraction number combina-tions, or two one-digit factors if they are multiplication or division number combinations. Examples include the following:

$$6 + 7 = 13 \qquad 12 - 8 = 4 \qquad 3 \times 5 = 15 \qquad 27 \div 9 = 3$$

Students study number combinations in the context of learning what the operations of arithmetic mean. For instance, addition can be thought of as an operation that tells us the total number in a set if we know the amount in each of two disjoint subsets. Multiplication can also be conceived as an operation that tells us the total amount when-ever we know two numbers: the number of equivalent disjoint subsets and the number in each subset.

Initially we should let younger students approach individual number combinations as problems to solve, often presented as open number sentences like $5 \times 4 = \bigcirc$. When our students are permitted to investigate these problems in cooperative groups, they build on each other's informal knowledge.

We must emphasize thinking during the study of number com-binations, and help our students make connections between them. Combinations for different operations are often related (some would say they are "close kin"); for example, $5 \times 7 = 35$ and $35 \div 7 = 5$ both have 5 and 7 as factors, and they have 35 as the total amount or product. Instead of always asking students to find a single num-ber as in $6 + \bigcirc = 13$, we should frequently pose more open-ended questions.

When two numbers are added, the total amount (their sum) is 13. What might the two numbers be? How many of the pairs of numbers include a six? What are the solutions to $\bigcirc + \bigcirc = 13$?

For addition combinations, Threlfall and Frobisher recommend that we stress patterns that students can use to generate new information.[36] Visual patterns, for example, can be constructed with counting cubes or Cuisenaire rods, and related to sequences of number combinations. Also, basic addition combinations that have 9 as the sum can be generated as follows.

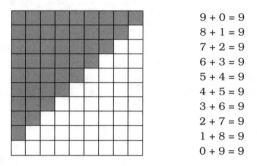

$$9 + 0 = 9$$
$$8 + 1 = 9$$
$$7 + 2 = 9$$
$$6 + 3 = 9$$
$$5 + 4 = 9$$
$$4 + 5 = 9$$
$$3 + 6 = 9$$
$$2 + 7 = 9$$
$$1 + 8 = 9$$
$$0 + 9 = 9$$

Other patterns can be related to compensation principles. For example, when one addend is *increased* by a particular number and the other addend is *decreased* by the same number, the sum remains the same. As our students consider this principle—possibly in a learning center—they can select number combination cards to place above and below relationship indicators.

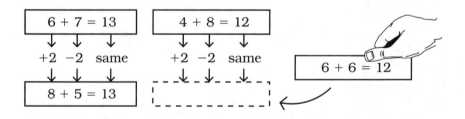

Similar activities can be planned for other principles, such as the fact that if, while one addend remains the same, the other addend is greater by a particular number, the sum will be greater by that number.

Before mastery activities are introduced our students need to be taught thinking strategies and more mature ways to determine a missing number. Isaacs and Carroll describe strategies which can help students understand and recall basic number combinations; they classify strategies in terms of focus: on counting, on parts and wholes, and on derived facts.[37] The following list is an adaptation of categories suggested by Isaacs and Carroll.

Counting

Counting on	addition, subtraction
Missing addend[38]	subtraction
Skip counting	multiplication, division
Repeated addition	multiplication, division

Observing Parts and Wholes

Make ten, and so many more	addition
	$6 + \mathbf{7} = (6 + \mathbf{4}) + \mathbf{3} = 10 + 3 = 13$

Deriving Combinations from Other Combinations

One/two more/less than a known combination	addition, subtraction
Use a double	addition
Compensation	addition, subtraction
Use the related addition combination	subtraction for $13 - 5$ think, $5 + ? = 13$
Use the related multiplication combination	division for $42 \div 6$ think, $6 \times ? = 42$
Same addends or factors (commutative)	addition, multiplication $5 \times 6 = 30$, so $6 \times 5 = 30$
Multiply in parts: rename, multiply, and then add or subtract.[39]	multiplication $7 = 5 + 2 \qquad 9 = 10 - 1$ $5 \times \mathbf{7} = 5 \times (\mathbf{5} + \mathbf{2}) =$ $(5 \times 5) + (5 \times 2)$ $7 \times \mathbf{9} = 7 \times (\mathbf{10} - \mathbf{1}) =$ $(7 \times 10) - (7 \times 1)$
Nines pattern: next product is one more ten, and one less unit	multiplication $5 \times 9 = 45$, so $6 \times 9 = 54$

Sometimes when we think a student was merely careless while attempting to recall specific number combinations, the student actually attempted one of the strategies listed above; however, the strategy was incorrectly applied. Perhaps the student attempted to count on, but miscounted. We need to assume that incorrect recall is rarely due to carelessness, and attempt to find out what is really going on. Remember, diagnosis should be continuous.

Mastery of the basic number combinations of arithmetic is the ability to recall missing sums, addends, products, and factors promptly and without hesitation. A student who has mastered $6 + 8 = 14$, when presented with "$6 + 8 = ?$" either orally or in writing, will recall 14 without counting or figuring it out. When a student attempts to find the product of two whole numbers (such as 36 and 457) by using a paper-and-pencil procedure, lack of mastery of the basic multiplication combinations requires time-consuming and distracting ways of finding the product. Lack of mastery of number combinations also greatly hampers mental computation and the ability to estimate.

If an older student has not mastered the basic number combinations, she probably persists in using counting or elaborate procedures to find needed numbers. She may understand the operations, yet she continues to require the security of counting or other time-consuming procedures when computing. She probably does not feel confident to simply recall the number. If such a student is involved in extensive practice activity, she reinforces use of less-than-adequate procedures. What she needs is practice *recalling* the missing number. How can we provide an instructional environment in which students like this one feel secure enough to try simply recalling missing numbers?

Games provide the safest environment for simple recall; when playing games, someone has to lose. Whereas the teacher always seems to want "the correct answer," in a game it is acceptable to lose at least part of the time. The competition in a game encourages a student to try simply recalling the number combination. Further, games often make possible greater attending behavior because of the materials involved. For instance, a student who rejects a paper-and-pencil problem such as "6 + 5 = ?" because it is a reminder of failure and unpleasantness, may attend with interest when the same question is presented with numerals painted on brightly colored cubes which can be moved about.

Obviously, what is intended is *not* an arithmetic game modeled after an old-fashioned spelling bee designed to eliminate less able students; nor is it a game designed to put a student under pressure in front of a large group of peers. The best games will be games involving only a few students, preferably students with rather comparable abilities. In such games a student can feel secure enough to try simple recall. We should choose games that provide immediate or early verification; students should learn promptly if they recalled correctly. Commercial games are available, but games can be made using simple materials—many of which are already in the classroom. Our students are quite capable of making up games and altering rules to suit their fancy when they are encouraged to do so. A homemade game using a mathematical balance would provide immediate verification for each student's response (Figure 3.5).

Games are also useful for retention once the number combinations are mastered, and research suggests that relatively infrequent use of games can maintain skill with number combinations.[40]

Calculators can supply answers, but they can also be used to help our students learn basic number combinations. For example, the constant function on a calculator can be used to help students generate products. For the products of 6 and numbers 2 through 9, chil-

FIGURE 3.5 Verification with a mathematical balance

dren press $\boxed{6}$ $\boxed{+}$ $\boxed{6}$ $\boxed{=}$, $\boxed{=}$, $\boxed{=}$, and so on. Students will not loose count if they repeatedly press the equals key and say: 2 sixes is 12, 3 sixes is 18, and so on.

Individuals can also use calculators as they practice recalling number combinations. For example, a student says "six times seven" as he presses $\boxed{6}$ $\boxed{\times}$ $\boxed{7}$. Then, he puts his hand behind his back and says "equals 42" *before* he presses $\boxed{=}$. The student receives immediate confirmation that he was correct. If he was incorrect, he should repeat the complete procedure immediately.

Our students need to understand the operations of arithmetic; yet in time they also need to be able to recall the basic number combinations. They need to make connections among combinations and acquire thinking strategies for finding missing numbers. Eventually, our students need practice—often in the form of games—to assure mastery of the basic number combinations.

TALKING AND WRITING MATHEMATICS

Both talking mathematics and writing mathematics are teaching strategies that can be used while teaching computation. They enhance learning by involving our students in expressions of meaning, and by giving them opportunities to relate the everyday language of their world to math language and to math symbols. They also provide opportunities for integrating mathematics with other subject areas.

Of the two strategies, the writings of students are typically more reflective. When students write prose as a part of instruction in mathematics they sometimes demonstrate understandings that are not adequate, or they use terms and symbols incorrectly. Be sure to read their writings diagnostically.[41]

Talking mathematics involves more risk taking on the part of students than does writing mathematics, at least at first. One activity that involves talking mathematics is for students to conduct an interview with an older adult to learn about specific paper-and-pencil algorithms they were taught and use now. Part of such an interview follows.

STUDENT: Grandpa, please subtract this for me. And think out loud so I will know how you are doing it.

$$\begin{array}{r} 253 \\ -179 \\ \hline \end{array}$$

GRANDPA: OK. Nine and four is 13. Write four here and put the one under the seven.

$$\begin{array}{r} 253 \\ -179 \\ \hline 4 \end{array}$$

Eight and seven is 15. Write seven here. . . .

STUDENT: (later) That's different! Does it always work? . . . Why does it work? . . .

When students explain mathematical topics in a journal, it can be considered an "academic learning log." Learning logs serve not only as records of student learning, but also help students clarify their thoughts.[42]

Journal writing can be done for different audiences. It should be first-person writing that focuses on something related to mathematics or learning mathematics. Often, journals are part of a written dialog with the teacher in which students express how they feel about mathematics, what they know with confidence, when they believe that knowledge can be used, and questions they may have.

We may want our students to keep two journals: one to write what they know or have learned, and another to tell how they feel about specific experiences in mathematics. Journal writing can help students focus on the topic at hand so they can ask appropriate questions; students who do not like to ask questions in class may be more likely to write their questions.

Journal writing is sometimes stimulated by prompts that we can provide. Examples of appropriate prompts include: "I learned _____." "I was pleased that I _____." "I am most proud of _____." And "I wish _____."[43]

Journals are not the only way to write mathematics. Some of the following activities require students to produce oral or written explanations related to computation.

- Write how you would teach your cousin to add decimals.
- Write a letter to a student who was absent, and explain what is most important to understand about multiplying decimals.
- Use a hand puppet to explain to your younger sister how to subtract two-digit numbers.
- Make a poster or a bulletin board that explains how to divide whole numbers.

These activities help students focus on what they are learning in mathematics.

- Write out definitions in your own words.
- In your own words write out the most important information about finding equivalent fractions.
- Write test questions about what you studied today.
- Describe any places you had difficulty, and how you worked it out.
- Write questions about what you do not understand. (Merely writing them may help reduce anxiety.)
- Respond to: "What I learned from my mistake."
- Use a Solve and Comment Page for practice. (See Figure 3.6.)

Students, individually or in groups, can respond to computations others have completed by talking and writing mathematics; both correctly and incorrectly worked-out examples can be included. Following is an example of a task that involves a paper with an error pattern similar to those illustrated in this book.

Score, analyze, and discuss each example.

For incorrect examples, describe in writing:
- what was done incorrectly,
- what should be done instead and why, and
- illustrate a correct procedure.

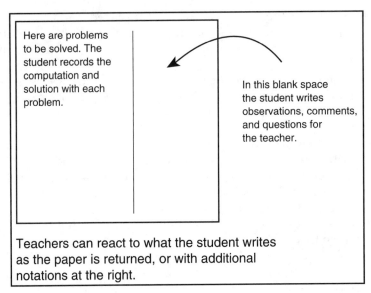

FIGURE 3.6   Solve and Comment Page

There are many reasons we want our students to talk and write mathematics.[44] Here is a list of additional things we can do to have our students write mathematics.

- Before a lesson, have students write in their journals to describe what they expect to happen. Later students can write how they felt during the lesson.
- Have students do reflective writing to prepare for a discussion.
- Encourage students to write a math autobiography. You can stimulate similar writings with sentence starters like these:

> **My best experience with math was _____.**
> **I liked math until _____.**
> **Math makes me feel _____.**
> **If I were a math teacher, I'd _____.**[45]

- Have students write word problems of their own. You can supply the data, or they can supply their own.
- Have students write and solve word problems for which a particular computational procedure would be appropriate.
- Let students write a story that teaches a math concept. For example, a young child could write a story to teach "the number 7" or "place value."
- Encourage students to write a report or a book on a mathematical topic. Examples include:

Numerations systems
Algorithms used by different peoples

Using Graphic Organizers for Instruction

Graphic organizers can enhance much of our instruction in mathematics, whether regular developmental instruction or intervention with students experiencing difficulty. When our students learn new ideas, graphic organizers can serve as patterns for organizing and representing relationships; they can also serve as a means of assessing student learning.

Many types of graphic organizers can be incorporated into the teaching of mathematics. Here are some examples.

Drawings. Children can draw pictures of things their family buys at the grocery store complete with price tags, and use them in constructing problems.

Charts. Fraction cards like $\boxed{\frac{2}{6}}$ and $\boxed{\frac{5}{8}}$ can be sorted in columns headed Less Than a Half, Names for One Half, and Greater Than a Half.

Overlapping circles. Phrase cards like $\boxed{100 - 99}$ and $\boxed{8 \div 8}$ and fraction cards can be placed in two overlapping circles, one labeled Fractions and the other labeled Names for One.

Webs and concept maps. Relationships among operations and among numbers are often shown with concept maps.[46] An example of a web to be completed with cards by young children appears in Figure 3.7.

FIGURE 3.7 A web for students to complete by sorting cards

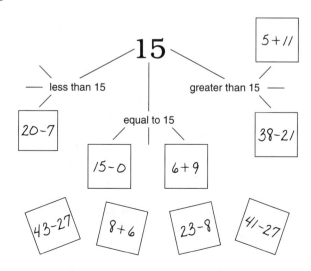

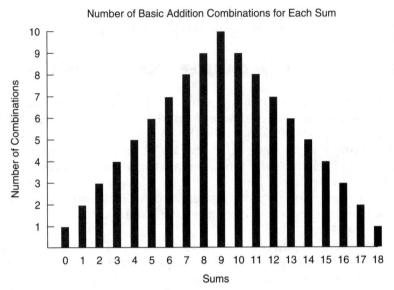

FIGURE 3.8   Graph for number of basic addition combinations for each sum

	Estimate	Paper	Mental	Calculator
Add				
Subtract				
Multiply				
Divide				

As you sort word problems, assume you have paper and pencil at hand, and it would take you about two minutes to locate a calculator.

FIGURE 3.9   Grid for sorting word problem cards by most appropriate method of computation and by operation needed to find the answer

Graphs.   Figure 3.8 illustrates a graph that students can make for basic addition combinations.

Grids.   Grids typically display categories determined by two characteristics. Figure 3.9 illustrates a grid in which word problems can be sorted by the operation required to determine the answer, and by the most appropriate method for the computation.

Procedural maps.   Figure 3.10 illustrates a procedural map for estimating the sum of two-digit numbers.

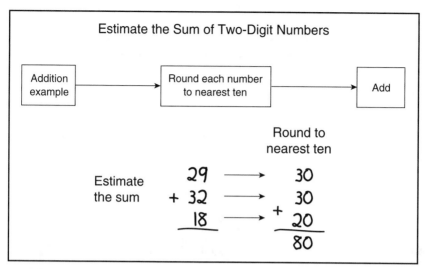

FIGURE 3.10 Procedural map for estimating the sum of two-digit numbers

FIGURE 3.11 Basic shapes for flowcharts

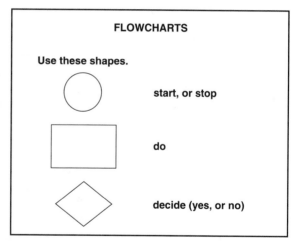

Flowcharts. Illustrations appear in Figures 3.11, 3.12, and 3.13.

Flowcharts are of particular interest for teaching computational procedures.

Number lines have uses that go beyond basic number and numeration work. For example, when teaching our students how to use basic number combinations for adding or subtracting with higher decade numbers, a pattern can be observed with number lines.

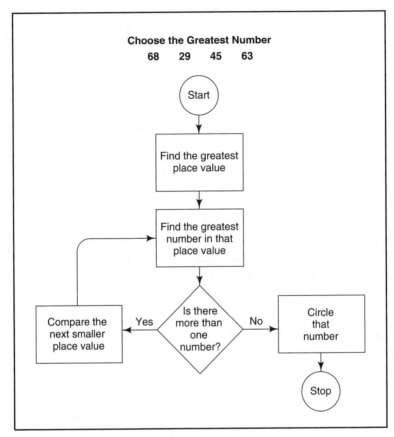

FIGURE 3.12   An example of a flowchart

This sequence illustrates a repeated number line shift.

$$5 + 8 = 13 \qquad\qquad 15 + 8 = \bigcirc \qquad\qquad 25 + 8 = \bigcirc$$

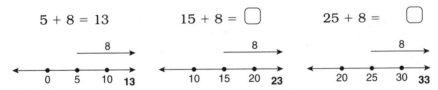

We can use concept maps and flowcharts for an overview of what will be studied, or as a way of summarizing what has already been taught. To use them to assess student understanding, have students write in empty blanks or boxes within the maps and charts.

To teach simple flowcharting procedures, make a chart available for reference that shows the basic shapes and how they are used. Figure 3.11 is an example of such a chart. When teaching simple flow-

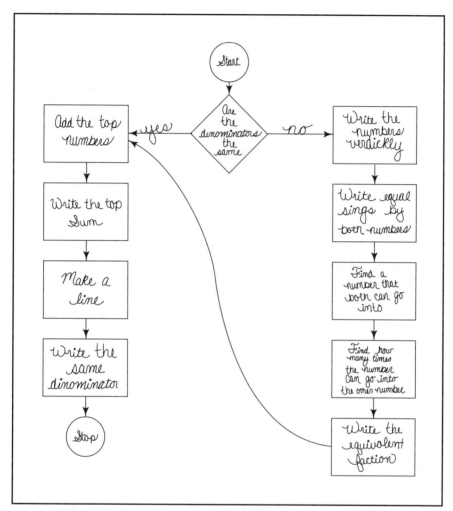

FIGURE 3.13   A fourth grader's flowchart for adding fractions

charting, focus on procedures for simple mathematical tasks. Figure 3.12 is an example of a flowchart developed to show how to choose the greatest of several whole numbers.

After our students have learned how to make a flowchart we can have pairs of students, and eventually individuals, create flowcharts for paper-and-pencil computation procedures. Figure 3.13 is a flowchart for adding fractions prepared by a fourth-grade boy. Make sure that student-generated flowcharts are tested; other students can follow the chart step by step to see if the chart is complete and accurate.

Near the end of the school year, some teachers have their students summarize computational procedures they have learned during the year by making flowcharts they can take with them to their new classroom.

USING ALTERNATIVE ALGORITHMS

If we are willing to accept the idea that there are many legitimate ways to subtract, divide, and so on, we could choose to introduce an algorithm that is fresh and new to those students who are experiencing difficulty. By doing so we may circumvent any mind-set of failure. We will also help students realize that there are many different ways of getting correct answers when computing.

Numerous examples of alternative algorithms are to be found in the literature of mathematics education. Several algorithms are described in these articles: Pearson describes pre- 1900 algorithms,[47] Carroll and Porter describe a variety of alternative procedures for whole-number operations,[48] and Philipp describes algorithms used by different cultures.[49]

Three examples of alternative algorithms follow. With students who experience difficulty learning to compute, we may find that a low-stress procedure such as the first algorithm is learned with relative ease. Like traditional algorithms, low-stress procedures can often be taught as sensible records of manipulations with sticks, blocks, or number rods. The advantage of such algorithms is that they separate fact recall from renaming, and thereby place fewer demands for remembering on the student who is computing.

Addition of Whole Numbers:
Hutchings's Low-Stress Method[50]

As illustrated in examples A and B, sums for number combinations are written with small digits to the left and to the right instead of in the usual manner.

When a column is added, the 1 ten is ignored and the one's digit is added to the next number. In example C, $5 + 9 = 14$, $4 + 8 = 12$,

$2 + 4 = 6$, and $6 + 7 = 13$. The remaining 3 ones are recorded in the answer. The tens are counted and also recorded. Multicolumn addition proceeds similarly, except the number of tens counted is recorded at the top of the next column.

Many students for whom regrouping in addition is difficult find this alternative rather easy to learn. It often brings success quickly, even with large examples. Other students, including those with perceptual problems, may be confused by the abundance of "crutches." This is especially true when it is not possible to write examples with large digits, which is the case with most published achievement tests.

Subtraction of Whole Numbers: The Equal Additions (or European-Latino) Method

A.
$$\begin{array}{r} 4\ 5\ '3 \\ -\ 1_{\bullet}\cancel{7}\ 8 \\ \hline 5 \end{array}$$

B.
$$\begin{array}{r} 4\ \cancel{5}\ 3 \\ _2\cancel{X}\ _{\bullet}\cancel{7}\ 8 \\ \hline 2\ 7\ 5 \end{array}$$

The principle of compensation is applied: when equal quantities are added to both the minuend and the subtrahend, the difference remains the same. In this computation, ten is added to the sum, i.e., to the 3 in the ones place. To compensate for this addition, 10 is also added to the known addend; the 7 in the tens place is replaced with 8. Similarly, 1 hundred is added to the sum; i.e., the 5 in the tens place becomes a 15. To compensate, 1 hundred is added to the known addend; the 1 in the hundreds place is replaced with 2.

Subtraction of Rational Numbers: The Equal Additions Method[51]

Problem:

$$-\ 7\tfrac{1}{4} \quad \text{add one } \left(\tfrac{4}{4}\right) \longrightarrow 7\tfrac{5}{4}$$
$$\underline{3\tfrac{3}{4}} \quad \text{add one } (1) \longrightarrow \underline{4\tfrac{3}{4}}$$

Difference:
$$3\tfrac{1}{2} \qquad\qquad\qquad\qquad 3\tfrac{2}{4}$$

The principle of compensation is applied. One is added to both the minuend and the subtrahend in order to subtract easily.

USING PEER TUTORING

Peer tutoring, a strategy we may find helpful when we teach computation, occurs when students instruct one another by challenging, explaining, and demonstrating concepts and procedures. Often the tutor learns even more than the student being tutored.

If we plan carefully, peer tutoring can foster many of the emphases of *Principles and Standards for School Mathematics:* problems will be solved, assessment will be conducted, mathematical ideas will be discussed, reasoning will justify procedures, manipulatives and drawings will be used for representations, and connections will be made with prior learning.[52] But these things will not happen unless we prepare carefully.

Barone and Taylor recommend at least a two-year age difference between tutors and their tutees.[53] They suggest ways to implement peer tutoring with young children; nevertheless, many of their ideas apply to peer tutoring by older students as well. We need to select engaging instructional activities to be taught, then prepare tutors by teaching them the activity before they teach it to their peers. We can even have tutors teach the activity to other tutors while we observe, and have tutors switch roles. After tutoring sessions it is helpful to have both tutors and tutees write in their journals.

HELPING INDIVIDUALS THROUGH COOPERATIVE GROUPS

Individual students who are learning to compute usually profit from involvement with other students while working on a problem or a task, especially when students work in a thoughtful and focused way. This is true for all students, including those who experience difficulty learning computational procedures. On-task behavior often improves and students become active information processors, not just passive receivers of information. Students who work cooperatively to solve problems communicate mathematical ideas as they work; they both challenge and help one another.

Students working in cooperative groups need to be responsible for the learning of each person within the group (perhaps there is to be a team score). But we need to hold each individual accountable for his or her own learning. Individuals also need to be held accountable for contributing to the group.

Typically, groups should be structured, heterogeneous groups—often groups of four students. Cooperative groups can be structured by the tasks we give them. Tasks related to computational knowledge and skills include the following.

- Discuss specific questions. For example, "What is the most important step in the procedure we studied? Why?"
- Solve a problem that involves deciding the appropriate method of computation, including procedures recently learned.
- Go over homework completed by individuals. Check answers with one another. Where answers differ determine why, and which is correct. Students often assume they are correct and have to be convinced by others that they are not.
- Review for a test. Assign a sample test for the group to complete together.

When possible, structure the tasks so that students not only explain procedures to one another, but also so that each student makes sure other participants in the group understand and can do the procedures.[54] And if an activity involves a calculator, make sure students take turns using the calculator.

Whenever tasks involve manipulatives, we must remember that our students do not learn by just using manipulatives; they learn by *thinking* about what they are doing when they use manipulatives. They need to reflect on what they are doing with manipulatives, and explain their reasoning to one another. It has been said that . . .

> We should never tell a child what that child might be able to tell us. Similarly, we should never tell a child what some other child might be able to tell the child for us.

We need to carefully observe our students as they work. Perhaps groups are working on an assignment to create a task or problem that requires a particular computation, or each group has been given a problem for which they are to demonstrate two or more solutions. We must focus on their thinking as we observe them—not on their answers alone.

Sample activities for cooperative groups of students are described in Appendix D. The activities focus on computational procedures.

USING PORTFOLIOS TO MONITOR PROGRESS DURING INSTRUCTION

Do our students have individual goals for learning mathematics? Can each student point to growth? Portfolios showcase student work and provide especially helpful insights into student growth and accomplishment.

Students may already have work folders for filing completed work or work in progress, but each of our students also needs to have a mathematics portfolio into which *selected* examples of mathematics work are placed. It is appropriate to require certain papers to be included in their portfolios, but students should be encouraged to select many or even most of the items—items *they* especially value or believe show growth or creativity.

During instruction we need to have our students reflect on work completed early in the year, and compare it with work completed more recently. One of the main purposes for mathematics portfolios is to "help students develop better self-assessment skills and become less reliant on the grades we assign to their work."[55] If we want students to understand why a certain computational procedure works, for instance, we may want to have students select the particular item from their work folder that *best* demonstrates their understanding of why the procedure works, and place it in their portfolio. Obviously, when we conference with parents, mathematics portfolios will be very useful.[56]

Our purposes for having students develop mathematics portfolios will determine many of the types of items included. We may want to suggest that students include several of the following.

- Papers showing more than one way to solve a problem
- Papers telling how the student knows which method of computation to use (estimate, paper and pencil, and so on) with examples for each method
- Papers showing why a traditional algorithm works
- Papers illustrating an alternative algorithm (or an algorithm invented by the student) and explaining why it works
- Papers that show how the student has corrected errors or misunderstandings
- Mathematical problems developed by the student; solutions may be included
- Papers displaying graphic organizers developed by the student; for example, a table of equivalent fractions
- Drawings of how manipulatives were used in solving a problem
- Individual or group reports of a project, such as a statistical survey with graphs
- Notes from an interview with someone about some aspect of mathematics
- Papers that show how mathematics is used in other subject areas
- Artwork involving geometric patterns or mathematical relationships
- Scale drawings
- Homework, especially solutions to nonroutine problems

- Performance assessment tasks given periodically
- Checklists completed by the teacher
- Mathematical autobiographies
- Writings describing how the student feels about mathematics class or "doing mathematics"
- Papers that respond to "What I Learned in Math Class Today"
- Papers that respond to "What I Learned from My Mistake," written by students who have adopted error patterns in specific computation procedures
- Notes from the teacher describing evidence the student understood a particular mathematical principle
- Self-assessment sheets for groups and for individuals

Or we may want to have our students select from their work folders the five best items relative to a specific topic, and place them in their mathematics portfolios along with a letter that explains why each was selected.

GUIDING INSTRUCTION

Teachers have found the following guidelines to be helpful. They provide a summary of principles to keep in mind when instructing students who are having difficulty learning to compute.

Focus on the Student

1. *Personalize instruction.* Even when students meet in groups for instruction, individuals must be assessed and programs must be planned for *individuals.* Some individual tutoring may be required.
2. *Believe the student is capable of learning.* A student who has met repeated failure needs to believe that she is a valued person and is capable of eventually acquiring the needed knowledge and skill. You must believe this, too, if you are to help.
3. *Make sure the student has the goals of instruction clearly in mind.* Make sure the student knows what is needed; he needs to know the direction instruction is heading. He needs to know where it will head eventually ("I'll be able to subtract and get the right answers") and where it is headed immediately ("I'll soon be able to rename a number many different ways").
4. *Encourage self-assessment.* From the beginning involve students in the assessment process. Let them help set goals for instruction.

5. *Ensure consistent expectations.* Make sure you and the student's parents have the same expectations in regard to what the student will accomplish. People in the United States tend to assume that difficulties with learning result from a lack of ability; in many other countries they are more likely to assume that difficulties are a result of insufficient effort. Be sure you and the student's parents are together in regard to such expectations.

6. *Provide the student with a means to observe any progress.* Portfolios and journals as well as charts and graphs can serve this function.

Teach Concepts and Skills

7. *Start with what the student knows and build on that knowledge.* She probably already knows more than you realize. Corrective instruction should build on a student's strengths; it should consider what she is ready to learn. Typically, students need to understand subordinate mathematical concepts before they can be expected to integrate them into more complex ideas.

8. *Emphasize ideas that help a student organize what he learns.* Students often assume the concept or procedure they are learning applies only to the specific task they are involved in at the time. Connect new learnings with what the student already knows. When organized, new learnings can be more easily retrieved from memory as the need arises; also, they can be applied more readily in new contexts. Stress ideas such as multiple names for a number, commutativity, identity elements, and inverse relations.

9. *Stress the ability to estimate.* A student who makes errors in computation will become more accurate with the ability to determine the reasonableness of answers.

Provide Instruction

10. *Base instruction on your diagnosis.* Take into account the patterns you observed while collecting data. What strengths can you build upon?

11. *Use a great variety of instructional procedures and activities.* Be sure to choose activities that differ from the way the student was previously taught, because he may associate previous instruction with fear and failure. Students develop ideas from experiences embodying the idea, and perceive the concept as that which is common to all of the experiences. Therefore, variety is often necessary for adequate concept formation.

12. *Involve students in higher-order thinking activities.* If paper-and-pencil computation is your instructional goal, you may want to focus on a large problem or task that is challenging and interesting to the student. If instruction is to be fruitful, your goal must be to thoroughly engage the student; prompt him to *think about* what is happening during instruction.

13. *Connect content to experiences out of school.* A student who can tie what she is learning to experiences out of school is likely to be motivated to learn and be able to apply what she does learn.

14. *Encourage the student to think out loud while working through a problem situation.* Have him show how and explain why certain materials and procedures are being used. Speaking out loud often enables a student to focus more completely on the task at hand.

15. *Ask leading questions that encourage reflection.* Allow sufficient time for the student to reflect.

16. *Let the student state his understanding of a concept or procedure in his own language.* Do not always require the terminology of textbooks. It may be appropriate to say, for example, "Mathematicians have a special name for that idea, but I rather like your name for it!"

17. *Sequence instruction in smaller amounts of content when needed.* Some students having difficulty need smaller "chunks." A large task may overwhelm such students. When instruction is based upon a sequence that leads to the larger task, these students can focus on more immediately attainable goals. Help them to see that immediate goals lead along a path going in the desired direction.

18. *Move toward symbols gradually.* Move from manipulatives to two-dimensional representations and visualizations to the use of symbols.

19. *Emphasize careful penmanship and proper alignments of digits.* A student must be able to read the work and tell the value assigned to each place where a digit is written. Columns can also be labeled if appropriate.

Use Concrete Materials

20. *Let the student choose from materials available.* Whenever possible, a student should be permitted to select a game or activity from materials that are available and lead toward the goals of instruction. Identify activities for which the student has needed prerequisite skills and which lead to the goals of instruction; then let her have some choice in deciding what she will do.

21. *Encourage a student to use aids as long as they are of value.* Peer group pressure often keeps students from using aids even when the teacher places aids on a table; the use of aids needs to be encouraged actively. Occasionally, a student needs to be prompted to try thinking a process through with just paper and pencil; but students often give up aids when they feel safe without them. After all, using aids is time consuming.

Provide Practice

22. *Make sure a student understands the process before assigning practice.* We have known for some time that, in general, drill reinforces and makes more efficient that which a student *actually* practices.[57] In other words, if a student counts on his fingers to find a sum, drill will only tend to help him count on his fingers more efficiently. He may find sums more quickly, but he is apt to continue any immature procedure he is using. Avoid extensive use of practice activities at a time when they merely reinforce processes that are developmental. By looking for patterns of error and by conducting data-gathering interviews in an atmosphere in which incorrect responses are accepted, you can usually learn enough to decide if the student is ready for practice.

23. *Select practice activities which provide immediate confirmation.* When looking for games and drill activities to strengthen skills, choose activities that let students know immediately whether the answer is correct. Many games, manipulatives, and teacher-made devices provide such reinforcement.

24. *Spread practice time over several short periods.* Typically, a short series of examples (perhaps five to eight) is adequate to observe any error pattern. Longer series tend to reinforce erroneous procedures. If a correct procedure is being used, frequent practice with a limited number of examples is more fruitful than occasional practice with a large number of examples.

In Chapters 4–12 you will read about many specific suggestions for instruction. The lists of selected resources (pp. 266–273) point to additional ideas.

REFLECTING ON INSTRUCTION IN COMPUTATION

Students need to learn to use different forms of computation. An estimate is often appropriate, but when an exact answer is needed mental computation, calculators, or paper-and-pencil algorithms can be used. Our students need to be able to do *all* of these calculations, and be able to decide when each is most appropriate.

They also need to understand operations so they will know which operation is required in a particular problem situation. Many other concepts and principles need to be understood, including numeration, equals, compensation principles, and properties of operations.

We can help our students understand these ideas by choosing concrete materials that are accurate mathematically, and planning engaging activities in which students reflect on what they do with the materials. Such activities are often springboards to acquisition of specialized mathematical vocabulary.

Ultimately, our students will need to both understand and recall basic number combinations. We need to teach thinking strategies before seeking mastery of addition and multiplication number combinations; when mastery is appropriate, games are often helpful. We also need to make sure that our students learn to use basic number combinations for addition and multiplication to answer subtraction and division questions.

We can enhance our mathematics instruction by having our students both talk and write mathematics, and by using peer tutoring or cooperative groups. Graphic organizers can often help our students organize and relate what they are learning to other concepts and to the world around them. Sometimes it is helpful if we teach an alternative algorithm.

The following chapters focus on paper-and-pencil computations. As you read you will examine papers of students, identify error patterns, suggest appropriate instruction, and receive feedback yourself.

REFERENCES

1. Rowan, T. (1995). Mathematics principles. *Curriculum Handbook.* Alexandria, VA: Association for Supervision and Curriculum Development, p. 4.124.
2. National Council of Teachers of Mathematics. (2000). *Principles and standards for school mathematics.* Reston, VA: The Council, p. 79.
3. Ibid, p. 78.
4. Kazemi, E. (1998). Discourse that promotes conceptual understanding. *Teaching Children Mathematics* 4(7), 410–414.
5. Sowder, J. (1997). Place value as the key to teaching decimal operations. *Teaching Children Mathematics* 3(8), 448–453.
6. Ashlock, R. B., Johnson, M. L., Wilson, J. W., & Jones, W. L. (1983). *Guiding each child's learning of mathematics.* New York: Macmillan, p. 482.
7. Fuson, K. C., Wearne, D., Hiebert, J. C., Murray, H. G., Human, P. G., Olivier, A. I., Carpenter, T. P., & Fennema, E. (1977). Children's conceptual structures for multidigit numbers and methods of multidigit addition and subtraction. *Journal for Research in Mathematics Education* 28(2), pp. 130–162.

8. Jones, G. A., Thornton, C. A., Putt, I. J., Hill, K. M., Mogill, A. T., Rich, B. S., & Van Zoest, L. R. (1996). Multidigit number sense: A framework for instruction and assessment. *Journal for Research in Mathematics Education 27*(3), pp. 310–336.
9. For example see K. Faulkner, L. Levi, & T. Carpenter (1999). Children's understanding of equality: A foundation for algebra. *Teaching Children Mathematics 6*(4), pp. 232–236.
10. National Council of Teachers of Mathematics. (2000). *Principles and standards for school mathematics.* Reston, VA: The Council, p. 34.
11. Adapted from R. B. Ashlock, M. L. Johnson, J. W. Wilson, & W. L. Jones (1983). *Guiding each child's learning of mathematics.* New York: Macmillan, pp. 478–485.
12. National Council of Teachers of Mathematics. (2000). *Principles and standards for school mathematics.* Reston, VA: The Council, p. 35.
13. Hiebert, J. (1999). Relationships between research and the NCTM standards. *Journal for Research in Mathematics Education 30*(1), p. 15.
14. Reys, R. E. (1999). Basic skills should include mental computation. *Mathematics Education Dialogues 3*(1), pp. 11–12.
15. Mochón, S. & Román, J. (1998). Strategies of mental computation used by elementary and secondary school children. *Focus on Learning Problems in Mathematics 20*(4), pp. 35–49.
16. Reys, B. J. (1986). Teaching computational estimation: Concepts and strategies. In H. L. Schoen and M. J. Zweng (Eds.), *Estimation and Mental Computation* (pp. 31–44). Reston, VA: National Council of Teachers of Mathematics.
17. See the May/June 1999 issue of *Mathematics Education Dialogues 2*(3), a publication of the National Council of Teachers of Mathematics.
18. Dessart, D J, DeRidder, C. M. & Ellington, A. J. (1999). The research backs calculators. *Mathematics Education Dialogues 2*(3), p. 6.
19. See K. Mackey (1999). Do we need calculators? *Mathematics Education Dialogues 2*(3), p. 3.
20. Ockenga, E. (1976). Calculator ideas for the junior high classroom. *The Arithmetic Teacher 23*(7), p. 519.
21. National Council of Teachers of Mathematics. (2000). *Principles and standards for school mathematics.* Reston, VA: The Council, p. 84.
22. National Council of Teachers of Mathematics. (2000). *Principles and standards for school mathematics.* Reston, VA: The Council, pp. 84–87.
23. Carroll, W. M. & Porter, D. (1997). Invented strategies can develop meaningful mathematical procedures. *Teaching Children Mathematics 3*(7), pp. 370.
24. Curcio, F. R. & Schwartz, S. L. (1998). There are no algorithms for teaching algorithms. *Teaching Children Mathematics 5*(1), pp. 26–30.
25. Reys, B. J. & Reys, R. E. (1998). Computation in the elementary curriculum: Shifting the emphasis. *Teaching Children Mathematics 5*(4), pp. 236–241.
26. Usnick, V. E. (1992). Multidigit addition: A study of an alternate sequence. *Focus on Learning Problems in Mathematics 14*(3), pp. 53–62.
27. National Council of Teachers of Mathematics. (2000). *Principles and standards for school mathematics.* Reston, VA: The Council, p. 87.
28. Stiger, J. W. & Stevenson, H. W. (1991, spring). How Asian teachers polish each lesson to perfection. *American Educator 15*(1), p. 44.
29. For an explanation and for illustrations of this strategy, see K. Cramer and L. Karnowski (1995). The importance of informal language in representing mathematical ideas. *Teaching Children Mathematics 1*(6), pp. 332–335.

30. National Council of Teachers of Mathematics. (2000). *Principles and standards for school mathematics*. Reston, VA: The Council, p. 63.

31. Steele, D. F. (1999). Learning mathematical language in the zone of proximal development. *Teaching Children Mathematics 6*(1), p. 41.

32. A helpful chart of roots, meanings, related words, and notes for teaching can be found in R. N. Rubenstein (2000). Word origins. Building communication connections. *Mathematics Teaching in the Middle School 5*(8), pp. 493–498.

33. For help accomplishing this, see R. Corwin, J. Storeygard, & S. Price (1996). *Talking mathematics: Supporting children's voices*. Portsmouth, NH: Heinemann.

34. Thompson, P. W. (1992). Notations, conventions, and constraints: Contributions to effective uses of concrete materials in elementary mathematics. *Journal for Research in Mathematics Education 23*(2), p. 146.

35. Battista, M. T. (1999). The mathematical miseducation of America's youth: Ignoring research and scientific study in education. *Phi Delta Kappan 80*(6), p. 428.

36. Threlfall, J. & Frobisher, L. (1999). Patterns in processing and learning addition facts. In A. Orton (Ed.), *Pattern in teaching and learning of mathematics* (pp. 49–66). New York: Cassell.

37. Isaacs, A. C. & Carroll, W. M. (1999). Strategies for basic-fact instruction. *Teaching Children Mathematics 5*(9), pp. 508–515.

38. It is easier for students to count *forward* than backward for the unknown addend. This is actually a how-many-more meaning for subtraction, and leads to the helpful practice of using related addition facts to answer subtraction questions.

39. Teaching distribution of multiplication over addition (multiplying "in parts") can help students proceed independently when solving untaught or forgotten basic multiplication facts; they can derive facts from multiplication facts they already know. Show the multiplication by partitioning an array.

40. For example see G. W. Bright, J. G. Harvey, & M. M. Wheeler (1980). Using games to maintain multiplication basic facts. *Journal for Research in Mathematics Education 11*(5), pp. 379–385.

41. See Whitin, D. J. & Whitin, P. E. (1998). The "write" way to mathematical understanding, In L. J. Morrow and M. J. Kenney (Eds.), *The teaching and learning of algorithms in school mathematics* (pp. 161–169). Reston, VA: National Council of Teachers of Mathematics.

42. Farris, P. J. (1993). *Language arts: A process approach*. Madison, WI: Brown and Benchmark Publishers.

43. A very helpful list of writing prompts is available in J. K. Stenmark (Ed.). (1991). *Mathematics assessment: Myths, models, good questions, and practical suggestions* (p. 48). Reston, VA: National Council of Teachers of Mathematics.

44. Connolly, P. (1989). Writing and the ecology of learning. In P. Connolly & T. Vilardi (Eds.), *Writing to learn mathematics and science* (pp. 10–11). New York: Teachers College Press.

45. Rose, B. (1989). Writing and mathematics. In P. Connolly & T. Vilardi (Eds.), *Writing to learn mathematics and science* (p. 24). New York: Teachers College Press.

46. Several examples are included in B. H. Bartels (1995). Promoting mathematics connections with concept mapping. *Mathematics Teaching in the Middle School 1*(7), pp. 542–549. Also see A. J. Baroody & B. H. Bartels (2000). Using concept maps to link mathematical ideas. Mathematics Teaching in the Middle School 5(9), pp. 604–609.

47. Pearson, E. S. (1986). Summing it all up: Pre-1900 algorithms. *The Arithmetic Teacher 33*(7), pp. 38–41.
48. Carroll, W. M. & Porter, D. (1998). Alternative algorithms for whole-number operations. In L. J. Morrow and M. J. Kenney (Eds.), *The teaching and learning of algorithms in school mathematics* (pp. 106–114). Reston, VA: National Council of Teachers of Mathematics.
49. Philipp, R. A. (1996). Multicultural mathematics and alternative algorithms. *Teaching Children Mathematics 3*(3), pp. 128–133.
50. Hutchings, B. (1976). Low-stress algorithms. In D. Nelson & R. E. Reys (Eds.), *Measurement in school mathematics* (pp. 218–239). Reston, VA: National Council of Teachers of Mathematics.
51. Signer, B. (1985, winter). The method of equal addition: It's rational! *Dimensions in Mathematics 5*, pp. 15–17.
52. National Council of Teachers of Mathematics. (2000). *Principles and standards for school mathematics*. Reston, VA: The Council.
53. Barone, M. M. & Taylor, L. (1996). Peer tutoring with mathematics manipulatives: A practical guide. *Teaching Children Mathematics 3*(1), pp. 8–15.
54. See Yakel, E., Cobb, P., Wood, T., Wheatley, G., & Merkel, G. (1990). The importance of social interaction in children's construction of mathematical knowledge. In T. Cooney Jr. & C. R. Hirsch (Eds.), *Teaching and learning mathematics in the 1990s* (pp. 12–21). Reston, VA: National Council of Teachers of Mathematics.
55. Lambdin, D. V. & Walker, V. L. (1994). Planning for classroom portfolio assessment. *The Arithmetic Teacher 41*(6), p. 318.
56. See J. Ensign (1998). Parents, portfolios, and personal mathematics. *Teaching Children Mathematics 4*(6), pp. 346–351.
57. See W. A. Brownell and C. B. Chazal (1935, September). The effects of premature drill in third grade arithmetic. *The Journal of Educational Research 29*, pp. 17–28ff; also in R. B. Ashlock & W. L. Herman, Jr. (1970). *Current research in elementary school mathematics*. New York: Macmillan, pp. 170–188.

PART TWO

⌐⌐

Helping Students Who Have Learned Error Patterns

In Part 2, you have the opportunity to identify patterns in student papers. You will be able to suggest what might be done to help our students who are experiencing difficulty.

Student papers are presented so you can study them and infer what the student was actually thinking and doing when completing the paper. Then you are referred to a page later in the chapter where the difficulty is discussed, and you have an opportunity to suggest instructional activities that may help the student. Finally, you are referred to a page where instructional activities for that student are described, and you can compare your suggestions with those of the author.

Note that some papers include a few correct answers, though the student's thinking will not always lead to a correct result. When this happens, students are encouraged to believe that their thinking is correct and their procedure is satisfactory. Teachers and parents find it even more difficult to realize there is an error pattern.

ᄂ

Chapter 4

Whole Numbers:
Addition and Subtraction

ロ刀

When planning instruction, we need to consider sufficient student data to divulge any *patterns* of incorrect and immature computations. We need to be alert to error patterns in student papers.

On the following pages, you will find examples of papers on which students practiced adding and subtracting whole numbers. With these simulated student papers, you have the opportunity to develop your own skill in identifying error patterns. These papers contain the error patterns of real students observed by teachers in ordinary school settings; they are like students in our own classrooms.

Look for a pattern of errors then check your findings by using the error pattern yourself with the examples provided. Be careful not to decide on the error pattern too quickly. (Students often make hasty decisions and, as a result, adopt the kind of erroneous procedures presented in this book.) When you think you see a pattern, verify your hypothesis by looking at the other examples on the student's paper.

You will read about each students' procedures and have opportunities to suggest needed instruction. It is always important for a teacher to have in mind more than one instructional strategy; therefore, try to suggest at least two different activities to help each student. Your suggestions can then be compared with the author's suggestions.

To further test your ability to identify patterns, turn to Appendix A where you will find additional student papers. A key is provided.

IDENTIFYING PATTERNS

Error Pattern N-C-1

There were 7 cookies on the plate, but Mother put 8 more cookies on the plate. How many cookies are on the plate now?

Gary said there are 14 cookies on the plate now. Look at his written work carefully. Can you find the error pattern he has followed?

Name _Gary_

A. $7 + 8 = 14$

B. $8 + 6 = 13$

C. $7 + 6 = 12$

D. $8 + 5 = 12$

Did you find Gary's error pattern? Check yourself by using his error pattern to determine these sums.

E. $7 + 7 =$ _____

F. $6 + 8 =$ _____

Next, turn to Pattern N-C-1 on page 106 to see if you were able to identify the error pattern. *Why* might Gary use such a procedure?

Error Pattern A-W-1

Collins has 74 marbles in one jar, and 56 marbles in his other jar. How many marbles does Collins have?

Mike came up with an answer that is over a thousand. Obviously, he is not estimating yet. Can you find the error pattern he followed?

Name _Mike_

A.
$$74$$
$$+56$$
$$\overline{1210}$$

B.
$$35$$
$$+92$$
$$\overline{127}$$

C.
$$67$$
$$+18$$
$$\overline{715}$$

D.
$$56$$
$$+97$$
$$\overline{1413}$$

Did you find his error pattern? Check yourself by using his error pattern to determine these sums.

E. 43
  $+65$

F. 88
  $+39$

Next, turn to Pattern A-W-1 on page 106 to see if you were able to identify the error pattern. How is Mike finding his answers? Why might he use such a procedure?

Error Pattern A-W-2

Mary gets some correct sums, but many of her answers are not even reasonable. What error pattern is Mary following in her written work?

Name _Mary_

A.
$$432$$
$$+265$$
$$697$$

B.
$$74$$
$$+43$$
$$18$$

C.
$$385$$
$$+667$$
$$9\ 1\ 16$$

D.
$$563$$
$$+545$$
$$1\ 1\ 8$$

Check to see if you found Mary's pattern by using her erroneous procedure to compute these examples.

E. 254
  $+535$

F. 618
  $+782$

Why might Mary or any student use such a procedure? Is she estimating? What can you say about her number sense? Next, turn to page 107 to see if you were able to identify her error pattern.

Error Pattern A-W-3

There were 56 students in Ms. Jones's gym class. Six more students were added to the class. How many students are in the class now?

When Carol adds she gets many of her answers correct, but she came up with 17 students for this problem. That is not even close. What is wrong? Can you find the error pattern she followed?

Name *Carol*

A.	B.	C.	D.	E.
56	18	8	42	85
+ 6	+30	+16	+56	+ 6
17	48	15	98	19

Did you find her error pattern? Check yourself by using her procedure to determine these sums.

F.	G.	H.
26	60	74
+ 3	+24	+ 5

What does Carol understand about numerals and estimating? What can you say about her "number sense"? Why might she be using such a procedure? To make sure you have identified her procedure, turn to page 108.

Error Pattern A-W-4

Dorothy does not seem to be thinking about what she is doing as she practices addition with paper and pencil. Her answers are quite unreasonable. Can you find her pattern of errors?

Name *Dorothy*

A.	B.	C.	D.
'75	'67	'84	'59
+ 8	+ 4	+ 9	6
163	111	183	125

Did you find Dorothy's procedure? What does Dorothy really understand about numerals and place value? What does she not yet understand? Will giving her more examples like this help her? Make sure you found her procedure by using her error pattern to compute these examples.

E. 46
+ 8

F. 98
+ 3

When you complete Examples E and F, turn to page 109 and see if you identified the pattern correctly. Why might Dorothy be using such a procedure?

Error Pattern S-W-1

Cheryl was very successful with paper-and-pencil subtraction until recently. Has she become careless, or is there another reason for her present difficulty? Look carefully at Cheryl's written work. What error pattern did she follow?

Note: Cheryl used a different procedure for one of the examples.

Name *Cheryl*

A. 32
− 16
  16

B. 245
− 137
  112

C. 524
− 298
  374

D. 135
− 67
  132

Did you find her error pattern? Check yourself by using her procedure for these examples.

E. 458
− 372

F. 241
− 96

What does Cheryl understand about subtraction? What does she understand about numerals and place value? What does she *not* understand? Why might a student use such a procedure? We call the

answer to a subtraction example a "difference." Would that have anything to do with her use of this procedure? Now turn to Pattern S-W-1
on page 110 to see if you were able to identify the error pattern.

Error Pattern S-W-2

George recently learned to regroup (or "rename"), and at first he got
correct answers. But soon there were difficulties when he met simple
problems like the following:

> Pat had 197 different marbles in his marble collection. But
> he traded 43 of them for baseball cards. How many dif-
> ferent marbles does he have now?

Look carefully at George's written work. Is he using estimation?
What does he understand about numeration and subtraction? What
does he *not* understand? What error pattern did he follow?

Name _George_

$$
\begin{array}{ccc}
\text{A.} & \text{B.} & \text{C.} \\
\begin{array}{r} 1\,9\,7 \\ -\ 4\ 3 \\ \hline 1\,4\,4 \end{array} &
\begin{array}{r} 1\,9\,6 \\ -\ 2\ 3 \\ \hline 1\ 4\,3 \end{array} &
\begin{array}{r} 3\,9\,4 \\ -\ 5\ 9 \\ \hline 3\ 2\,5 \end{array}
\end{array}
$$

Did you find his error pattern? Check yourself by using his procedure for these examples.

$$
\begin{array}{cc}
\text{D.} & \text{E.} \\
\begin{array}{r} 2\,7\,3 \\ -\ 3\,8 \\ \hline \end{array} &
\begin{array}{r} 2\,8\,5 \\ -\ 6\,3 \\ \hline \end{array}
\end{array}
$$

Why might a student use such a procedure? Now turn to Pattern
S-W-2 on page 111 to see if you identified the error pattern.

Error Pattern S-W-3

Donna's answers seem reasonable to her, and most of them are correct. But she keeps getting incorrect answers when she subtracts.
Look carefully at her written work. Do you find an error pattern?

Name *Donna*

A.
$$147$$
$$- 20$$
$$\overline{120}$$

B.
$$624$$
$$-323$$
$$\overline{301}$$

C.
$$527$$
$$-304$$
$$\overline{203}$$

D.
$$805$$
$$-201$$
$$\overline{604}$$

Did you find her pattern? Check yourself by using her procedure for these examples.

E.
$$446$$
$$-302$$

F.
$$760$$
$$-230$$

Why might a student use such a procedure? Has Donna learned something that she is using inappropriately? Now turn to Pattern S-W-3 on page 112 to see if you actually found Donna's pattern of errors.

Error Pattern S-W-4

Barbara seemed to be doing well with subtraction until recently. Look carefully at her written work. Can you find a pattern of errors?

Name *Barbara*

A.
$$6\overset{8}{\cancel{7}}\overset{1}{\cancel{3}}$$
$$-248$$
$$\overline{445}$$

B.
$$\overset{2}{\cancel{3}}25$$
$$-151$$
$$\overline{174}$$

C.
$$\overset{5}{\cancel{7}}\overset{1}{2}\overset{}{6}$$
$$-349$$
$$\overline{287}$$

D.
$$\overset{2}{\cancel{4}}\overset{1}{3}\overset{}{4}$$
$$-276$$
$$\overline{68}$$

What does she know how to do? What does she *not* understand? Do you think she is using estimation? Make sure you found the pattern by using her procedure for these examples.

E. 436
-172

F. 625
-348

What might have caused Barbara to begin using such a procedure? Turn to Pattern S-W-4 on page 112 to see if you actually found Barbara's pattern of errors.

DESCRIBING INSTRUCTION

Error Pattern N-C-1
(from Gary's paper on page 100)

If you discovered Gary's procedure, you completed Examples E and F as shown.

E. $7 + 7 = \underline{\quad 13 \quad}$ F. $6 + 8 = \underline{\quad 13 \quad}$

During an interview with his teacher, Gary admitted he uses his fingers to count addition sums. So his teacher gave him an addition example and said, "Lots of boys and girls use their fingers. Show me how you use *your* fingers." Gary counted out the first addend, then used the last finger already used as the first finger for counting out the second addend.

If you were Gary's teacher, what would you do? What help would you provide? Briefly describe two instructional activities you believe would correct his error pattern and provide the understanding needed.

1. _____

2. _____

After you describe at least two activities, turn to page 113 to see if your suggestions are among those listed.

Error Pattern A-W-1
(used by Mike on page 100)

Using the error pattern, Examples E and F would be computed as shown.

E. $\begin{array}{r} 43 \\ +65 \\ \hline 108 \end{array}$ F. $\begin{array}{r} 88 \\ +39 \\ \hline 1117 \end{array}$

If your responses are the same as these, you were able to identify Mike's erroneous computational procedure. The ones were added and recorded, then the tens were added and recorded (or vice versa). The sum of the ones and the sum of the tens were each recorded without regard to place value in the sum. Note that Mike may have applied some knowledge of place value in his work with the two addends, *i.e.*, he may have treated the 88 in Example F as 8 tens and 8 ones, and his answer as 11 tens and 17 ones. It is also true that Mike may have merely thought "8 plus 9 equals 17, and 8 plus 3 equals 11." I have found many students who think through such a problem in this way; some of these students also emphasize that you add 8 and 9 first because "you add the ones first."

Mike has the idea of adding ones with ones—possibly from work with bundles of sticks and single sticks. He apparently knows he should consider all of the single sticks together. He *may* know a rule for exchanging or regrouping 10 single sticks for one bundle of 10, but, if he does, he has not applied the rule to these examples. Previous instruction may not have given adequate emphasis to the mechanics of recording sums.

Cox found, in her study of systematic errors among children in regular second- through sixth-grade classrooms, that 67% of the children who made systematic errors when adding two two-digit numbers with renaming made this particular error.[1]

If you were Mike's teacher, how would you help him? Describe two instructional activities that might correct the error pattern.

1. _____

2. _____

When you have completed your responses, turn to page 114 to see if your suggestions are among the alternatives described.

Error Pattern A-W-2
(from Mary's paper on page 101)

If you used Mary's error pattern, you completed Examples E and F as they are shown.

E.
$$
\begin{array}{r}
2\ 5\ 4 \\
+5\ 3\ 5 \\
\hline
7\ 8\ 9
\end{array}
$$

F.
$$
\begin{array}{r}
3\ 2 \\
6\ 1\ 8 \\
+7\ 8\ 2 \\
\hline
1\ 1\ 1\ 2
\end{array}
$$

This pattern is a reversal of the procedure used in the usual algorithm—without regard for place value. Addition is performed from left to right, and, when the sum of a column is 10 or greater, the left figure is recorded and the right figure is placed above the next column to the right.

If you were Mary's teacher, what corrective procedures might you follow? Describe two instructional activities that might help Mary add correctly.

1. _____

2. _____

When your responses are complete, turn to page 115 and see if your suggestions are among the alternatives described.

Error Pattern A-W-3

(from Carol's paper on page 102)

If you found Carol's error pattern, your results are the same as the erroneous computation shown.

F.
$$
\begin{array}{r}
2\ 6 \\
+\ \ \ 3 \\
\hline
1\ 1
\end{array}
$$

G.
$$
\begin{array}{r}
6\ 0 \\
+2\ 4 \\
\hline
8\ 4
\end{array}
$$

H.
$$
\begin{array}{r}
7\ 4 \\
+\ \ \ 5 \\
\hline
1\ 6
\end{array}
$$

Carol misses examples in which one of the addends is written as a single digit. When working such examples, she adds the three digits as if they were all units. When both addends are two-digit numbers, she appears to add correctly. However, it is quite probable that Carol is not applying any knowledge of place value with either type of example. She may be merely adding units in every case. (When both addends are two-digit numbers, she adds units in straight columns. When one addend is a one-digit number, she adds the three digits along a curve.) If this is the way Carol is thinking, she will probably experience even more failure and frustration when she begins to add and subtract examples that require renaming.

How would you help Carol? Describe at least two instructional activities you believe would correct Carol's error pattern.

1. _____

2. _____

After you have described at least two activities, turn to page 116 and compare your suggestions with those listed there.

Error Pattern A-W-4

(from Dorothy's paper on page 102)

Using Dorothy's error pattern, Examples E and F would be computed as shown below.

E.
$$
\begin{array}{r}
\overset{\text{'}}{4}\,6 \\
+\ \ 8 \\
\hline
1\ 3\ 4
\end{array}
$$

F.
$$
\begin{array}{r}
\overset{\text{'}}{9}\,8 \\
+\ \ 3 \\
\hline
1\ 3\ 1
\end{array}
$$

Dorothy is not having difficulty with basic number combinations, but higher decade addition situations are confusing her. She tries to use the regular addition algorithm; however, when she adds the tens column she adds in the one-digit number again.

If Dorothy has been introduced to the multiplication algorithm, she may persist in seeing similar patterns for computation whenever numerals are arranged as she has seen them in multiplication examples. Changing operations when the arrangement of digits is similar is difficult for some children. An interview with Dorothy may help you determine if she really knows how to add problems like these. When working with a child who tends to carry over one situation into her perception of another, avoid extensive practice at a given time on any single procedure.

How would you help Dorothy? Describe at least two instructional activities that would help Dorothy replace her erroneous pattern with a correct procedure.

1. _____

2. _____

When both activities are described, turn to page 117 and compare your suggestions with those recorded there.

Error Pattern S-W-1

(from Cheryl's paper on page 103)

Using the error pattern, Examples E and F would be computed as shown below.

E.
$$\begin{array}{r} 458 \\ -372 \\ \hline 126 \end{array}$$

F.
$$\begin{array}{r} 241 \\ -96 \\ \hline 255 \end{array}$$

Did you identify the error pattern? As a general rule, the ones are subtracted and recorded, then the tens are subtracted and recorded, and so on. Apparently Cheryl is considering each position (ones, tens, and so on) as a separate subtraction problem. In Example E she probably did not think of the numbers 458 and 372, but only of 8 and 2, 5 and 7, and 4 and 3. Further, in subtracting single-digit numbers, she does not conceive of the upper figure (minuend) as the number in a set and the lower figure (subtrahend) as the number in a subset. When subtracting ones Cheryl may think of the larger of the two numbers as the number of the set, and the smaller as the number to be removed from the set. Or she may merely compare the two single-digit numbers much as she would match sets one to one or place rods side by side to find a difference. In Example F, she would think "1 and 6, the difference is 5." She uses the same procedure when subtracting tens and hundreds. Cheryl may have merely overgeneralized commutativity for addition, and assumed that subtraction is also commutative.

Note that Example A on page 103 is correct. This example includes much smaller numbers than the other examples. It may be that Cheryl counted from 16 to 32, or she may have used some kind of number line. If she did think of 32 as "20 plus 12" in order to subtract, it may be that she applies renaming procedures only to smaller numbers that she can somehow conceptualize, but she breaks up larger numbers in the manner described above.

Has Cheryl heard rules in the classroom or at home that she is applying in her own way? Perhaps she has heard "Always subtract the little number from the big one" and "Stay in the column when you subtract."

Children frequently adopt this error pattern. For children in regular classrooms who were subtracting a two-digit number from a two-digit number with renaming, Cox found that 83% of the children with systematic errors used this particular procedure.[2]

If you were Cheryl's teacher, what would you do? Describe two instructional activities that might help Cheryl correct the error pattern.

1. _____

2. _____

After you have finished writing your responses, turn to page 118 to see if your suggestions are among the alternatives described.

Error Pattern S-W-2

(from George's paper on page 104)

Did you identify the error pattern George used?

D.
$$2\overset{6}{\cancel{7}}{}^{\prime}3$$
$$-\ 3\ 8$$
$$\overline{2\ 3\ 5}$$

E.
$$2\overset{7}{\cancel{8}}{}^{\prime}5$$
$$-\ 6\ 3$$
$$\overline{2\ 1\ 1\ 2}$$

George has learned to "borrow," or rename, in subtraction. In fact, he renames whether he needs to or not. It is possible that George would be able to rename one ten as 10 ones, and it is also possible that he could interpret the answer (in Example E) as 2 hundreds, 1 ten, and 12 ones. But his final answer does not take account of conventional place-value notation.

You have observed that the answer to Example D is correct. George's procedure is correct for a subtraction example that requires renaming tens as ones. However, George has overgeneralized. He does not distinguish between examples that require renaming and examples that do not require renaming. The fact that some of his answers are correct may reinforce his perception that the procedure he is using is appropriate for all subtraction examples.

Many children rename the minuend when it is unnecessary. In Cox's study, when children in regular classrooms subtracted a two-digit number from a two-digit number with no renaming, 75% of the children who used a systematic erroneous procedure did rename the minuend, although it was inappropriate to do so.[3]

How would you help George with his problem? Describe two instructional activities that would help George replace his error pattern with a correct computational procedure.

1. _____

2. _____

After you complete your two descriptions, turn to page 119 and compare what you have written with the suggestions presented there.

Error Pattern S-W-3

(from Donna's paper on page 105)

Did you find Donna's error pattern?

E. 446
   −302
   ─────
    104

F. 760
   −230
   ─────
    530

Although Donna subtracts 0 − 0 = 0 correctly, she consistently writes "0" for the missing addend (difference) whenever the known addend (subtrahend) is zero. She may be confusing this situation with multiplication combinations in which zero is a factor. At any rate, she writes nine of the basic subtraction combinations incorrectly because of this one difficulty.

We ought to be able to help Donna with a problem of this sort. How would you help her? Describe two instructional activities you think would enable Donna to subtract correctly.

1. _____

2. _____

Did you describe at least two activities? (It is important to have more than one possible instructional procedure in mind when working remedially with a child.) If so, turn to page 120 and compare your suggestions with the suggestions described there.

Error Pattern S-W-4

(from Barbara's paper on page 105)

Did you find Barbara's error pattern?

E. 436
   −172
   ─────
    264

F. 625
   −348
   ─────
    187

Barbara appeared to be doing well with subtraction until recently, when renaming more than once was introduced. She apparently had been thinking something like "Take 1 from 4 and put the 1 in front of the 3" (Example E). Now she has extended this procedure so that, in Example F, she thinks, "In order to subtract (*i.e.*, in order to use a simple subtraction combination), I need a 1 in front of the 5 and a 1 in front of the 2. Take *two* 1s from the 6. . . ." Note that if Barbara had not been showing her work with crutches of some sort, it would have been much more difficult to find the pattern.

Help is needed—promptly—before she reinforces her error pattern with further practice. How would you help her? Describe two instructional activities you think would make it possible for Barbara to subtract correctly, even in examples such as these.

1. _____

2. _____

When you have described two instructional activities, turn to page 122 and compare your suggestions with those listed there.

When students learn one algorithm without adequate conceptual grounding and are then taught another algorithm, they sometimes confuse the two procedures. Carlos learned the equal-additions algorithm (also called the European-Latino algorithm), but was later taught the procedure commonly taught in the United States. What he is doing now makes no sense mathematically, for he is combining the algorithms in a mechanical way.[4] Can you figure out what he is doing?

$$\begin{array}{r} {}^{1}_{3}\ {}^{15} \\ 45 \\ -\ 29 \\ \hline 66 \end{array} \qquad \begin{array}{r} {}^{1}_{4}\ {}^{12} \\ 52 \\ -34 \\ \hline 88 \end{array} \qquad \begin{array}{r} {}^{1}\ {}^{5}\ {}^{12} \\ 62 \\ -\ 17 \\ \hline 75 \end{array}$$

CONSIDERING ALTERNATIVES

Error Pattern N-C-1
(from pages 100 and 106)

It was noted that this child counted out the first addend, then used the last finger already used as the first finger for counting out the second addend.

E. $7 + 7 = \underline{/3}$ F. $6 + 8 = \underline{13}$

You suggested instructional activities to help this child. Are any of these among your suggestions?

1. *Make sets of marks.* Let the child make a set of marks for the first addend, then a set for the second addend. Ask, "Are there 10?" Let the child circle 10 marks, and count on to find the total number.
2. *Use an all-new set.* Explain that the finger which was counted twice cannot be a part of both sets. For the second number, an *all-new* set is needed.
3. *Count sets of objects and fingers.* Put a row of objects on the table and let the child count off a set for the first addend, then a set for the second addend. (Note when the first set is complete and the fact that the next object is part of a new set.) The total amount in both sets can then be counted. Repeat the same activity, but let the child use his fingers to make sets.

Error Pattern A-W-1

(from pages 100 and 106)

See if your suggestions are among those listed below.

E.
$$
\begin{array}{r}
43 \\
+\,65 \\
\hline
108
\end{array}
$$

F.
$$
\begin{array}{r}
88 \\
+\,39 \\
\hline
1117
\end{array}
$$

Note: Be sure to extend your diagnosis by interviewing the student. Let Mike "think out loud" for you. Unless you do this, you will not even know whether he is adding the ones or the tens first.

1. *Use bundles of 10 and single sticks.* Show both addends, then "make a 10" as may have been done in past instruction. Emphasize that we always need to start with the single sticks. Apply a rule for exchanging or regrouping if it is possible. Then make 10 bundles of 10, if possible. With paper and pencil, record what is done *step by step*.
2. *Provide the student with a set of numerals (0–9) and a frame for the answer.* Each box of the frame should be of a size that will enclose only one digit. Let the student use the cardboard or plastic numerals to record sums for problems. This activ-

ity should help the student remember to apply the rule for exchanging.

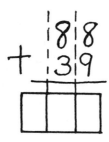

3. *Play chip-trading games.* To develop the idea for exchanging many for one, play games in which the values of chips are defined in terms of our numeration place-value pattern. However, it is easier to begin with bases less than 10. A child rolls a die and receives as many units as indicated on the die. He then exchanges for higher valued chips according to the rule of the game (five for one if base five, 10 for one if base ten). Play proceeds similarly. The first child to get a specific chip of a high value wins. Such games are described in *Chip Trading Activities, Book I.*[5]

Error Pattern A-W-2
(from pages 101 and 107)

What instructional activities do you suggest to help Mary correct the error pattern illustrated? See if your suggestions are among those described.

E.
$$254$$
$$+535$$
$$\overline{789}$$

F.
$$6\overset{3}{1}\overset{2}{8}$$
$$+782$$
$$\overline{1112}$$

1. *Estimate sums.* Even *before* computing, the sum can be estimated. For instance, in Example F it can be determined in advance that the sum is more than 1,300.
2. *Use base-ten blocks and show the sum.* Have her use base-ten blocks to show both addends, and challenge her to show the total amount with as few pieces of wood as possible. (Ten of one size can always be traded for the next larger size.) Then have her examine her written work again. Can she make up a rule to help her remember to make 10 if she can?

3. *Use a gamelike activity with a pattern board, base blocks, and a bank.* Help students understand place values, and begin computation with units by making the algorithm a written record of moves in a gamelike activity. A pattern board serves as an organizing center. Appendix C describes such activities and includes an illustration for addition with whole numbers.

Error Pattern A-W-3

(from pages 102 and 108)

Are your suggestions among those listed?

F.   26   G.   60   H.   74
   + 3   + 24   + 5
   ─────   ─────   ─────
    1 1   84   16

Note: An interview with Carol may provide very helpful information. Is she able to explain the examples that were worked correctly? Does she identify tens and units? Does she reason that units must be added to units, and tens must be added to tens?

1. *Play Pick-a-Number.* This game stresses the different values a digit may signify in various positions. Use cards with 0–9. Each player draws a form like this:

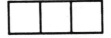

One player picks a card and reads the number, and each player writes that number in one of the spaces. Repeat until all blanks are full. The player showing the greatest number wins.

2. *Show each addend.* After the student shows both addends with base-ten blocks or with bundles of 10 and single sticks, have her collect the units and record the total number of units. She may then collect the tens and record the total number of tens.

3. *Draw a line to separate tens and units.* This procedure may help with the mechanics of notation if the student understands the need to add units to units and tens to tens.

$$
\begin{array}{c|c}
T & U \\
 & 3 \\
+\ 2 & 6 \\
\hline
2 & 9
\end{array}
\qquad
\begin{array}{c|c}
T & U \\
6 & 0 \\
+\ 2 & 4 \\
\hline
8 & 4
\end{array}
\qquad
\begin{array}{c|c}
T & U \\
7 & 4 \\
+\ & 5 \\
\hline
7 & 9
\end{array}
$$

Error Pattern A-W-4

(from pages 102 and 109)

You have suggested instructional activities for helping Dorothy (or any student) using this error pattern. Are your suggestions among those listed?

E.
$$
\begin{array}{r}
{}^{1}4\ 6 \\
+\quad 8 \\
\hline
1\ 3\ 4
\end{array}
$$

F.
$$
\begin{array}{r}
{}^{1}9\ 8 \\
+\quad 3 \\
\hline
1\ 3\ 1
\end{array}
$$

Note: The following suggestions assume the student is *not* confusing these higher decade situations with multiplication.

1. *Explain the process naming units and tens.* Let the student explain the addition to you in terms of units (or ones) and tens. If her understanding of place value is adequate, this procedure may be sufficient to clear up the difficulty. It may be necessary to have her use base-ten blocks or a place-value chart.
2. *Label units and tens.* Have the student label each column. The use of squared paper may also help if only one digit is written in each square.

$$
\begin{array}{|c|c|}
\hline
T & U \\
\hline
1 & \\
\hline
4 & 6 \\
\hline
+ & 8 \\
\hline
5 & 4 \\
\hline
\end{array}
$$

3. *Make higher decade sequences.* Help the student discover the pattern illustrated, then have her complete similar sequences. She may want to make up a few patterns all on her own.

$$
\begin{array}{c}
6 \\
+8 \\
\hline
14
\end{array}
\qquad
\begin{array}{c}
16 \\
+8 \\
\hline
24
\end{array}
\qquad
\begin{array}{c}
26 \\
+8 \\
\hline
34
\end{array}
\qquad
\begin{array}{c}
36 \\
+8 \\
\hline
44
\end{array}
\ \cdots\ \bullet
$$

Error Pattern S-W-1
(from pages 103 and 110)

Are your activities among those described?

$$
\text{E.}\quad
\begin{array}{c}
458 \\
-372 \\
\hline
126
\end{array}
\qquad\qquad
\text{F.}\quad
\begin{array}{c}
241 \\
-\ 96 \\
\hline
255
\end{array}
$$

Note: Be sure to extend your diagnosis by interviewing the student and letting her think out loud as she works similar examples. Does she use the erroneous procedure only with greater numbers? Does she, on her own initiative, question the reasonableness of her answers? (In Example F, the result is greater than the minuend.)

1. *Use bundles of 100, bundles of 10, and single sticks.* Let the student show the "number altogether," that is, the minuend or sum shown by the upper numeral. Pose the problem of removing the number of sticks shown by the lower numeral. Any verbal problems presented in this context should describe take-away rather than comparison situations. Trading or exchanging as needed could be done at a bank. (If more than one child is having this difficulty, pose the problem to a pair of children who will work on the task together.) Eventually, guidance should be provided to help the student remove units first, then tens, and so on.

2. *Use a learning center for renaming.* For Cheryl and others with similar difficulties, a simple learning center could be set up to help them rename a minuend and select the most useful name for that number in a specific subtraction problem. One possibility is to have a sorting task in which the child decides which cards show another name for a given number and

which show an entirely different number. A second task would be to consider all the different names for the given number and decide which of the names would be most useful for computing subtraction examples that have the given number as the minuend. Ask, "Which name will let us use the subtraction number combinations we know?"

$$\begin{array}{r} 352 \\ -128 \end{array}$$ $350+2$ $340+12$

3. *Use base-ten blocks.* Proceed as in Activity 1.
4. *Use a place-value chart.* Proceed similarly.

Error Pattern S-W-2

(from pages 104 and 111)

Are the activities you suggested for George similar to any of the activities described?

D.
$$\begin{array}{r} 2\ \overset{6}{\cancel{7}}\ \overset{1}{3} \\ -\quad 3\ 8 \\ \hline 2\ 3\ 5 \end{array}$$

E.
$$\begin{array}{r} 2\ \overset{7}{\cancel{8}}\ \overset{1}{5} \\ -\quad 6\ 3 \\ \hline 2\ 1\ 1\ 2 \end{array}$$

Note: Helpful instruction will emphasize (1) the ability to distinguish between subtraction problems requiring regrouping in order to use basic subtraction combinations and subtraction problems not requiring regrouping, and (2) mechanics of notation.

1. *Use a physical representation for the minuend (sum).* If the minuend of Example E is represented physically (with base blocks or bundles of sticks), questions can be posed such as "Can I take away 3 units *without* trading?" or "When do I need to trade and when is it not necessary for me to trade?"

2. *Replace computation with* yes *or* no. Focus on the critical skill of distinguishing by presenting a row of subtraction problems for which the differences are *not* to be computed. Have the child simply write yes or no for each example to indicate the decision whether regrouping is or is not needed. If this is difficult, physical materials should be available for the child to use. (See Activity 1.)

3. *Use a number line and estimate.* Let the student use a number line to help with the estimate. A number line showing at least hundreds and tens may be helpful for this purpose. Ask, "Will the answer be more than a hundred? less than a hundred?"

Error Pattern S-W-3
(from pages 105 and 112)

You have described two instructional activities you think would help students like Donna with this zero difficulty. Are any of your suggestions among those listed?

E.
$$
\begin{array}{r}
446 \\
-302 \\
\hline
104
\end{array}
$$

F.
$$
\begin{array}{r}
760 \\
-230 \\
\hline
530
\end{array}
$$

1. *Use base blocks or bundled sticks to picture the computation.* Show the sum (the minuend) of a given subtraction problem.

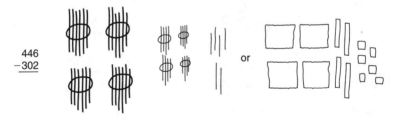

$$
\begin{array}{r}
446 \\
-302 \\
\hline
\end{array}
$$

Sit beside the student and arrange the materials so that units are to the right and hundreds to the left as in the algorithm. For Example E, let the student remove the number (of sticks or blocks) shown by the given addend, beginning with the units. After the student removes a subset of 2 units, you record the fact that 4 units remain. After the student removes an empty set of tens, you record the fact that 4 tens remain, and so on. For another example, you remove the subset while the *student* records the number remaining each time.

2. *Try a sorting game.* If the student has been introduced to the multiplication combinations for zero, there may be confusion between the zero property for multiplication and the zero properties for other operations. For the zero combinations of arithmetic, prepare cards similar to the ones shown.

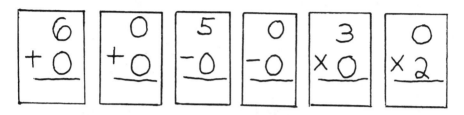

(Vertical notation is suggested in this case because it appears in the algorithm. It may be appropriate to include division number sentences as well, e.g., $0 \div 3 = \square$.) To create an individual activity or a game for two, the cards can be sorted into two sets—those with zero for the answer and those that do not have zero for an answer.

3. *Use a calculator.* Have the student try several examples of adding a zero, subtracting a zero, and multiplying by zero. Then ask her to state a generalization or rule for each operation. Have her compare the rules to see how they are alike or different.

Error Pattern S-W-4

(from pages 105 and 112)

Do you find, among the suggestions listed, your suggestions for helping Barbara?

E.
$$\overset{3}{\cancel{4}}\overset{1}{3}6$$
$$-172$$
$$\overline{264}$$

F.
$$\overset{4}{\cancel{5}}\overset{1}{2}5$$
$$-348$$
$$\overline{187}$$

1. *Teach both situations, one column at a time.* Present problem situations involving subtraction with two two-digit numbers—situations that involve regrouping a ten as ones, and situations that do not. Make sure students can distinguish between these situations and do the computation required before introducing two three-digit numbers. Again, teach both situations together and focus on distinguishing between situations that require regrouping a hundred as tens from those that do not.[6]

    Note: Asking a student to check his computation may accomplish little in this situation. "Adding up" may only confirm that individual subtraction combinations have been correctly recalled. The following activities are suggested to help a student keep in mind the *total quantity* from which a lesser number is being subtracted.

2. *Use base-ten blocks to show the sum (minuend).* Pointing to the known addend (subtrahend) ask, "Do we need to trade so we can remove this many? What trading must we do?" As appropriate, trade a ten for ones and *immediately* record the action; as appropriate, trade a hundred for tens and record that action. Stress the need to proceed step by step. Let the student trade and remove blocks while you record the action, then reverse the process. While you trade and remove blocks (thinking aloud as you do), let the student make the record.

3. *Use a gamelike activity with a pattern board, base blocks, and a bank.* Help students understand place values and the algorithm itself by making it a written record of moves in a gamelike activity. A pattern board serves as an organizing center. Appendix C describes such activities and includes an illustration for subtraction with whole numbers.

CONCLUSION

Help students learn to choose when an estimate is needed and when an exact answer is needed; and help them learn to choose the most appropriate way to get that exact answer when they are to add or subtract whole numbers. Many times the most appropriate procedure is a paper-and-pencil procedure.

As you help each student learn addition and subtraction procedures, focus on concepts and number sense. Help students make a habit of asking, "Is it reasonable?" Continuously emphasize estimation. And help students monitor their own learning, possibly by keeping a journal.

During instruction, make sure each student is aware of his strengths. Help the student take note of progress as it is made. Proceed in very small steps, if necessary, to ensure successful experiences.

Diagnosis is a continuous process. It continues even during instructional activity as you observe a student at work. Keep looking for patterns.

REFERENCES

1. Cox, L. S. (1975). Systematic errors in the four vertical algorithms in normal and handicapped populations. *Journal for Research in Mathematics Education* 6(4), pp. 202–220.
2. Ibid.
3. Ibid.
4. See P. Ron (1998). My family taught me this way. In L. J. Morrow and M. J. Kenney (Eds.), *The teaching and learning of algorithms in school mathematics* (pp. 115–119). Reston, VA: National Council of Teachers of Mathematics.
5. Davidson, P. S., Galton, G. K., & Fair, A. W. (1972). Chip trading activities: Book I. Fort Collins, CO: Scott Resources, Inc. Available from suppliers of materials for elementary school mathematics. This book of instructions is part of *Chip Trading Activities,* a sequence of games, problems, and other activities involving the trading of colored chips. The activities emphasize concepts of place value, patterns of numeration, decimal notation, regrouping in addition and subtraction, the multiplication and division processes, and numeration systems other than base ten.
6. To read about the experience of one teacher, see P. Temple, (1999). Learning subtraction. *Teaching Children Mathematics* 6(1), p. 4.

Chapter 5

Whole Numbers: Multiplication and Division

⌐⌐

In this chapter you will find examples of papers on which students practiced multiplying and dividing whole numbers. These papers may be like some you will encounter in your own classroom.

Look for a pattern, then check your findings by using the procedure with the examples provided for that purpose. When you think you see the pattern, make sure by looking at the other examples on the paper.

After you read about each student's procedure, you will have an opportunity to suggest needed instruction. Keep in mind the suggestions from Chapter 3. Try to suggest at least two different activities to help each student. Then compare your suggestions with the author's suggestions.

IDENTIFYING PATTERNS

Error Pattern M-W-1

Bob is proud of the fact that he really knows his basic multiplication combinations, and when his math group was multiplying by one-digit numbers he always got the correct answer. But now he often gets an incorrect product.

> The new park is in the shape of a parallelogram measuring 46 meters along the base and having a height of 26 meters. What is the area of the new park?

Look carefully at Bob's written work for this and other problems. His place value columns are aligned carefully, but he is having difficulty. What error pattern is he following?

Name *Bob*

A.
$$\overset{2}{4}6$$
$$\times\ \ 24$$
$$\overline{\ \ 184}$$
$$\underline{\ 102}$$
$$\overline{\ 1204}$$

B.
$$'76$$
$$\times\ \ 32$$
$$\overline{\ \ 152}$$
$$\underline{\ 228}$$
$$\overline{\ 2432}$$

C.
$$\overset{5}{4}8$$
$$\times\ \ 57$$
$$\overline{\ \ 336}$$
$$\underline{\ 250}$$
$$\overline{\ 2836}$$

Did you find his error pattern? Check yourself by using his procedure for Examples D and E.

D.
$$98$$
$$\times\ 56$$

E.
$$86$$
$$\times\ 45$$

Do you think Bob is using estimation, or can you tell? What does he *not* yet understand? Turn to Pattern M-W-1 on page 130 to see if you identified the error pattern.

Error Pattern M-W-2

Previously, Joe experienced some success multiplying by a one-digit factor; however, this practice paper suggests a difficulty. The products are not correct, and it is important that Joe receive help before he does more practice exercises. It is a common error pattern. Can you find it?

Name *Joe*

A.
$$\overset{2}{2}7$$
$$\underline{\times 4}$$
$$168$$

B.
$$\overset{2}{3}4$$
$$\underline{\times 6}$$
$$304$$

C.
$$\overset{3}{4}5$$
$$\underline{\times 7}$$
$$495$$

Did you find his error pattern? What does Joe understand correctly? What does Joe need to understand and apply in this situation? Check yourself by using his procedure for Examples D and E.

D.
$$\begin{array}{r} 6\,8 \\ \times\quad 5 \\ \hline \end{array}$$

E.
$$\begin{array}{r} 2\,9 \\ \times\quad 3 \\ \hline \end{array}$$

After you finish Examples D and E, turn to page 131 to see if you were able to identify the error pattern. What could possibly have caused Joe to learn such a procedure?

Error Pattern M-W-3

Doug seems to multiply correctly by a one-digit multiplier, but now he is having trouble with two- and three-digit multipliers. Can you find his error pattern?

Name _Doug_

A.
$$\begin{array}{r} 3\overset{1}{\,1\,}3 \\ \times\quad 4 \\ \hline 1\,2\,5\,2 \end{array}$$

B.
$$\begin{array}{r} 2\,1\,0 \\ \times\,1\,5 \\ \hline 2\,1\,0 \end{array}$$

C.
$$\begin{array}{r} 5\overset{1}{\,2\,}4 \\ \times\,3\,4 \\ \hline 1\,5\,7\,6 \end{array}$$

D.
$$\begin{array}{r} 4\overset{1}{\,3\,}3 \\ \times\,2\,2\,6 \\ \hline 8\,7\,8 \end{array}$$

Did you find his pattern? What does Doug do correctly? He seems to be confused by two-and three-digit multipliers. What is he confusing with the multiplication algorithm?

Check yourself by using Doug's error pattern for Examples E and F.

E. $6\ 2\ 1$
    $\times \quad 2\ 3$

F. $5\ 1\ 7$
    $\times \ 4\ 6\ 3$

After Examples E and F are completed, turn to page 131 to learn if you have correctly identified Doug's procedure. What instruction might you initiate with Doug or any student using such a procedure?

Error Pattern D-W-1

Jim attempts several problems involving quotients. Example A is worded as follows:

> At the factory, there are 176 sponges to be placed 2 in a bag. How many bags will be needed?

Jim's quotient for this problem is not even reasonable. Obviously, he is not using estimation. What he is actually doing may surprise you. Can you find his error pattern?

Name _Jim_

A. $2\overline{)176}$ quotient 233

B. $4\overline{)824}$ quotient 221

C. $3\overline{)713}$ quotient 231

Did you find the erroneous procedure? Check yourself by using Jim's procedure for Examples D and E.

D. $3\overline{)639}$

E. $4\overline{)518}$

Why might Jim be using this procedure? Do you suppose the teacher could have said anything that he is applying inappropriately?

After completing Examples D and E, turn to Pattern D-W-1 on page 132 and learn if you correctly identified Jim's error pattern. What instructional procedures might you use to help Jim or any other student using this procedure?

Error Pattern D-W-2

Clearly, Gail does not understand division as a relationship between two factors and a reasonable product. Her division computation is neat, with columns aligned, but the quotients she computes are usually incorrect. Look carefully at her written work. Can you find the error pattern she has followed?

Name *Gail*

A.
$$
\begin{array}{r}
44 \\
2\overline{)88} \\
8 \\
\hline
8 \\
8 \\
\hline
\end{array}
$$

B.
$$
\begin{array}{r}
14 \\
4\overline{)164} \\
16 \\
\hline
4 \\
4 \\
\hline
\end{array}
$$

C.
$$
\begin{array}{r}
67 \\
3\overline{)228} \\
21 \\
\hline
18 \\
18 \\
\hline
\end{array}
$$

D.
$$
\begin{array}{r}
39 \\
5\overline{)465} \\
45 \\
\hline
15 \\
15 \\
\hline
\end{array}
$$

Did you find the incorrect procedure? Check yourself by using the error pattern to compute these examples.

E.
$$3\overline{)75}$$

F.
$$6\overline{)516}$$

Why might Gail be using this procedure? Turn to Pattern D-W-2 on page 133 and see if you identified her error pattern. Can you think of a way to help Gail?

Error Pattern D-W-3

John has been doing well with much of his work in division, but recently he began having difficulty. Can you find his error pattern?

Name _John_

A.
$$\begin{array}{r} 6\,5\,\text{R}\,1 \\ 7\overline{)4\,5\,6} \\ 4\,2 \\ \hline 3\,6 \\ 3\,5 \\ \hline 1 \end{array}$$

B.
$$\begin{array}{r} 9\ \ 4\,\text{R}\,2 \\ 6\overline{)5\,4\,2\,6} \\ 5\,4 \\ \hline 2\,6 \\ 2\,4 \\ \hline 2 \end{array}$$

C.
$$\begin{array}{r} 6\ \ 7\ \text{R}\,4 \\ 8\overline{)4\,8\,6\,0} \\ 4\,8 \\ \hline 6\,0 \\ 5\,6 \\ \hline 4 \end{array}$$

D.
$$\begin{array}{r} 5\ \ 4\ \text{R}\,3 \\ 8\overline{)4\,0\,3\,5} \\ 4\,0 \\ \hline 3\,5 \\ 3\,2 \\ \hline 3 \end{array}$$

Do you think John is using estimation? Try his procedure with these examples.

E. $9\overline{)2\,7\,2\,1}$ F. $6\overline{)4\,2\,5\,0}$

After you complete Examples E and F, turn to page 134 to see if you correctly identified John's error pattern. Why might John be using such a procedure? What instructional procedures might you use to help him?

DESCRIBING INSTRUCTION

Error Pattern M-W-1
(used by Bob on page 125)

Did you find the error pattern Bob used?

Consider Example E. When multiplying 5 ones times 6 ones, Bob recorded the 3 tens as a reminder above the 8 tens so he would add 3 tens to the product of 5 and 8 tens. However, the reminder recorded when multiplying by ones was *also* used when multiplying by tens.

D.
$$
\begin{array}{r}
\overset{4}{9}\,8 \\
\underline{5\,6} \\
5\,8\,8 \\
\underline{4\,9\,0} \\
5\,4\,8\,8
\end{array}
$$

E.
$$
\begin{array}{r}
\overset{3}{8}\,6 \\
\underline{4\,5} \\
4\,3\,0 \\
\underline{3\,5\,4} \\
3\,9\,7\,0
\end{array}
$$

Note that the answers to Example B on page 125 and Example D above are correct. Bob's error pattern may have gone undetected because he gets enough correct answers—enough positive reinforcement—to convince him that he is using a correct procedure. There may have been enough correct answers to cause Bob's busy teacher to conclude that Bob was merely careless. But Bob is *consistently* applying an erroneous procedure.

How would you help Bob with this problem? Describe two instructional activities that would help Bob replace this error pattern with a correct computational procedure.

1. _____

2. _____

When you have written descriptions of two instructional activities, turn to page 134 and compare what you have written with the suggestions presented there.

Error Pattern M-W-2
(from Joe's paper on page 125)

Did you find the error pattern Joe uses?

D.
$$
\begin{array}{r}
\overset{4}{6}\,8 \\
\times\ \ 5 \\
\hline
5\,0\,0
\end{array}
$$

E.
$$
\begin{array}{r}
\overset{2}{2}\,9 \\
\times\ \ 3 \\
\hline
1\,2\,7
\end{array}
$$

Joe is using an erroneous procedure that is all too frequently adopted by students. He adds the number associated with the crutch *before* multiplying the tens figure, whereas the algorithm requires that the tens figure be multiplied first. In Example D, he thought "6 plus 4 equals 10 and 5 times 10 equals 50" instead of "5 times 6 equals 30 and 30 plus 4 equals 34." It may be that when Joe learned the addition algorithm involving regrouping, his teacher reminded him repeatedly, "The first thing you do is to add the number you carry." Many teachers drill children on such a rule, and it is little wonder that children sometimes apply the rule in inappropriate contexts.

The fact that students frequently use Joe's procedure does not lessen your obligation to help Joe multiply correctly. How would *you* help him? Describe two different instructional activities you think would enable Joe to replace his error pattern with a correct computational procedure.

1. _____

2. _____

When you have finished writing both descriptions, turn to page 137 and compare what you have written with the suggestions offered there.

Error Pattern M-W-3
(from Doug's paper on page 126)

Did you find Doug's error pattern? If so, you completed Examples E and F as they are shown.

E.

$$
\begin{array}{r}
6\,2\,1 \\
\times\ \ 2\,3 \\
\hline
1\,2\,4\,3
\end{array}
$$

F.

$$
\begin{array}{r}
5\,\overset{2}{1}\,7 \\
\times\ 4\,6\,3 \\
\hline
2\,0\,8\,1
\end{array}
$$

The procedure used by Doug is a blend of the algorithm for multiplying by a one-digit multiplier and the conventional addition algorithm. Each column is approached as a separate multiplication. When the multiplicand has more digits than the multiplier, the leftmost digit of the multiplier continues to be used.

You may meet Doug in your own classroom. How would you help him? Describe at least two instructional activities you believe would enable Doug to multiply by two- and three-digit numbers correctly.

1. _____

2. _____

After your descriptions are written, turn to page 138 and see if your suggestions are among those listed there.

Error Pattern D-W-1

(used by Jim on page 127)

Did you find the erroneous procedure Jim used?

D.

$$
3\overline{)6\,3\,9}\ \ ^{2\ 1\ 3}
$$

E.

$$
4\overline{)5\,1\,8}\ \ ^{1\ 4\ 2}
$$

Example D is correct and it does not give many clues to Jim's thinking. However, the fact that Example D *is* correct is a reminder that erroneous procedures sometimes produce correct answers, thereby making the error pattern more difficult for the teacher to identify.

Example E illustrates Jim's thinking more completely. Apparently Jim ignores place value in the dividend and quotient, and he thinks of each digit as "ones." Furthermore, he considers one digit of the dividend and the one-digit divisor as two numbers "to be divided." The greater of the two (whether the divisor or a digit within the dividend) is divided by the lesser and the result is recorded. Jim has probably learned something like "a smaller number goes into a larger number." Interestingly, the remainder is ignored.

How would you help Jim with his problem? Describe two instructional activities that you think would help Jim replace this erroneous procedure with a correct computational procedure.

1. _____

2. _____

After you have written descriptions of two appropriate instructional activities, compare your activities with the suggestions on page 140.

Error Pattern D-W-2

(from Gail's paper on page 128)

Using Gail's incorrect procedure, Examples E and F would be computed as shown.

E.

$$3\overline{)75} \\ \underline{60} \\ 15 \\ \underline{15}$$ gives quotient 52

F.

$$6\overline{)516} \\ \underline{480} \\ 36 \\ \underline{36}$$ gives quotient 68

Did you find the error pattern? In the ones column Gail records the first quotient figure she determines, and in the tens column she records the second digit she determines. In other words, the answer is recorded right to left. In the usual algorithms for addition, subtraction, and multiplication of whole numbers, the answer is recorded right to left. Perhaps Gail assumes it is appropriate to do the same with the division algorithm.

The fact that Example A is correct illustrates again that correct answers are sometimes obtained with incorrect procedures, thereby positively reinforcing an error pattern.

It is quite probable that, for Example E, Gail thinks "7 divided by 3" (or perhaps "3 times what number is 7") rather than "75 divided by 3." The quotient for a shortcut expression such as "7 divided by 3" would indeed be 2 units. Shortcuts in thinking and the standard algorithm for division may have been introduced too soon.

What would you do if you were Gail's teacher? What corrective steps might you take? Describe two instructional activities that you believe would help Gail correct the erroneous procedure.

1. _____

2. _____

If you have finished your responses, turn to page 141 and see if your suggestions are among the alternatives listed there.

Error Pattern D-W-3
(from John's paper on page 129)

If you found John's error pattern, you completed Examples E and F as they are shown.

E.

$$9\overline{\smash{\big)}2721} \quad \begin{array}{r} 3\ \ 2\,{}_{R3} \\ \hline 2721 \\ 27 \\ \hline 21 \\ 18 \\ \hline 3 \end{array}$$

F.

$$6\overline{\smash{\big)}4250} \quad \begin{array}{r} 7\ \ 8\,{}_{R2} \\ \hline 4250 \\ 42 \\ \hline 50 \\ 48 \\ \hline 2 \end{array}$$

John has difficulty with examples that include a zero in the tens place of the quotient. Whenever he cannot divide in the tens place, he proceeds to the ones place, but without recording a zero to show that there are no tens. He may believe that "zero is nothing." Also, careless placement of figures in the quotient may contribute to John's problem.

How would you help John? Describe at least two instructional activities you believe would help John correct his pattern of error.

1. _____

2. _____

When you have completed both descriptions, turn to page 142 and compare your suggestions with those listed there.

CONSIDERING ALTERNATIVES

Error Pattern M-W-1
(from pages 125 and 130)

How would you help a student such as Bob correct the error pattern illustrated? Are the activities you described similar to any of those listed?

D.
$$\overset{4}{9}\,8$$
$$\underline{5\,6}$$
$$5\,8\,8$$
$$\underline{4\,9\,0}$$
$$5\,4\,8\,8$$

E.
$$\overset{3}{8}\,6$$
$$\underline{4\,5}$$
$$4\,3\,0$$
$$\underline{3\,5\,4}$$
$$3\,9\,7\,0$$

Note: The following activities emphasize place value, the distributive property, and proper mechanics of notation.

1. *Use more partial products and no reminder.* The algorithm that follows can be related to an array partitioned twice. When the student is able to use this algorithm with ease, let him try to combine the first two partial products (and also the last two) by *remembering* the number of tens (and the number of hundreds). Do not encourage use of a written reminder in this situation.

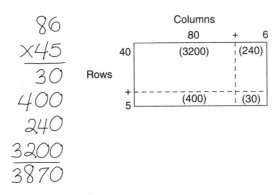

2. *Make two problems.* Have the student multiply by ones and then by tens in two separate problems. As he computes the product in this way, encourage him to try remembering his reminder number (rather than writing it) "because they are sometimes confusing in multiplication and division." When he can compute each easily without recording a reminder, you will probably want to suggest that he convert to a more standard algorithm.

3. *Record tens within partial products.* Instead of writing a "reminding number" above the example, use lightly-written, half-sized numerals within each of the partial products to record the number of tens to be remembered.

$$86 \rightarrow \quad 86 \rightarrow \quad 86$$
$$\times 45 \qquad \times 45 \qquad \times 45$$
$$ \qquad \overset{3}{}0 \qquad 4\overset{3}{3}0$$

$$86 \rightarrow \quad 86 \rightarrow \quad 86$$
$$\times 45 \qquad \times 45 \qquad \times 45$$
$$4\overset{3}{3}0 \qquad 4\overset{3}{3}0 \qquad 4\overset{3}{3}0$$
$$\overset{2}{}4 \qquad 3\overset{2}{4}4 \qquad 3\overset{2}{4}4$$
$$\phantom{4\overset{3}{3}0} \qquad \phantom{4\overset{3}{3}0} \qquad 3870$$

4. *Apply the commutative and associative principles.* This technique should be especially helpful if the student has difficulty in processing open number sentences like $5 \times 80 = ?$; $40 \times 6 = ?$; and $40 \times 80 = ?$ These number sentences are parts of Example E and suggest a prerequisite skill for such examples; namely, application of the commutative and associative principles where one of the factors is a multiple of a power of 10. The error pattern may result, in part, from thinking of all digits as ones and the inability to think of tens, hundreds, and so on, when using multiplication number combinations. After the associative principle is introduced with one-digit factors (perhaps with the aid of a three-dimensional arrangement of cubic units), let the student think through examples such as:

$$40 \times 6 = (4 \times 10) \times 6$$
$$= (10 \times 4) \times 6$$
$$= 10 \times (4 \times 6)$$
$$= 10 \times 24$$
$$= 240$$

When the student generalizes this procedure, he will be able to compute the product of a one-digit number and a multiple of a power of 10 *in one step.*

Caution There is a very real danger in proceeding to a standard algorithm too quickly. Often, a new, more efficient procedure is best introduced as a shortcut for an already understood algorithm. Whenever zeros help a student think in terms of place value, do not insist that the units zero in the second and succeeding partial products be dropped.

Use Reminders

Written reminder numbers are to be encouraged if they are useful and help the student understand what he is doing. But they can be confusing when multiplying by a two-digit multiplier. Also, questions such as 5 × 86 = ☐ ☐ occur within division computation, where use of a written reminder is impractical. For these reasons, students should be encouraged to remember numbers in multiplication, rather than writing a reminder.

Error Pattern M-W-2

(from pages 125 and 131)

You have described two instructional activities for helping Joe and other students who have adopted the error pattern illustrated. Are your suggestions included in the activities described?

D.
$$\begin{array}{r} \overset{4}{6}\,8 \\ \times \quad 5 \\ \hline 5\,0\,0 \end{array}$$

E.
$$\begin{array}{r} \overset{2}{2}\,9 \\ \times \quad 3 \\ \hline 1\,2\,7 \end{array}$$

1. *Use partial products.* Such an algorithm is easily developed as a step-by-step record of what is done when an array is partitioned. Help the student determine the order in which the multiplication and addition occur, lead him to generalize, and state the sequence.

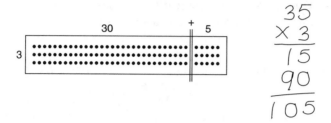

$$
\begin{array}{r}
35 \\
\times\ 3 \\
\hline
15 \\
90 \\
\hline
105
\end{array}
$$

2. *Write the reminder below the bar.* Instead of the student writing a reminder in the conventional way, have him make a small numeral below the bar to remind him to add *just before* recording a product.

$$
\begin{array}{r}
29 \\
\times\quad 3 \\
\hline
{}^{2}\ 7
\end{array}
\qquad
\begin{array}{r}
29 \\
\times\quad 3 \\
\hline
\overset{2}{8}\ 7
\end{array}
$$

Error Pattern M-W-3

(from pages 126 and 131)

Are either of the instructional activities you suggested among those listed?

E.
$$
\begin{array}{r}
621 \\
\times\quad 23 \\
\hline
1243
\end{array}
$$

F.
$$
\begin{array}{r}
5\overset{2}{1}7 \\
\times\ 463 \\
\hline
2081
\end{array}
$$

1. *Use the distributive property.* Have the student rewrite the problem as two problems. Later, the two products can be related to partial products in the conventional algorithm.

$$
\begin{array}{r}
621 \\
\times\quad 23 \\
\hline
\end{array}
\longrightarrow
\begin{array}{r}
621 \\
\times\quad 20 \\
\hline
?
\end{array}
\qquad
\begin{array}{r}
621 \\
\times\quad 3 \\
\hline
?
\end{array}
$$

If the student does not understand why the sum of the two multiplication problems is the same number as the product in the original problem, partition an array and label the parts. If the student does not understand the concept of an array, begin with small numbers.

2×3

Then use rectangles to represent arrays with greater numbers.

23×621

621

20 +	(20×621)
3	(3×621)

2. *Use a paper mask.* To help the student focus on multiplying the entire upper figure (multiplicand) by one place value at a time, cover the multiplier so only one digit will show at a time. After multiplication by the units digit is completed, the mask can be moved to the left so that only the tens digit is visible. Later, the hundreds digit can be highlighted. With each digit, emphasize the need to do a complete multiplication problem. Also stress proper placement of each partial product.

3. *Use a calculator.* Use a calculator to compute each partial product. Make sure the correct values are multiplied; for 23×621, multiply 3×621 then 20×621.

Error Pattern D-W-1
(from pages 127 and 132)

How might you help Jim correct the erroneous procedure in the illustration? Are the instructional activities you described similar to any of the activities listed?

D.
$$3\overline{\smash{)}639} = 213$$

E.
$$4\overline{\smash{)}518} = 142$$

Note: To help the student who has adopted such an error pattern, select activities that emphasize place values in the dividend and stress the total quantity of the dividend. Procedures that can be understood in relation to concrete referents are needed instead of an assortment of rules to be applied in a mechanical way. In essence, a division algorithm needs to be reintroduced.

1. *Use manipulatives to redevelop the algorithm.* Teach the algorithm as a step-by-step record of activities with manipulatives. For the problem $54 \div 3 = ?$ the dividend can be shown as 5 tens and 4 units using base-ten blocks, Cuisenaire rods, or single sticks and bundles. See the gamelike activity for division described in Appendix C.
2. *Estimate quotient figures.* Use open number sentences such as $3 \times ? \le 54$ with the rule that the number to be found is the largest multiple of a power of 10 that will make the number sentence true.
3. *Focus on skill in multiplying multiples of powers of 10 by a single digit.* This skill, used in the above activities, may need to be developed independently of a division algorithm. Patterns can be observed from such data as the following display.

$2 \times 3 = 6$	$2 \times 3 = 6$
$2 \times 30 = 60$	$20 \times 3 = 60$
$2 \times 300 = 600$	$200 \times 3 = 600$

Have the student describe the pattern orally. Consider this conversation.

STUDENT: You find the numbers (digits) for the multiplication fact, then you count the zeros and write the same number of zeros. Then you are done.

TEACHER: That's a great rule, but does it always work? Try your rule with these examples, then use your calculator to see if the rule always works.

Error Pattern D-W-2

(from pages 128 and 133)

Illustrations of Gail's error pattern in division of whole numbers are shown here. Are the instructional activities you suggested to help this student among those described?

E.

$$
\begin{array}{r}
5\,2 \\
3\overline{)7\,5} \\
6\;0 \\
\hline
1\;5 \\
1\;5 \\
\hline
\end{array}
$$

F.

$$
\begin{array}{r}
6\;8 \\
6\overline{)5\,1\,6} \\
4\;8\;0 \\
\hline
3\;6 \\
3\;6 \\
\hline
\end{array}
$$

1. *Emphasize place value in estimating quotient figures.* Let the student use open number sentences such as $3 \times ? \le 70$ and $3 \times ? \le 15$ while thinking through Example E. Number sentences should be completed remembering the following: When dividing 7 tens, the missing number is the largest multiple of 10 that will make the number sentence true. For $3 \times ? \le 70$, $? = 20$. Similarly, when dividing 15 ones, the missing number is the largest multiple of one that will make the number sentence true.

2. *Use a different algorithm.* At least temporarily, choose an algorithm that will show the value of each partial quotient. In each of the algorithms shown, the 8 in the quotient of Example F is shown as 80, thereby emphasizing proper placement of quotient figures. After the student is able to use such algorithms, a transition to the standard computational procedure can be made, if desired, by recording quotients differently. In Example F-3, the first quotient figure would be recorded as 8 in the tens place instead of as 80.

F-1

$$
\begin{array}{l}
6\overline{)5\,1\,6} \\
4\;8\;0 = 8\,0 \times 6 \\
3\;6 \\
3\;6 = \quad 6 \times 6 \\
\hline
\quad\quad 8\,6 \times 6
\end{array}
$$

F-2

$$
\begin{array}{r|l}
6\overline{)5\,1\,6} & \\
4\;8\;0 & 8\,0 \\
3\;6 & \\
3\;6 & 6 \\
\hline
& 8\,6
\end{array}
$$

F-3

$$
\begin{array}{r}
8\;6 \\
\hline
6 \\
8\;0 \\
6\overline{)5\,1\,6} \\
4\;8\;0 \\
\hline
3\;6 \\
3\;6 \\
\hline
\end{array}
$$

3. *Develop skill in multiplying numbers by powers of 10.* This skill is necessary for meaningful use of any of the division algorithms. A series of equations can be written to facilitate observation of patterns.

$$6 \times 4 = 24$$
$$6 \times 40 = 240$$
$$6 \times 400 = 2400$$

4. *Estimate the quotient before computing.* Frequently, quotients resulting from the erroneous algorithm are quite unreasonable. If intelligent estimating is followed by computing, and the estimate and the quotient are then compared, the student may rethink her computational procedure.

Error Pattern D-W-3
(from pages 129 and 134)

You have suggested activities for helping John, who is using the error pattern illustrated. Are your suggestions among those listed?

E.

```
      3  2 r3
   9)2 7 2 1
     2 7
       2 1
       1 8
         3
```

F.

```
      7  8 r2
   6)4 2 5 0
     4 2
         5 0
         4 8
           2
```

1. *Use lined paper turned 90°.* It may be that letting the student use vertically lined paper (or cross-sectioned paper) will clear up the problem. The omission of one digit becomes very obvious when such forms are used for practice.

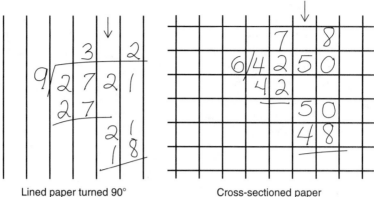

Lined paper turned 90°   Cross-sectioned paper

2. *Use the pyramid algorithm.* At least temporarily, use an algorithm that emphasizes place value. If the pyramid algorithm has been learned by the student earlier in the instructional program, ask him to solve some of the troublesome examples using it to see if he can figure out why he is having difficulty now. If the pyramid algorithm is new to the student, he may enjoy trying a new procedure that is a bit easier to understand.

$$\begin{array}{r} 6\ 0\ 7\ \text{r}\ 4 \\ \hline 7 \\ 6\ 0\ 0 \\ 8\overline{)4\ 8\ 6\ 0} \\ \underline{4\ 8\ 0\ 0} \\ 6\ 0 \\ \underline{5\ 6} \\ 4 \end{array}$$

3. *Estimate the quotient before beginning computation.* Have the student determine how many digits are in the quotient, then record an estimated quotient. This may be sufficient to overcome the problem, especially if careless writing of quotient figures is a major cause of the difficulty.

4. *Use base-ten blocks and a gamelike activity.* Teach the algorithm as a step-by-step record of activities with base-ten blocks, using the gamelike activity for division described in Appendix C. For Example E (2721 ÷ 9 = ?) the two 10-blocks cannot be distributed among nine sets; and it is therefore necessary to exchange the two 10-blocks for an equal number—an equal amount of wood—for 20 unit-blocks. But before exchanging, *make sure the student records in the algorithm with a zero that no 10-blocks are being distributed* among the nine sets.

CONCLUSION

Keep looking for patterns while teaching multiplication and division procedures. Continuously emphasize the need for reasonable answers. Build on students' strengths.

Notice how your students use language—the specific meanings they associate with words and phrases during diagnosis and instruction.

When students use manipulatives, be sure they connect what they observe with the written procedure you are teaching. Vary instruction by including enjoyable games and puzzles when possible.

Chapter 6

Fractions: Concepts and Equivalence
⌐⌐

Papers in this chapter involve fraction concepts and equivalent fractions. However, the procedures students used resulted in many incorrect answers.

Can you find the patterns that characterize each student's responses? Check your findings by using the error pattern with the examples provided for that purpose. Be careful not to decide on the error pattern too quickly. Verify your hypothesis by looking at the other examples on the student's paper.

Then read about the procedure the student used and suggest needed instruction. It is always important for a teacher to have in mind more than one instructional strategy, so try to suggest at least two different activities to help each student. Your suggestions can then be compared with the author's suggestions.

If this book is to help you with your teaching of school mathematics, you will need to "play the game." Take time to try out the error pattern before turning to another part of the book. Write out brief descriptions of instructional activities before moving ahead to see what suggestions are recorded later. Do not be content just to read about patterns of error; as a teacher you also learn by *doing*, and by *thinking* about what you are doing. Take time to respond by writing in the designated places.

IDENTIFYING PATTERNS

Error Pattern F-C-1
Gretchen completed her worksheet with ease, but only one example is correct. What does she understand? What does she *not* yet understand?

145

At times she has used an erroneous procedure. Can you find her error pattern?

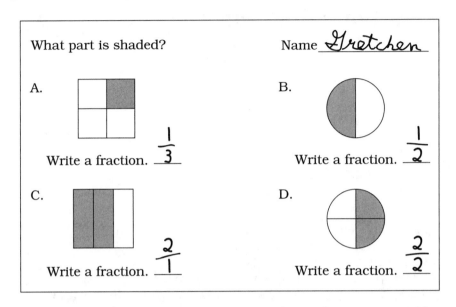

What part is shaded?   Name _Gretchen_

A.

Write a fraction. $\dfrac{1}{3}$

B.

Write a fraction. $\dfrac{1}{2}$

C.

Write a fraction. $\dfrac{2}{1}$

D.

Write a fraction. $\dfrac{2}{2}$

Why do you think Gretchen responded correctly to Example B? Make sure you found her error pattern by using her procedure for these.

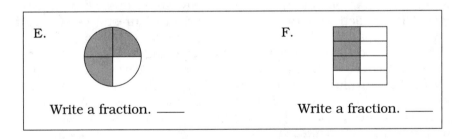

E.

Write a fraction. _____

F.

Write a fraction. _____

Now, turn to Pattern F-C-1 on page 149 and see if you identified her procedure. How will you help Gretchen so that she will have correct associations for fraction symbols?

Error Pattern F-C-2

Carlos was asked to complete a worksheet to demonstrate understanding of certain fraction concepts. What does he understand? What does he *not* yet understand? Find his error pattern.

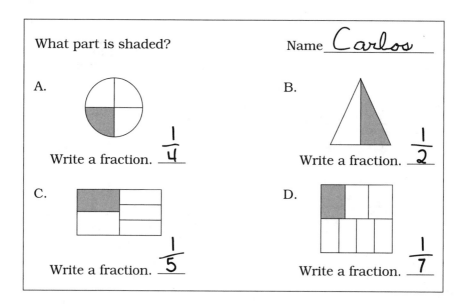

Make sure you know what Carlos is doing by using his procedure for these examples.

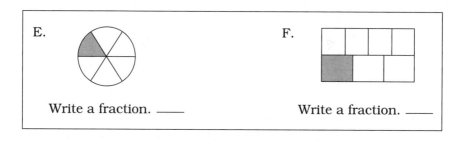

Now, turn to Pattern F-C-2 on page 150 and see if you identified his procedure. Why might he be responding in this way?

Error Pattern F-E-1

Jill needs to determine the simplest terms for each fraction. Some are already in simplest terms, but some fractions need to be changed to simpler terms.

What procedure is she using? This is a difficult error pattern to find. You may have to interview Jill and listen to her explanation of how she changed each fraction.

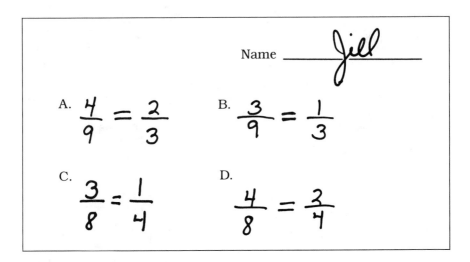

Even though she was using an error pattern, Jill actually did change some fractions to simplest terms. Find out if you correctly identified Jill's procedure by using her error pattern to complete Examples E and F.

E.
$$\frac{3}{4} =$$

F.
$$\frac{2}{8} =$$

Next, turn to page 151 where Jill's pattern is described. How might you help Jill or others using such a pattern?

Error Pattern F-E-2

If Sue understands basic fraction concepts and what *equals* means she certainly is not applying that knowledge. She appears to be following some rules she constructed somehow, perhaps from phrases she heard in the classroom.

Sue tried to change each fraction to lowest or simplest terms, but her results are quite unreasonable. Can you find her error pattern?

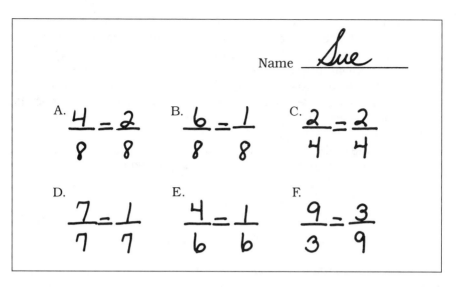

Use Sue's procedure with these fractions to learn if you found her pattern.

G. $\dfrac{3}{6} =$

H. $\dfrac{6}{4} =$

After Examples G and H are completed, turn to page 152 to see if you found Sue's error pattern. How would you help Sue or any student using such a procedure? Where would you begin?

DESCRIBING INSTRUCTION

Error Pattern F-C-1
(from Gretchen's paper on page 146)

If you completed Examples E and F using the procedure Gretchen used, you completed them as follows.

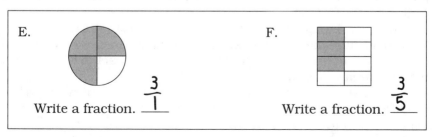

Apparently Gretchen understands that the number of shaded parts is indicated by the numerator. She then counts the number of parts not shaded, and records that number (rather than the total number of equivalent parts) as the denominator for her fraction.

Gretchen's response to Example B (on page 146) is not consistent with the procedure she used. She may have memorized a specific connection between a semi-circular shape and one half; for her, a semi-circular region may be "what one half looks like."

Briefly describe two instructional activities you believe would provide the understanding needed, and help Gretchen correct her error pattern.

1. _____

2. _____

Now, turn to page 152 to see if your suggestions are among those listed.

Error Pattern F-C-2

(from Carlos's paper on page 147)

If you completed Examples E and F using the procedure Carlos used, you completed them as follows.

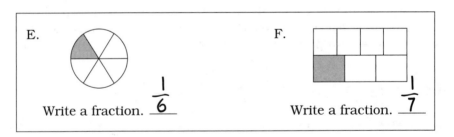

Carlos associates the denominator of the fraction with the total number of parts indicated, and the numerator with the number of shaded parts.

However, he apparently fails to understand that these associations apply *only* when *all* shaded parts are equivalent. Each fractional part needs to be the same part of the whole unit; each needs to cover the same area within the unit region.

Carlos needs to make sure that all parts are equivalent. When they are not equivalent, he needs to determine how much of the unit region each individual shaded part covers, and write a fraction with this in mind.

Briefly describe two instructional activities you believe would help Carlos and provide the understanding needed.

1. _____

2. _____

Now, turn to page 153 to see if your suggestions are among those listed.

Error Pattern F-E-1

(from Jill's paper on page 148)

Did you find Jill's error pattern?

$$\text{E.} \quad \frac{3}{4} = \frac{1}{2} \qquad \text{F.} \quad \frac{2}{8} = \frac{1}{4}$$

Jill's computation appears almost random though, interestingly, several answers are correct. She obviously does not recognize which fractions are already in simplest terms. She explains her procedure as follows:

> "4 goes to 2, and 9 goes to 3"
> "3 goes to 1, and 9 goes to 3"

For Examples E and F,

> "3 goes to 1, and 4 goes to 2"
> "2 goes to 1, and 8 goes to 4"

Jill simply associates a specific whole number with each given numerator or denominator. *All* 3s become 1s and *all* 4s become 2s when fractions are to be reduced or changed to simplest terms. This procedure is a very mechanical one, requiring no concept of a fraction; however, it does produce correct answers part of the time.

Concepts such as the equivalence of rational numbers develop *very slowly* over time. If students are taught computational procedures before they develop adequate concepts of fractions and equivalent fractions, they are apt to experience difficulty.

Jill has a very real problem. How would you help her? Describe two instructional activities that would help Jill replace this erroneous procedure with a correct procedure.

1. _____

2. _____

After two activities have been described, turn to page 155 and compare what you have written with the suggestions listed there.

Error Pattern F-E-2

(from Sue's paper on page 149)

Did you correctly identify Sue's pattern of errors? Many teachers would assume she had responded randomly.

$$\text{G.} \quad \frac{3}{6} = \frac{2}{6} \qquad\qquad \text{H.} \quad \frac{6}{4} = \frac{1}{6}$$

Sue considers the given numerator and denominator as two whole numbers, and divides the greater by the lesser to determine the new numerator, ignoring any remainder; then the greater of the two numbers is copied as the new denominator. Perhaps she has observed, in the fractions she has seen, that the denominator is usually the greater of the two numbers.

How would you help Sue? She is not unlike many other children who develop mechanistic and unreasonable procedures in arithmetic classes. Describe at least two instructional activities that you believe would help Sue learn to correctly change fractions to lowest or simplest terms.

1. _____

2. _____

When you have described at least two activities, turn to page 157 and compare your suggestions with those listed there.

CONSIDERING ALTERNATIVES

Error Pattern F-C-1

(from pages 146 and 149)

This error pattern (See E) was explained, "Three parts are shaded, so that number goes on top; one part is not shaded, so write that number below."

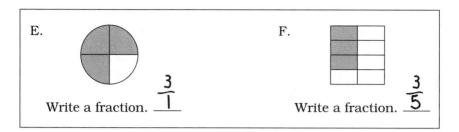

E.

Write a fraction. $\dfrac{3}{1}$

F.

Write a fraction. $\dfrac{3}{5}$

It is critical that students understand the way a fractional (or a decimal) part of a quantity is related to the unit. You suggested instructional activities. Are any activities you suggested similar to those described here?

1. *Start with the whole.* Have the student "build" the fraction for a given unit region by thinking about the whole unit. "How many equal-sized parts are there *altogether* in the whole square (circle, etc.)? Write that number." Then have the student put a "roof" over that number, and write the number of shaded parts on top. Be sure to have the student read each fraction she makes, and read them top-to-bottom: "one of four parts, that's one fourth; two of three parts, that's two thirds; and so on." A set can be used in place of a unit region—possibly with two colors.

2. *Color parts, then record.* For each of these rectangular strips, have the student record the total number of equal-sized parts, then make a line above each numeral (to show that it is the total number of equal-sized parts), and then color one or more parts in each strip. Finally, have the student write the number of *colored* parts above the total number of parts. Ask, "How much of each strip is colored?"

Error Pattern F-C-2
(from pages 147 and 150)

Example F was explained, "One part is shaded so write one on top, and there are seven parts so write seven for the bottom number." The student does this even when the parts do not have the same area.

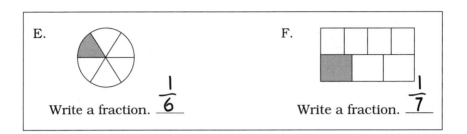

E.   Write a fraction. $\frac{1}{6}$

F.   Write a fraction. $\frac{1}{7}$

Are the instructional activities you suggested similar to any of the activities described here?

1. *Select fourths.* Give the student partially shaded regions similar to these, and have the student select all that show one fourth. Have the student explain (to you or to another student) why each shaded region does or does not show one fourth.

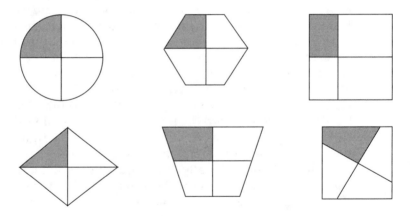

2. *Focus on equal area.* In using fractional parts of a unit region as the model for a fraction, the parts do not have to be the same shape, but they *do* have to be the same size; that is, they must have the same area. They have to cover the same amount of surface. Have the student identify which of the following regions are divided into equal-sized parts, and which are not so divided.

Error Pattern F-E-1

(from pages 148 and 151)

The error pattern illustrated was explained: "3 goes to 1, and 4 goes to 2." Are the instructional activities you suggested similar to any of the activities described here?

E. $\dfrac{3}{4} = \dfrac{1}{2}$ F. $\dfrac{2}{8} = \dfrac{1}{4}$

Note: It may be wise to extend the diagnosis to determine if the student is able to interpret a fraction as parts of a region or a set. If the student cannot, instruction should begin with the concept of a fraction. The following activities assume the student has a basic understanding of a fraction even though a mechanical rule for changing a fraction to simplest terms was adopted.

1. *Use fractional parts of regions.* Begin with reference to the unit, then show the given number with fractional parts. Do *not* restrict the instruction to pie shapes, but use rectangular shapes as well. Pose the question, "Can we use larger parts to cover exactly what we have?" Record several "experiments" and note the ones that are already in simplest terms. Then look for a mathematical rule for changing, *i.e.,* dividing both numerator and denominator by the same number.

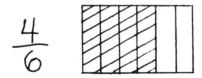

$\dfrac{4}{6}$

2. *Build an array with fractional parts of a set.* With discs of two colors, make a row for a given fraction.

2 of the 3 discs are white

$\dfrac{2}{3} \longrightarrow \bigcirc \bigcirc \oslash$

Then, build an array by forming additional rows of discs— rows identical to the first. As each row is formed, count the columns and the discs. Record the equivalent fractions.

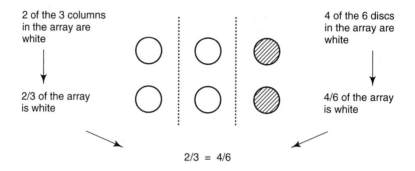

2/3 = 4/6

3. *Look for a pattern in a list.* Present a list of *correct* examples similar to the following, and have the student look for a pattern (a mathematical rule) for changing. Test out the suggested pattern on other examples. When a correct procedure is found, use it to help determine the fractions that can be changed to simpler terms and those already in simplest terms.

$$\frac{6}{8} = \frac{3}{4}$$

$$\frac{4}{6} = \frac{2}{3}$$

Note: Two equivalent fractions, decimals, and/or percents can be thought of as two pictures of the same number—but "wearing different clothes."

4. *Make sets of equivalent fractions.* Students can do this by subdividing a region, then continuing to subdivide it again and again. Record the resulting sets of equivalent fractions in order, with the lesser numerator first; then use the sets for finding simplest terms. Look for a relationship between any one fraction and the first fraction in the set.

$$\frac{2}{3} \quad \frac{4}{6} \quad \frac{6}{9} \quad \frac{8}{12} \ldots$$

5. *Play a game.* Play a board game in which players race their pieces forward along a track made up of sections, each of which is partitioned into twelfths. Players roll special dice, draw cards with fraction numerals, or draw unit regions for fractions. Possible fractions include 1/2, 2/3, 5/6, 3/4, and so forth. Moves forward are for the equivalent number of twelfths. An example of this kind of game can be found in the *Fraction Bars* program.[1]

Error Pattern F-E-2
(from pages 149 and 152)

In order to change to lowest terms, Sue divided the greater number by the lesser to determine the new numerator, and copied the greater number as the new denominator. Which of the instructional activities you suggested are among the activities described?

G.
$$\frac{3}{6} = \frac{2}{6}$$

H.
$$\frac{6}{4} = \frac{1}{6}$$

There is some evidence that this student is only manipulating symbols in a mechanistic way and not even interpreting fractions as part of unit regions. For example, her statement that 3/6 = 2/6 suggests that an understanding of 3/6 or 2/6 as parts of a unit just is not present, or, if it is, it is a behavior associated with something like fraction pies, and it is not applied in other contexts. Also, she probably thinks of *equals* as "results in" instead of "is the same as." It may be wise to interview her to determine how she conceptualizes *fractions* and *equals* before planning instruction.

1. *Match numerals with physical or diagrammatic representations.* To encourage the interpretation of a fraction in terms of real world referents, help the student learn and reinforce these abilities:
    a. Given a physical representation or a diagram for a fraction, the student writes the fraction or picks out a numeral card showing "how much." In an activity of this sort be sure the student understands the given frame of reference, *i.e.*, the unit.
    b. Given a fraction, the student represents the fraction with blocks, parts of a unit region, sets, etc., or draws an appropriate diagram.
2. *Find equivalent numerals on number lines.* Have the student place number lines side by side so that whole numbers

match, then look for different fractions that name the same number.

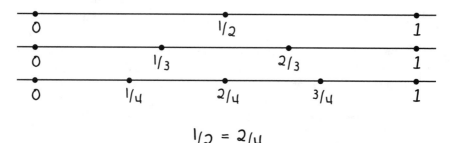

$$1/2 = 2/4$$

3. *Order fraction cards.* Give the student a set of cards, each with a different fraction but the same denominator. Then, let the student sequence the cards, thereby focusing on the fact that $3/6 \neq 2/6$. (It may be necessary to emphasize that the equality sign means "is the same as.") Encourage the student to refer to physical representations or to diagrams as necessary to verify decisions.

4. *Play "Can you make a whole?"* The student has a need to recognize fractions that can be changed to a mixed number. Give her a set of cards with a fraction on each. Some of the cards should have proper or common fractions; others should have improper fractions. The student can play a game by sorting individual cards into two piles, those which will "make a whole" (those equal to or greater than 1) and those which will "not make a whole." Then after a playing partner or teacher challenges the student by picking two of the sorted cards, the student must use physical representations to prove that the fractions are sorted correctly. If two students are playing, they should take turns sorting and challenging. More specific game rules and scoring procedures (if any) can be agreed upon by the students involved.

CONCLUSION

Many manipulatives and diagrams are available for modeling quantities expressed as fractions and decimals. Equivalent parts of unit regions, fraction bars, and number lines are examples. Use a variety of models, so that students associate numerals with quantities and not with particular representations.

As you help each student learn procedures for changing a fraction to equivalent fractions, focus on concepts and number sense.

Help students make a habit of asking, "Is it reasonable?" Ask questions like "Are both numbers more than a half?" "This number is almost one; is this number almost one also?" Continuously emphasize estimation.

Remember that diagnosis continues even during instructional activities as you observe students at work. Keep looking for patterns.

REFERENCE

1. Bennet, A. B. Jr., & Davidson, P. S. (1973). *Fraction Bars*. Ft. Collins, CO: Scott Resources, Inc. The materials can be purchased from many supply houses for elementary school mathematics.

Chapter 7

Fractions and Decimals: Addition and Subtraction

Evidences of purely mechanical procedures abound. Such procedures cannot be explained by a student with mathematical principles or physical aids. Students who use mechanical procedures "push symbols around" whenever there are examples to be computed and right answers to be determined. Many of the students represented here have been introduced to the standard short-form algorithms too soon. Some students lack very basic understandings of numeration or the algorithm itself, while others have become careless and confused. Sadly, each student has practiced an erroneous procedure.

Here are examples of papers on which students practiced addition and subtraction with fractions and decimals. Look for a pattern in each paper, then make sure you found the student's procedure by looking at all of the examples on the paper. Check your findings by using the procedure with the examples provided for that purpose.

Accompanying many of the error patterns is a discussion of reasons some students may learn to compute that way. If the procedure produces the correct answer part of the time, the validity of the pattern is confirmed in the student's mind.

After you read about each student's erroneous procedure, suggest needed instruction. Keep in mind instruction as described in Chapter 3. Try to propose at least two different activities to help each student, then compare your suggestions with those in this book.

Additional student practice papers for addition and subtraction with fractions and decimals are in Appendix A where you can further test your ability to identify patterns. A key is provided.

IDENTIFYING PATTERNS

Error Pattern A-F-1

> Wes sold bagels from bags of 30 bagels. On Monday, he sold $\frac{4}{5}$ of a bag, then on Tuesday he sold $\frac{2}{3}$ of a different bag. How many full bags of bagels did he sell?

If Robbie was using estimating skills, he could have thought, "Four fifths is almost one, and two thirds is more than a half. So, their sum is about one and a half." He would have known that six eighths is not a reasonable answer.

Look at Robbie's written work. He is using a common error pattern. Can you find it?

Name **Robbie**

A. $\dfrac{4}{5} + \dfrac{2}{3} = \dfrac{6}{8}$

B. $\dfrac{1}{4} + \dfrac{2}{3} = \dfrac{3}{7}$

C. $\dfrac{7}{8} + \dfrac{5}{6} = \dfrac{12}{14}$

D. $\dfrac{3}{7} + \dfrac{1}{2} = \dfrac{4}{9}$

Did you find the pattern? Make sure by using the pattern to compute these examples.

E. $\dfrac{3}{4} + \dfrac{1}{5} =$

F. $\dfrac{2}{3} + \dfrac{5}{6}$

What does Robbie understand? What does Robbie *not* yet understand? Can you think of a situation in which Robbie's procedure would actually be correct for the total needed? Think about sports.

Turn to page 168 and see if you identified the pattern correctly. Why might Robbie be using such a procedure?

Error Pattern A-F-2

Look at Dave's paper. Do you think he is using estimation skills? His error pattern is all too common. Can you find it?

Name **Dave**

A.
$$\frac{3}{4} + \frac{2}{3} = \frac{5}{12}$$

B.
$$\frac{6}{8} + \frac{1}{3} = \frac{7}{24}$$

C.
$$\frac{2}{3} + \frac{5}{6} = \frac{7}{18}$$

D.
$$\frac{3}{5} + \frac{2}{3} = \frac{5}{15} = \frac{1}{3}$$

Did you find Dave's procedure? Check yourself by using his procedure to compute Examples E and F.

E.
$$\frac{1}{3} + \frac{3}{5} =$$

F.
$$\frac{3}{8} + \frac{4}{5}$$

Dave's difficulty may involve a previous learning which he recalls and applies (inappropriately) when adding examples like these.

Turn to page 169 and see if you identified the procedure correctly.

Error Pattern A-F-3

Robin knows she must change unlike fractions so they have a common denominator before she can add the numbers. In fact, she is able to find a common denominator.

Beyond that, her procedure appears to make no sense at all. Even so, she is following a regular error pattern.

Can you find her procedure?

Name __Robin__

A.

$$\frac{1}{2} = \frac{1}{4}$$

$$+\frac{1}{4} = \frac{1}{4}$$

$$\frac{2}{4}$$

B.

$$\frac{2}{5} = \frac{2}{10}$$

$$+\frac{1}{2} = \frac{1}{10}$$

$$\frac{3}{10}$$

C.

$$\frac{3}{5} = \frac{3}{15}$$

$$+\frac{1}{3} = \frac{1}{15}$$

$$\frac{4}{15}$$

Did you find Robin's procedure? Check yourself by using her procedure to compute Examples D and E.

D.

$$\frac{3}{4}$$

$$+\frac{1}{2}$$

E.

$$\frac{4}{5}$$

$$+\frac{1}{4}$$

What does Robin actually understand? What does Robin *not* yet understand as indicated by her work?

Turn to page 169 and see if you identified the procedure correctly.

Error Pattern S-F-1

Andrew was able to add with fractions and mixed numbers, but he seems to have difficulty subtracting with mixed numbers.

Clearly, Andrew is *not* using estimating skills. For Example B, he could have thought, "If I subtract two thirds, the results cannot be what I started with." If he pictured a number line in his head for Example C, he would have moved from six to five *and beyond* because, "the answer has to be less than five."

Andrew is using an error pattern similar to a common pattern for subtraction of whole numbers. Can you find the error pattern in his work?

Name *Andrew*

A.
$$7\frac{1}{2}$$
$$-\ 3$$
$$\overline{4\frac{1}{2}}$$

B.
$$8\frac{1}{3}$$
$$-\ \frac{2}{3}$$
$$\overline{8\frac{1}{3}}$$

C.
$$6$$
$$-\ 1\frac{1}{4}$$
$$\overline{5\frac{1}{4}}$$

D.
$$3\frac{1}{4}$$
$$-\ 2\frac{3}{4}$$
$$\overline{1\frac{3}{4}}$$

Did you find the pattern? Make sure by using his procedure to compute these examples.

E.
$$5\frac{1}{5}$$
$$-\ 3\frac{3}{5}$$

F.
$$1$$
$$-\ \frac{1}{3}$$

What does Andrew actually understand? What does he *not* yet understand?

Turn to page 170 and see if you identified the procedure correctly. Why might Andrew be using such a procedure?

Error Pattern S-F-2

Chuck began with this problem:

> Riva selected a piece of scrap lumber that was $8\frac{3}{4}$ feet long. She cut off a board that was $6\frac{1}{8}$ feet long. How long was the remaining piece of lumber?

Chuck chose the correct operation, but followed an error pattern in his computation. Look carefully at his written work and find his procedure.

Name __Chuck__

A. $8\frac{3}{4} - 6\frac{1}{8} = 2\frac{2}{4}$ B. $5\frac{3}{8} - 2\frac{2}{3} = 3\frac{1}{5}$

C. $9\frac{1}{5} - 1\frac{3}{8} = 8\frac{2}{3}$ D. $7\frac{2}{5} - 4\frac{7}{10} = 3\frac{5}{5}$

Did you find the procedure? Make sure by using his error pattern to compute these examples.

E. $6\frac{2}{3} - 3\frac{1}{6} =$ F. $4\frac{5}{8} - 1\frac{3}{4} =$

What do you think Chuck actually *does* understand about fractions, mixed numbers, and subtraction? What does he *not* yet understand?

Turn to page 171 and see if you identified the procedure correctly.

Error Pattern S-F-3

If Ann understands what *equals* means, she is not using that knowledge. She appears to have constructed her own procedure using different phrases she heard. Can you determine the faulty procedure she is using?

Name __Ann__

A.
$$2\frac{3}{4} = 2\frac{11}{4}$$
$$-1\frac{1}{2} = 1\frac{3}{4}$$
$$\overline{\qquad 1\frac{8}{4}}$$

B.
$$11\frac{1}{6} = 11\frac{67}{48}$$
$$-3\frac{7}{8} = 3\frac{31}{48}$$
$$\overline{\qquad 8\frac{36}{48}}$$

C.
$$9\frac{1}{3} = 9\frac{28}{3}$$
$$-\frac{2}{3} = \frac{2}{3}$$
$$\overline{\qquad 9\frac{26}{3}}$$

Did you find the error pattern? Make sure by using her procedure to compute these examples.

D.
$$5\frac{3}{8}$$
$$-2\frac{1}{2}$$

E.
$$4\frac{1}{3}$$
$$-1\frac{4}{5}$$

What does Ann understand about fractions and mixed numbers, and about subtraction? What does she *not* yet understand?

Turn to page 171 and see if you identified the procedure correctly. How would you help Ann?

Error Pattern A-D-1

Harold knows his addition number combinations. Does he use estimation skills?

Examine his work carefully. Can you find the error pattern he is following?

Name *Harold*

A.
```
   .8
 +.4
 ─────
  .12
```

B.
```
   .6
 +.9
 ─────
  .15
```

C.
```
   .4
 +.3
 ─────
  .7
```

D.
```
   .5
 +.8
 ─────
  .13
```

Did you find the pattern? Make sure by using Harold's procedure to compute these examples.

E.
```
   .3
 +.5
 ─────
```

F.
```
   .7
 +.7
 ─────
```

What does he actually understand about decimals? What does he *not* yet understand?

Turn to page 172 and see if you identified the procedure correctly. Why might Harold be using such a procedure?

Error Pattern S-D-1

Les has learned to align place value columns correctly, yet he sometimes has difficulty when subtracting with decimals. Can you determine his procedure?

Name _Les_

A.
$$87 - .31 = ?$$

B.
$$99.4 - 27.86 = ?$$

C.
$$200 - .65 = ?$$

$$\begin{array}{r} 87 \\ -\ .31 \\ \hline 87.3\ 1 \end{array}$$

$$\begin{array}{r} 99.4 \\ -27.86 \\ \hline 71.66 \end{array}$$

$$\begin{array}{r} 200 \\ -\ \ .65 \\ \hline 200.65 \end{array}$$

Find out if you correctly determined Les's error pattern by using his procedure to complete Examples D and E.

D.
$$60 - 1.35 = ?$$

E.
$$24.8 - 2.26 = ?$$

What does he actually understand about subtraction? What does he *not* yet understand?

If you completed Examples D and E, turn to page 173 and check your responses. How might you help Les or others using such a procedure?

DESCRIBING INSTRUCTION

Error Pattern A-F-1
(from Robbie's paper on page 161)

Did you find Robbie's error pattern?

E.
$$\frac{3}{4} + \frac{1}{5} = \frac{4}{9}$$

F.
$$\frac{2}{3} + \frac{5}{6} = \frac{7}{9}$$

Robbie adds the numerators to get the numerator for the sum, then adds the denominators to get the denominator for the sum—an all-too-prevalent practice. It is likely that Robbie has already learned to multiply fractions and he is following a similar procedure for adding fractions.

How would you help Robbie? Describe two instructional activities that would help him replace his error pattern with a correct computational procedure.

1. _____

2. _____

After you complete your two descriptions, turn to page 174 and compare what you have written with the suggestions presented there.

Error Pattern A-F-2
(from Dave's paper on page 162)

Did you find the error pattern Dave is using?

E. $\dfrac{1}{3} + \dfrac{3}{5} = \dfrac{4}{15}$ F. $\dfrac{3}{8} + \dfrac{4}{5} = \dfrac{7}{40}$

Dave may remember that you often have to multiply when adding fractions like these, although he does not apply any understanding of common denominators or renaming fractions. He merely adds the numerators to get the numerator for the sum, and multiplies the denominators to get the denominator for the sum.

How would you help Dave? Describe two instructional activities that you think would help Dave replace his error pattern with a correct computational procedure.

1. _____

2. _____

When you have finished describing both instructional activities, turn to page 175 and compare your suggestions with those listed there.

Error Pattern A-F-3
(from Robin's paper on page 163)

Did you find Robin's procedure?

D.
$$\frac{3}{4} = \frac{3}{4}$$
$$+\ \frac{1}{2} = \frac{1}{4}$$
$$\frac{4}{4}$$

E.
$$\frac{4}{5} = \frac{4}{20}$$
$$+\ \frac{1}{4} = \frac{1}{20}$$
$$\frac{5}{20}$$

Robin is able to determine the least common denominator and she uses it when changing two fractions so they will have the same denominator. However, she merely copies the original numerator. Apparently, Robin is able to add like fractions correctly.

How would you help Robin with her difficulty? Describe two instructional activities that you believe would help her learn to add unlike fractions correctly.

1. _____

2. _____

When you have described both activities, turn to page 176 and compare your suggestions with those listed there.

Error Pattern S-F-1
(from Andrew's paper on page 164)

Did you find Andrew's error pattern?

E.
$$5\frac{1}{5}$$
$$-\ 3\frac{3}{5}$$
$$2\frac{2}{5}$$

F.
$$1$$
$$-\ \frac{1}{3}$$
$$1\frac{1}{3}$$

In every case the whole numbers are subtracted as simple subtraction problems, perhaps even before attention is given to the column of common fractions. Where only one fraction appears in the problem (Example F), the fraction is simply "brought down." If two fractions appear, Andrew records the difference between them, ignoring whether the subtrahend or the minuend is the greater of the two.

How would you help Andrew? Describe two instructional activities you think would help Andrew correct his erroneous procedures.

1. _____

2. _____

When both descriptions are completed, turn to page 177 and compare your suggestions with those listed there.

Error Pattern S-F-2

(from Chuck's paper on page 165)

Did you find Chuck's error pattern?

E.
$$6\frac{2}{3} - 3\frac{1}{6} = 3\frac{1}{3}$$

F.
$$4\frac{5}{8} - 1\frac{3}{4} = 3\frac{2}{4}$$

Chuck is subtracting by first finding the difference between the two whole numbers and recording that difference as the new whole number. He then finds the difference between the two numerators and records that difference as the new numerator. Finally, he finds the difference between the two denominators and records that number as the new denominator. The procedure is similar to addition as seen in Error Pattern A-F-1. However, students using this procedure for subtraction necessarily ignore the order of the minuend and the subtrahend.

Someone needs to come to Chuck's aid. How would you help him? Describe two instructional procedures you believe would help Chuck subtract correctly when given examples such as these.

1. _____

2. _____

When you have described two instructional activities, turn to page 178 and compare your suggestions with those listed there.

Error Pattern S-F-3

(from Ann's paper on page 166)

Did you find the pattern?

D.
$$5\frac{3}{8} = 5\frac{43}{8}$$
$$-2\frac{1}{2} = 2\frac{5}{8}$$
$$\overline{\qquad 3\frac{38}{8}}$$

E.
$$4\frac{1}{3} = 4\frac{13}{15}$$
$$-1\frac{4}{5} = 1\frac{9}{15}$$
$$\overline{\qquad 3\frac{4}{15}}$$

Ann has difficulty changing mixed numbers to equivalent mixed numbers that have a common denominator. She does determine a common denominator, but she computes each new numerator by multiplying the original denominator times the whole number and adding the original numerator. She merely copies the given whole number.

You probably recognize part of the procedure as the way to find the new numerator when changing a mixed number to a fraction, but doing this makes no sense when changing a mixed number to an equivalent mixed number with a specified denominator.

How would you help Ann? Describe two instructional activities you believe will help her subtract correctly when she encounters examples such as these.

1. _____

2. _____

If you have described two activities, turn to page 179 and compare what you have written with the suggestions recorded there.

Error Pattern A-D-1
(from Harold's paper on page 167)

Did you find Harold's error pattern?

E.
$$.3$$
$$+.5$$
$$\overline{\quad .8}$$

F.
$$.7$$
$$+.7$$
$$\overline{\quad .14}$$

Harold seemingly adds these decimals as we would add whole numbers, but the placement of the decimal point in the sum is a problem. In every case he merely places the decimal point at the left of the sum. Or perhaps he thinks something like, "Apples added to apples are apples, and tenths added to tenths are tenths." So in Example F, the 14 is "crowded" into tenths. He might even explain, "Seven tenths plus seven tenths is 14 tenths."

We ought to be able to help Harold with a problem of this sort. How would *you* help him? Describe at least two instructional activities you believe would enable Harold to add such examples correctly.

1. _____

2. _____

After you have recorded both activities, turn to page 180 and compare your suggestions with the suggestions listed there.

Error Pattern S-D-1

(from Les's paper on page 168)

Did you determine the procedure Les is using?

D.
$$60 - 1.35 = ?$$

$$\begin{array}{r} 60 \\ -\ 1.35 \\ \hline 59.35 \end{array}$$

E.
$$24.8 - 2.26 = ?$$

$$\begin{array}{r} 24.8 \\ -\ 2.26 \\ \hline 22.66 \end{array}$$

When presented with "ragged" decimals such as these, Les simply brings down the extra digits at the right. Apparently, when there are no ragged decimals he is able to subtract correctly.

What would you do to help Les? Describe two activities you believe would help him subtract correctly when confronted with ragged decimals.

1. _____

2. _____

When your activities have been described, turn to page 182 and compare your ideas with the suggestions listed there.

CONSIDERING ALTERNATIVES

Error Pattern A-F-1
(from pages 161 and 168)

What instructional activities do you suggest to help Robbie correct the error pattern illustrated? See if your suggestions are among those illustrated.

E. $\dfrac{3}{4} + \dfrac{1}{5} = \dfrac{4}{9}$ F. $\dfrac{2}{3} + \dfrac{5}{6} = \dfrac{7}{9}$

Note: Because the error pattern is so similar to the multiplication algorithm, Robbie may be a student who tends to carry over one situation into his perception of another. If so, avoid extensive practice at a given time on any single procedure.

1. *Emphasize both "horizontal" and "vertical."* When adding *un-like* fractions, it is usually best to write the example vertically so the renaming can be recorded more easily. Give the student experience deciding which of the several examples should be written vertically to facilitate computation and which can be computed horizontally.

2. *Use unit regions and parts of unit regions.* Let the student first represent each addend as fractional parts of a unit region. It will be necessary for him to exchange some of the fractional parts so they are all of the same size (same denominator). The fractional parts can then be used to determine the total number of units. This procedure should be related step-by-step to the mechanics of notation in a written algorithm, probably as an example written vertically so the renaming can be noted more easily.

3. *Contrast ratio situations.* The algorithm used by Robbie *is* appropriate when adding win-loss ratios for different sets of games. (If he wins six of eight games, then he wins three of four more games, altogether he has won nine of 12 games.) Describe fraction (ratio) situations for the student, and have him decide which ones require a common denominator for addition.

4. *Discuss counting as a strategy.* Show how counting is appropriate when the denominators are the same, but is not appropriate when they are different.

5. *Estimate answers before computing.* This may require some practice locating fractions on a number line and ordering fractions written on cards. Use phrases like "almost a half" and "a

little less than one" when discussing problems. In Example F, more than a half is added to a little less than one. The result should be about one and a half.

> At the heart of flexibility in working with rational numbers is a solid understanding of different representations for fractions, decimals, and percents.
>
> Principles and Standards for School Mathematics, NCTM[1]

Error Pattern A-F-2

(from pages 162 and 169)

How would you help a student such as Dave who uses the error pattern illustrated? Are your suggestions included among the activities described?

E. $\dfrac{1}{3} + \dfrac{3}{5} = \dfrac{4}{15}$ F. $\dfrac{3}{8} + \dfrac{4}{5} = \dfrac{7}{40}$

1. *Stress that adding requires common denominators.* It makes sense to add the numerators only if the denominators are *already* the same. Explain that the reason we sometimes multiply denominators is to find a number we can use as the denominator for both fractions. Shift the focus away from getting an answer to two questions:

   • What number can I use for both denominators?
   • What equivalent fractions use that denominator?

2. *Use a number line to focus on equivalent fractions.* Prepare a number line from zero to one, with rows of labels for halves, thirds, fourths, and so on. Have the student find and state the many fractions for the same point. State that each point shows a number, and the fractions are different names for the same number. When we find an equivalent fraction, we are finding a different name for the same number.

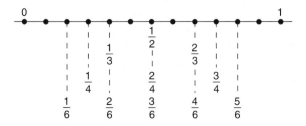

3. *Estimate answers before computing.* Consider each fraction. Is it closest to zero, to one half, or to one? (The student may need to check a number line for reference at first.) In Example E, one number is a bit less than one half, while the other number is a bit more than one half. Their sum should be about one rather than 4/15—which is closer to zero.

Error Pattern A-F-3
(from pages 163 and 169)

Robin uses the error pattern illustrated. Are your suggestions for helping Robin among the activities described?

$$\text{D.} \quad \frac{3}{4} = \frac{3}{4}$$
$$+ \quad \frac{1}{2} = \frac{1}{4}$$
$$\frac{4}{4}$$

$$\text{E.} \quad \frac{4}{5} = \frac{4}{20}$$
$$+ \quad \frac{1}{4} = \frac{1}{20}$$
$$\frac{5}{20}$$

Note: Apparently Robin can find the least common denominator. She also can add like fractions. Corrective instruction should focus on the specific process of changing a fraction to higher terms with a designated denominator; e.g., $\frac{3}{4} = \frac{?}{20}$.

1. *Show that two fractions are or are not equal.* The equals sign tells us that numerals or numerical expressions on either side are names for the same number (the same fractional part, the same point on a number line). Help Robin find ways to tell if two different fractions name the same number, and have her "prove" in *more than one way* that both fractions show the same amount. Examples of varied procedures that can be used include stacking fractional parts of a unit region, using a number line which is labelled with different fractions (halves, thirds, fourths, and so on), finding a name for one $\left(\frac{n}{n}\right)$ that could be used to change one of the fractions to the other, and for $\frac{a}{b} = \frac{c}{d}$ showing that $ad = bc$.

2. *Use the multiplicative identity.* Emphasize the role of one by outlining $\frac{n}{n}$ with the numeral "1" as illustrated. Make sure the

student notes that both terms of a fraction are multiplied, and therefore, *both* terms in the new fraction are different than the original fraction.

$$\frac{3}{4} = \frac{3 \times \boxed{2}}{4 \times \boxed{2}} = \frac{6}{8}$$

3. *Use games involving equivalent fractions.* Let the student play games in which equivalent fractions are matched, possibly adaptations of rummy or dominoes. Such games provide an excellent context for discussing how to determine if two fractions name the same number.
4. *Use a shield.* Within the algorithm, use a shield as illustrated to help focus on the task of changing a fraction to higher terms. Make sure the student understands that the procedure for changing a fraction is the same as that used *within* this algorithm.

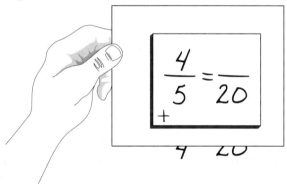

Error Pattern S-F-1
(from pages 164 and 170)

Are your suggestions for helping Andrew among the suggestions listed?

E.
$$\begin{array}{r} 5\frac{1}{5} \\ -\ 3\frac{3}{5} \\ \hline 2\frac{2}{5} \end{array}$$

F.
$$\begin{array}{r} 1 \\ -\ \frac{1}{3} \\ \hline 1\frac{1}{3} \end{array}$$

Note: You will want to interview this student and have him think out loud as he works similar examples. Does he question the reasonableness of his answers? In Example F, the result is greater than the sum (minuend).

1. *Use fractional parts of a unit region.* Interpret the example as "take-away" subtraction and use fractional parts to show *only* the sum. If the student subtracts the whole numbers first, demonstrate that this procedure does not work because not enough remains so the fraction can be subtracted. Conclude that the fraction must be subtracted before the whole number. Let the student exchange one of the units for an equivalent set of fractional parts in order to take away the quantity indicated by the subtrahend.

2. *Record the renaming.* Record the exchange of fractional parts (suggested above) as a renaming of the sum. The sum is renamed so the fraction can be subtracted easily.

$$\begin{array}{r} 4\,\frac{6}{5} \\ \cancel{5}\,\cancel{\frac{1}{5}} \\ -\,3\,\frac{3}{5} \\ \hline 1\,\frac{3}{5} \end{array}$$

3. *Practice specific prerequisite skills.* Without computing, the student can decide which examples require renaming and which do not. The skill of renaming a mixed number in order to subtract can also be practiced.

Error Pattern S-F-2
(from pages 165 and 171)

Do you find, among the suggestions listed, your suggestions for helping Chuck?

E. $6\frac{2}{3} - 3\frac{1}{6} = 3\frac{1}{3}$ F. $4\frac{5}{8} - 1\frac{3}{4} = 3\frac{2}{4}$

Note: Extended diagnosis is probably wise. Most of the subordinate skills you may have identified for addition with fractions apply equally to subtraction.

1. *Distinguish between horizontal and vertical.* When subtracting with unlike fractions and with mixed numerals, it is usually best to write the example vertically so the renaming can be recorded more easily. Let the student practice deciding which of several examples should be written vertically to facilitate computation and which can be computed horizontally.

2. *Use fractional parts of a unit region.* As you work with the student, or a group of students, let them use fractional parts to show *only* the sum, then set apart the amount indicated by the known addend. Students will soon discover that it is necessary to deal with the fraction before the whole number. They will often need to exchange in order to set apart the amount required. This task can help students relate problems more adequately to the operation of subtraction. However, it can become a cumbersome procedure, so choose examples carefully. (An appropriate example might be $3\frac{1}{6} - 1\frac{2}{3}$.) Step-by-step, relate the activity with fractional parts to the vertical algorithm.

Error Pattern S-F-3
(from pages 166 and 171)

Are your suggestions for helping Ann among the suggestions listed?

D.
$$5\frac{3}{8} = 5\frac{43}{8}$$
$$-2\frac{1}{2} = 2\frac{5}{8}$$
$$\overline{\quad\quad\quad 3\frac{38}{8}}$$

E.
$$4\frac{1}{3} = 4\frac{13}{15}$$
$$-1\frac{4}{5} = 1\frac{9}{15}$$
$$\overline{\quad\quad\quad 3\frac{4}{15}}$$

Note: Corrective instruction should focus on changing a mixed number to an equivalent mixed number, one in which the fraction has a specified denominator.

1. *Prove that mixed numbers are or are not equal.* Emphasize that the whole number and fraction together constitute a mixed number, and that "equals" written between two mixed numbers says that they name the same number (show the same amount, name the same point on a number line). Two mixed numbers can be shown to be equal with unit regions and fractional parts, or with an appropriately labeled number line.

2. *Make many names for a mixed number.* With the help of an aid such as unit regions and fractional parts, let the student generate as many names as possible for a given mixed number. For example:

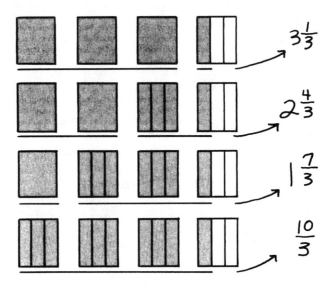

Then, for an example like $3\frac{1}{3} - 1\frac{2}{3} = ?$ ask, "Which is the most useful name for $3\frac{1}{3}$?"

3. *Point to different trading patterns.* Liken the regrouping within this algorithm to the regrouping done with whole numbers when different bases are used. Chip trading activities with varied trading rules have a structure similar to the process of changing a mixed number to an equivalent mixed number.

Error Pattern A-D-1
(from pages 167 and 172)

You have described two activities for helping Harold with the difficulty illustrated. Are either of your suggestions among those listed?

E.
$$\begin{array}{r} .3 \\ +.5 \\ \hline .8 \end{array}$$

F.
$$\begin{array}{r} .7 \\ +.7 \\ \hline .14 \end{array}$$

Note: Some teachers will be tempted to simply tell the student that in problems like Example F the decimal point should go between the two digits in the sum. However, such directions only compound the problem. This student needs a greater understanding of decimal numeration and the ability to apply such knowledge. Tell students to "line up place values" when they compute with decimals. Do not tell them to "line up decimal points"—that is just a result of lining up place values. Research has shown that much of the difficulty students have with decimals stems from a lack of conceptual understanding.[2]

Further diagnosis is probably wise. When the addends also include units, does the student regroup tenths as units (as in the first example) or does he think of two separate problems—one to the right of the point and one to the left of the point (as in the second example)?

$$
\begin{array}{r}
6.7 \\
+8.5 \\
\hline
15.2
\end{array}
\qquad \text{or} \ ? \qquad
\begin{array}{r}
6.7 \\
+8.5 \\
\hline
14.12
\end{array}
$$

1. *Use blocks or rods.* Define one size as a unit. Then let the student show each addend with blocks or rods one tenth as large as the unit. After he combines the two sets, he can exchange tenths for a unit, if possible, so he will have "as few blocks as possible for this much wood" (or a similar expression for the particular materials used). He should compare the results of this activity with his erroneous procedure.

2. *Use a number line.* Mark units and tenths clearly on a number line and show addition with arrows. Compare the sum indicated on the number line with the sum resulting from computation.

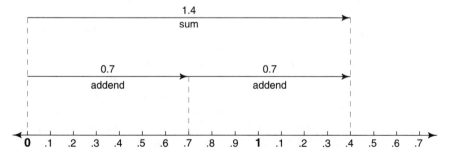

3. *Use vertically lined or cross-sectioned paper.* Theme paper can be turned 90° to use as vertically lined paper. Let the student compute with only one digit placed in a column. If cross-sectioned paper is used, only one digit should be written within each square.

4. *Use metersticks.* Use metersticks to reintroduce decimals and the names for the value of each place.

Error Pattern S-D-1
(from pages 168 and 173)

You described ways to help Les or other students who subtract as il-lustrated when they encounter ragged decimals. Are your suggestions among those listed?

D.
$$60 - 1.35 = ?$$

E.
$$24.8 - 2.26 = ?$$

$$
\begin{array}{r}
6\,0 \\
-\ 1.35 \\
\hline
5\,9.35
\end{array}
$$

$$
\begin{array}{r}
24.8 \\
-\ 2.26 \\
\hline
2\,2.66
\end{array}
$$

Note: Usually the need to add or subtract decimals arises from measurement situations, and measurements should al-ways be expressed in the same units and with the same preci-sion if they are to be added or subtracted. Ragged decimals are inappropriate. At the same time, ragged decimals sometimes oc-cur in situations with money (e.g., $4 − $.35). They also appear on some standardized tests, and many teachers believe students need to be taught a procedure for computing with them even if examples are somewhat contrived.

1. *Use a place-value chart.* A place-value chart can be relabeled for use with decimals (e.g., tens, ones, tenths, and hundredths). For a given example, let the student first show the sum (minu-end) and then work through the regrouping necessary to sub-tract as would be done with whole numbers. Point out that the regrouping is being done *as if* additional zeros were written to the right of the decimal point. Suggest that by affixing zeros ap-propriately, the examples can be computed without the confu-sion of ragged decimals. If it will simplify things, encourage the student to affix zeros when adding as well as when subtract-ing. (Be sure students *affix* zeros; they do not add them.)
2. *Use base-ten blocks.* For use with decimals, the unit must be defined differently from the way it is used with whole num-bers, so you may choose to use blocks that are not lined. Use them as the place-value chart is used.

3. *Use money.* Use pennies, dimes, dollar bills, and ten-dollar bills much as you would use a place-value chart. Stress the fact that the dollar bill is the unit; the dimes and pennies are tenths and hundredths of one dollar.

CONCLUSION

Students with deficient fraction concepts who are introduced to addition and subtraction procedures too soon commonly develop inadequate procedures. Many such error patterns were observed in this chapter. The fact that operations with fractions are difficult for students worldwide, along with lessened use, are reasons some educators are beginning to argue that we no longer need to include fractions within the curriculum.[3] Other educators point to their value in preparation for learning algebra.

Teach computational procedures so that they make sense to students. Those students who tend toward the use of rote procedures sometimes use part of one learned procedure within a procedure they are creating. For example, they may use parts of the procedure for multiplying fractions when they add fractions. Always be on the alert for similar patterns during instructional activities, and keep emphasizing the need for reasonable answers.

Sometimes students create procedures in which they state that one quantity is equal to an entirely different quantity. Keep emphasizing the fact that two equivalent fractions or mixed numbers are names for *the same number.* If the two are shown at different points on a number line, they are not the same.

When students add and subtract with decimals, stress that place values must be aligned. Also remind students that only one digit appears in each place.

Vary instruction as much as possible. Build on each student's strengths, and watch students gain in confidence.

REFERENCES

1. National Council of Teachers of Mathematics. (2000). *Principles and standards for school mathematics.* Reston, VA: The Council, p. 215.
2. For example, see T. P. Carpenter, M. K. Corbitt, H. S. Kepner, Jr., M. M. Lindquist, & R. E. Reys (1981). Decimals: Results and implications from national assessment. *Arithmetic Teacher 28*(8), pp. 34–37.
3. Groff, P. (1996). It is time to question fraction teaching. *Mathematics Teaching in the Middle School 1*(8), pp. 604–607.

Chapter 8

Fractions and Decimals: Multiplication and Division

⌐⌐

It is challenging to teach multiplication and division with fractions and decimals so that the algorithms make sense to students—especially procedures with fractions. Troublesome misconceptions frequently intervene. For instance, students often believe that if you multiply your answer will be bigger, and if you divide your answer will be smaller.

But instruction *can* focus on making sense of procedures by using manipulatives and applying mathematical ideas understood when learning about operations with whole numbers. Multiplication and division papers in this chapter involve many misconceptions. Accordingly, the procedures often produce incorrect answers. Can you find the patterns that characterize each student's responses?

Check your findings by using the error pattern with the additional examples, then read about the student's procedure and suggest needed instruction. It is important for a teacher to have in mind more than one instructional strategy, so try to suggest at least two to help each student. Then compare your suggestions with those in this book.

As you plan instruction, keep the meanings of the two operations in mind along with their relationship to one another. Also remember the varied two- and three-dimensional representations available for teaching about fractions and decimals.

In Appendix A there are additional student papers so you can further test your ability to identify patterns. A key is provided.

IDENTIFYING PATTERNS

Error Pattern M-F-1

> Four fifths of the bushes are azaleas. Three fourths of the azaleas are pink. What part of the bushes are pink azaleas?

If Dan were using good number sense and estimating skills, he would know that one times one is one, and less-than-one times less-than-one is something less than one. Furthermore, only a part (first factor) of the second factor is less than the second factor. Look at Dan's written work. His products are not at all reasonable.

Name _Dan_

A.
$$\frac{4}{5} \times \frac{3}{4} = 166$$

B.
$$\frac{1}{2} \times \frac{3}{8} = 68$$

C.
$$\frac{2}{9} \times \frac{1}{5} = 100$$

D.
$$\frac{2}{3} \times \frac{4}{6} = 132$$

Dan appears to be using a procedure he constructed from phrases he heard and parts of procedures he observed. Can you determine what procedure he is using?

Make sure you found Dan's procedure by using it to compute these examples.

E.
$$\frac{3}{4} \times \frac{2}{3} =$$

F.
$$\frac{4}{9} \times \frac{2}{5} =$$

What does Dan actually understand? What does he *not* yet understand?

Turn to page 190 and see if you identified the pattern correctly. Why might Dan be using such a procedure?

Error Pattern M-F-2

Do you think Lynn is using estimating skills? Does she understand that multiplication with fractions is commutative?

In Example D, two times almost-one ($\frac{4}{5}$) is likely to be almost-two. The product will certainly be *more* than one, and her product is less than one. Most of her products are not reasonable.

Can you find the procedure she is following?

Name *Lynn*

A. $\dfrac{1}{8} \times 1 = \dfrac{1}{8}$ B. $\dfrac{2}{3} \times 3 = \dfrac{6}{9}$

C. $\dfrac{1}{4} \times 6 = \dfrac{6}{24}$ D. $\dfrac{4}{5} \times 2 = \dfrac{8}{10}$

Lynn may be confusing this situation with something else she has learned. Can you find the procedure she used? Check yourself by using her error pattern to compute these examples.

E. $\dfrac{3}{8} \times 4 =$ F. $\dfrac{5}{6} \times 2 =$

Now that you have completed Examples E and F, turn to page 191 and see if you identified the procedure correctly.

Error Pattern D-F-1

When Linda divides with fractions, her answers are sometimes correct, but frequently they are not correct.

She does not appear to be using good number sense and estimating skills. If she were, she might think, for Example C, "How many halves ($\frac{2}{4}$) are in about one half ($\frac{6}{10}$)? There should be about one, not one and one half ($\frac{3}{2}$)."

Can you find the procedure she is following?

Name *Linda*

A. $\dfrac{4}{6} \div \dfrac{2}{2} = \dfrac{2}{3}$ B. $\dfrac{6}{8} \div \dfrac{2}{8} = \dfrac{3}{1}$

C. $\dfrac{6}{10} \div \dfrac{2}{4} = \dfrac{3}{2}$ D. $\dfrac{7}{5} \div \dfrac{3}{2} = \dfrac{2}{2}$

Linda may be confusing this situation with something else she learned.

See if you found her procedure. Use her error pattern to compute these examples.

E. $\dfrac{4}{12} \div \dfrac{4}{4} =$ F. $\dfrac{13}{20} \div \dfrac{5}{6} =$

Next, turn to page 192 and see if you identified the procedure correctly.

Error Pattern D-F-2

Does Joyce understand the operation of division?

Is she using good number sense and estimating skills? If she is, she might think, for Example A, "Is there less than one half ($\frac{3}{8}$) in more-than-a-half ($\frac{2}{3}$)? Yes, so the answer should be at least one; but my answer ($\frac{9}{16}$) is less than one."

Can you find the error pattern she is using?

Name _Joyce_

A. $\dfrac{2}{3} \div \dfrac{3}{8} = \dfrac{3}{2} \times \dfrac{3}{8} = \dfrac{9}{16}$

B. $\dfrac{2}{5} \div \dfrac{1}{3} = \dfrac{5}{2} \times \dfrac{1}{3} = \dfrac{5}{6}$

C. $\dfrac{3}{4} \div \dfrac{1}{5} = \dfrac{4}{3} \times \dfrac{1}{5} = \dfrac{4}{15}$

See if you found her error pattern. Use her procedure to compute these examples.

D. $\dfrac{5}{8} \div \dfrac{2}{3} =$

E. $\dfrac{1}{2} \div \dfrac{1}{4} =$

When you complete Examples D and E, turn to page 192.

Error Pattern M-D-1

> Dried fruit costs $6.45 a pound. How much do 3 pounds of dried fruit cost?

Marsha seems to have difficulty with some multiplication problems involving decimals, but she solves other examples correctly.

If she were estimating Example C, she might think, "A number less than one times 21 has to be less than 21. But my answer is much more than 21."

Can you find her pattern of errors?

Name *Marsha*

A.
$$\begin{array}{r} \$\,6.45 \\ \times\ \ \ 3 \\ \hline \$19.35 \end{array}$$

B.
$$\begin{array}{r} 32.7 \\ \times\ \ \ .5 \\ \hline 16.35 \end{array}$$

C.
$$\begin{array}{r} 21.8 \\ \times\ .4 \\ \hline 87.2 \end{array}$$

D.
$$\begin{array}{r} 4.35 \\ \times\ 2.3 \\ \hline 1305 \\ 870\ \ \\ \hline 100.05 \end{array}$$

See if you found Marsha's error pattern. Use her procedure to compute these examples.

E.
$$\begin{array}{r} 40.5 \\ \times\ \ \ .6 \\ \hline \end{array}$$

F.
$$\begin{array}{r} 6.7 \\ \times\ \ 3 \\ \hline \end{array}$$

When you complete Examples E and F, turn to page 193. How might you help Marsha or any other student using such a procedure?

Error Pattern D-D-1

When Ted started dividing decimals, his answers were usually correct. But he frequently gets the wrong quotient. Can you find his pattern of errors?

Name __Ted__

A.
$$
\begin{array}{r}
3.91 \\
6\overline{\smash{\big)}23.5} \\
\underline{18} \\
55 \\
\underline{54} \\
1
\end{array}
$$

B.
$$
\begin{array}{r}
9.62 \\
4\overline{\smash{\big)}38.6} \\
\underline{36} \\
26 \\
\underline{24} \\
2
\end{array}
$$

C.
$$
\begin{array}{r}
1.644 \\
5\overline{\smash{\big)}8.24} \\
\underline{5} \\
32 \\
\underline{30} \\
24 \\
\underline{20} \\
4
\end{array}
$$

How much does Ted understand about decimal place values? What does he understand about remainders in division examples?

Use Ted's procedure with these examples to see if you found his error pattern.

D. $3\overline{\smash{\big)}2.57}$

E. $.7\overline{\smash{\big)}9.35}$

Now turn to page 193 and see if you identified the procedure correctly. How might you help Ted or any other student using this error pattern?

DESCRIBING INSTRUCTION

Error Pattern M-F-1
(from Dan's paper on page 185)

Did you find Dan's error pattern?

E. $\dfrac{3}{4} \times \dfrac{2}{3} = 89$

F. $\dfrac{4}{9} \times \dfrac{2}{5} = 200$

Dan begins by multiplying the first numerator and the second denominator and recording the units digit of this product. If there is a tens digit, he remembers it to add later (as in multiplication of whole numbers). He then multiplies the first denominator and the second numerator, adds the number of tens remembered, and records this as the number of tens in the answer. The procedure involves a sort of cross multiplication and the multiply-then-add sequence from multiplication of whole numbers.

Dan uses this error pattern consistently. He has somehow learned to multiply fractions this way. How would you help him learn the correct procedure? Describe two instructional activities you believe would help.

1. _____

2. _____

After two activities have been described, turn to page 194 and compare what you have written with the suggestions listed there.

Error Pattern M-F-2
(from Lynn's paper on page 186)

Did you find the procedure Lynn is using?

E. $\dfrac{3}{8} \times 4 = \dfrac{12}{32}$ F. $\dfrac{5}{6} \times 2 = \dfrac{10}{12}$

Lynn has learned that when you are multiplying and you have a fraction, you have to multiply *both* the numerator and the denominator of the fraction. Of course, when multiplying both terms by the same number she is actually multiplying the fraction by *one* rather than by the whole number in the example. It may be that she multiplied both numerator and denominator by the same number when she practiced changing a fraction to higher terms, and she continues to use this familiar pattern.

How would you help Lynn? Describe two activities that you believe would enable her to multiply correctly.

1. _____

2. _____

If you have described two such activities, turn to page 195 and compare your suggestions with the ideas listed there.

Error Pattern D-F-1

(from Linda's paper on page 187)

Did you find the error pattern Linda is using?

E.
$$\frac{4}{12} \div \frac{4}{4} = \frac{1}{3}$$

F.
$$\frac{13}{20} \div \frac{5}{6} = \frac{2}{3}$$

Linda divides the first numerator by the second numerator and records the result as the numerator for the answer. She then determines the denominator for the answer by dividing the first denominator by the second denominator. In both divisions she ignores remainders. Note that Examples A, B, and E are correct. It may be that she learned her procedure while the class was working with such examples. The common denominator method of dividing fractions may be part of the background because her procedure is similar; however, she fails to change the fractions to equivalent fractions with the same denominator before dividing.

This is a tricky error pattern, producing both correct answers and absurd answers with zero numerators and denominators. Linda obviously needs help. How would you help her? Describe two instructional activities you think would enable her to replace her error pattern with a correct computational procedure.

1. _____

2. _____

When you have noted your descriptions, turn to page 196 and compare them with the suggestions listed there.

Error Pattern D-F-2

(from Joyce's paper on page 188)

Did you find the procedure Joyce is using?

D.
$$\frac{5}{8} \div \frac{2}{3} = \frac{8}{5} \times \frac{2}{3} = \frac{16}{15}$$

E.
$$\frac{1}{2} \div \frac{1}{4} = \frac{2}{1} \times \frac{1}{4} = \frac{2}{4}$$

Joyce knows to invert and multiply, but she inverts the dividend (or product) instead of the divisor. It *does* make a difference.

Dividing fractions seems to involve such an arbitrary rule. How would *you* help Joyce? Describe two instructional activities you believe would help her divide correctly.

1. _____

2. _____

When you have described both activities, turn to page 197 and compare your ideas with the activities described there.

Error Pattern M-D-1
(from Marsha's paper on page 189)

If you used Marsha's error pattern, you completed Examples E and F as they are shown.

E.
$$\begin{array}{r} 40.5 \\ \times\ \ .6 \\ \hline 24.30 \end{array}$$

F.
$$\begin{array}{r} 6.7 \\ \times\ \ 3 \\ \hline 2.01 \end{array}$$

In her answer, Marsha places the decimal point by counting over from the left instead of from the right in the product. She frequently gets the correct answer (as in Examples A, B, and E), but much of the time her answer is not the correct product.

If you were Marsha's teacher, what corrective procedures might you follow? Describe two instructional activities that you think would help Marsha multiply decimals correctly.

1. _____

2. _____

When your responses are complete, turn to page 198 and see if your suggestions are among the alternatives described.

Error Pattern D-D-1
(from Ted's paper on page 190)

If you found Ted's error pattern, your results are the same as the erroneous computations shown.

D.
$$3 \overline{)2.57} \quad \begin{array}{r} .852 \\ \hline \end{array}$$

```
        .852
     _____
  3 | 2.57
      24
      __
       17
       15
       __
        2
```

E.
```
          13.34
        _____
  .7 | 9.35
       7
       _
       23
       21
       __
        25
        21
        __
         4
```

Ted misses examples because of the way he handles remainders. If division does not "come out even" when taken as far as digits given in the dividend, Ted writes the remainder as an extension of the quotient. He may believe this is the same as writing R2 after the quotient for a division problem with whole numbers. Some students, having studied division with decimals, use a procedure similar to Ted's when dividing whole numbers. For example, 600 divided by 7 is computed as 85.5.

How would you help Ted? Describe at least two instructional activities you believe would correct his error pattern.

1. _____

2. _____

After you have described at least two activities, turn to page 199 and compare your suggestions with the suggestions listed there.

CONSIDERING ALTERNATIVES

Error Pattern M-F-1
(from pages 185 and 190)

How would you help a student such as Dan correct the error pattern illustrated? Are the activities you described similar to any of those presented here?

E.

$$\frac{3}{4} \times \frac{2}{3} = 89$$

F.

$$\frac{4}{9} \times \frac{2}{5} = 200$$

Note: The student's products are most unreasonable and continued diagnosis is wise. Does this student understand the equals sign as meaning "the same as"? What kind of meaning does he associate with common fractions? Does he believe that products are *always* greater numbers?

1. *Use fractional parts of unit regions.* When interpreting an example like $\frac{3}{4} \times \frac{2}{3} = ?$ as $\frac{3}{4}$ of $\frac{2}{3} = ?$, picture a rectangular region partitioned into thirds and shade two of them. This represents $\frac{2}{3}$ of one. Next, partition the unit so the student can see $\frac{3}{4}$ of the $\frac{2}{3}$. What part of the unit is shown as $\frac{3}{4}$ of $\frac{2}{3}$? Be sure he relates the answer to the unit rather than just the $\frac{2}{3}$. Record the fact that $\frac{3}{4}$ of $\frac{2}{3} = \frac{6}{12}$ and solve other problems with drawings. Then redevelop the rule for multiplying fractions by observing a pattern among several examples completed with fractional parts of unit regions.

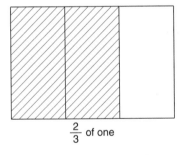

$\frac{2}{3}$ of one

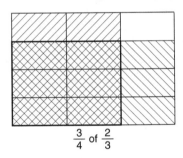

$\frac{3}{4}$ of $\frac{2}{3}$

2. *Estimate before computing.* Students often assume that the result of multiplying will be a larger number. Ask if $\frac{2}{3}$ is less than one or more than one. Is $\frac{1}{4}$ of $\frac{2}{3}$ less than one or more than one? $\frac{2}{4}$ of $\frac{2}{3}$? $\frac{3}{4}$ of $\frac{2}{3}$? Will $\frac{3}{4}$ of $\frac{2}{3}$ be less than $\frac{2}{3}$ or more than $\frac{2}{3}$? It will be helpful if the student expects his answer to be less than $\frac{2}{3}$. Of course, a student must understand fraction concepts before he can be expected to learn to estimate.

Error Pattern M-F-2
(from pages 186 and 191)

How would you help Lynn correct the error pattern illustrated? Are your ideas similar to those listed?

E. $\dfrac{3}{8} \times 4 = \dfrac{12}{32}$ F. $\dfrac{5}{6} \times 2 = \dfrac{10}{12}$

1. *Make the whole number a fraction.* Show Lynn that when multiplying both terms by the same number, she is multiplying by one (in the form $\frac{n}{n}$) and not by the number given. Have her put 1 under the whole number. Both numbers will be fractions and the child can then use the procedure for multiplying fractions; e.g., $\frac{3}{8} \times \frac{4}{1} = \frac{12}{8}$.

2. *Use a number line.* On a number line which is labeled appropriately, have the student draw arrows to show the multiplication. Emphasize that the product tells how many sixths (or whatever denominator is being used). For $2 \times \frac{5}{6}$ or for $\frac{5}{6} \times 2$:

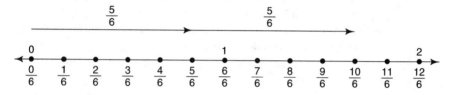

3. *Use addition.* Reverse the factors and have the child solve the addition problem suggested.

$$\dfrac{3}{8} \times 4 = 4 \times \dfrac{3}{8}$$

$$4 \times \dfrac{3}{8} = \dfrac{3}{8} + \dfrac{3}{8} + \dfrac{3}{8} + \dfrac{3}{8} = \dfrac{12}{8}$$

Error Pattern D-F-1

(from pages 187 and 192)

What instructional activities do you suggest to help Linda correct the error pattern illustrated? See if your suggestions are among those described.

E. $\dfrac{4}{12} \div \dfrac{4}{4} = \dfrac{1}{3}$ F. $\dfrac{13}{20} \div \dfrac{5}{6} = \dfrac{2}{3}$

Note: Selection of appropriate activities will depend somewhat on which algorithm for division with fractions the student was taught originally.

1. *Discover a pattern.* Introduce the Invert and Multiply Rule by presenting a varied selection of examples complete with correct answers; e.g., $\frac{7}{12} \div \frac{3}{5} = \frac{35}{36}$. Let the student compare the problems and answers and look for a pattern among the division examples. Be sure each hypothesized rule is tested by checking it against all examples in the selection. After the pattern has been found, make sure the student verbalizes the rule and makes up a few examples to solve.

2. *Estimate answers with paper strips and a number line.* Using a number line and the measurement model for division, make a strip of paper about as long as the dividend and another about as long as the divisor. Ask how many strips the length of the divisor strip can be made from the dividend strip. For $\frac{5}{8} \div \frac{2}{5} = ?$, the answer might be about one and one half. For Example F, the estimate might be a little less than one.

Error Pattern D-F-2
(from pages 188 and 192)

How would you help a student such as Joyce who uses the error pattern illustrated? Are your suggestions included among those listed?

D.
$$\frac{5}{8} \div \frac{2}{3} = \frac{8}{5} \times \frac{2}{3} = \frac{16}{15}$$

E.
$$\frac{1}{2} \div \frac{1}{4} = \frac{2}{1} \times \frac{1}{4} = \frac{2}{4}$$

Note: Determine whether the student consistently inverts the dividend, or alternates between the divisor and the dividend. You may also want to make sure the student has no difficulty distinguishing between right and left.

1. *Compare results.* Have the student compare inverting the dividend with inverting the divisor. Do both procedures produce the same result? Then explain that it is the divisor "there on the right" that is to be inverted. Have the student suggest a

way of remembering to invert the fraction on the right and not the other fraction when dividing. (Be careful. Remember the student in Chapter 2 who used the piano.)

2. *Use parts of a unit region.* Because inverting the dividend and inverting the divisor produce different answers, the student can use a manipulative aid to determine which result is correct. Parts of a unit region may be appropriate if the example is interpreted as measurement division. For $\frac{1}{2} \div \frac{1}{4} = ?$ have the student first place $\frac{1}{2}$ of a unit on top of a unit region. This shows the dividend or product. Then explain that just as $6 \div 2 = ?$ asks, "How many 2s are in 6?" so $\frac{1}{2} \div \frac{1}{4} = ?$ asks, "How many $\frac{1}{4}$s are in $\frac{1}{2}$?" Have the student cover the $\frac{1}{2}$ of a unit with $\frac{1}{4}$s of a unit. In all, exactly *two* $\frac{1}{4}$s are equal to $\frac{1}{2}$. The correct result is two, not $\frac{2}{4}$; it is the result obtained by inverting the divisor on the right.

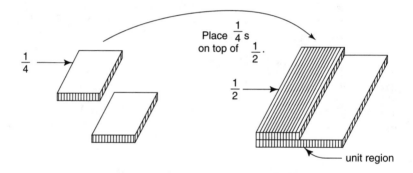

Place $\frac{1}{4}$ s on top of $\frac{1}{2}$.

$\frac{1}{4}$

$\frac{1}{2}$

unit region

3. *Use paper strips and a number line.* These can be used as described in the previous error pattern, but used in this case to determine which fraction should be inverted for the correct result.

Error Pattern M-D-1

(from pages 189 and 193)

Illustrations of Marsha's error pattern in multiplication of decimals are shown here. Are the instructional activities you suggested to help her among those described?

E.
$$\begin{array}{r} 40.5 \\ \times\ \ \ .6 \\ \hline 24.30 \end{array}$$

F.
$$\begin{array}{r} 6.7 \\ \times\ \ \ 3 \\ \hline 2.01 \end{array}$$

1. *Estimate before computing.* Use concepts like less than and
more than in estimating the product before computing. For
Example E, a bit more than 40 is being multiplied by about a
half. The product should be a bit more than 20. There is only
one place where the decimal point could go if the answer is to
be a bit more than 20. Similarly, in Example F, 6.7 is between
6 and 7; therefore, the answer should be between 18 and 21.
Again, there is only one place the decimal point can be written
for the answer to be reasonable. For 3.452 × 4.845, it can be
easily seen that the product must be between 12 (i.e., 3 × 4)
and 20 (i.e., 4 × 5), and there will be only one sensible place
to write the decimal point.
2. *Look for a pattern.* Introduce the rule for placing the decimal
point in the product by presenting a varied selection of examples complete with correct answers. As the student compares
the examples, ask her to look for a pattern. Be sure she
checks her pattern against all examples in the selection.
When the correct pattern or rule is established, let the student verbalize the rule and use it with a few examples she
makes up herself.

Error Pattern D-D-1
(from pages 190 and 193)

Are your suggestions for helping Ted among the suggestions listed?
He has the difficulty illustrated.

D.
```
     .852
  3)2.57
    24
    17
    15
     2
```

E.
```
     13.34
  .7)9.35
    7
    23
    21
    25
    21
     4
```

1. *Label columns on lined paper.* Turn theme paper 90° and write
each column of digits between two vertical lines. Then label

each column with the appropriate place value. This may help discourage moving digits around mechanically. In Example D, 2 hundredths is not the same as 2 thousandths.

2. *Study alternatives for handling remainders.* By using simple examples and story problems, first show that for division of *whole* numbers there are at least three different ways to handle remainders:

a. As the amount remaining after distributing. Either a measurement or partitioning model for division can be used.

$$
\begin{array}{r}
6\,4 \\
6\,\overline{)3\,8\,7} \\
3\,6 \\
\hline
2\,7 \\
2\,4 \\
\hline
3
\end{array}
$$

ANSWER: 64 (groups, or in each group) with 3 left over

b. As a fraction within the quotient expressed as a mixed number. A partitioning model for division is usually used here.

$$
\begin{array}{r}
9\,3\,{}^{1}\!/_{4} \\
4\,\overline{)3\,7\,3} \\
3\,6 \\
\hline
1\,3 \\
1\,2 \\
\hline
1
\end{array}
$$

ANSWER: $93\frac{1}{4}$ for each of the 4

c. As an indicator that the quotient should be rounded up by one, often in relation to the cost of an item. For example, pencils priced at 3 for 29¢ would sell for 10¢ each.

$$
\begin{array}{r}
9 \\
3\,\overline{)2\,9} \\
2\,7 \\
\hline
2
\end{array}
$$

ANSWER: 10¢ each

Next, consider remainders for division of decimals similarly. If the remainder in Example D is viewed as the amount leftover after distributing, 0.02 would remain. If it is viewed as a common fraction within the quotient, the quotient would be 0.85 $\frac{2}{3}$ or 0.857.

CONCLUSION

As you emphasize multiplication and division meanings, you may find it helpful to review those meanings with whole numbers before talking about fractions and decimals. For example, "For 8 divided by 2 we can think, how many 2s in 8? And for $\frac{1}{2}$ divided by $\frac{1}{3}$ we can think, how many $\frac{1}{3}$s in $\frac{1}{2}$?"

Before letting students practice procedures for multiplying and dividing with fractions, take time for them to estimate many of the products and quotients. "Will almost one times one half be greater than a half or less than a half? Why?" Students can discuss several examples and describe answers that are reasonable.

Be alert for any student who believes that a product must be a greater number. Frequently students infer this from their work with whole numbers.

Make sure students use what they know about the relationship between multiplication and division as they estimate reasonable quotients, and verify the results of their computation. Ask questions like, "Will the number be greater than one or less than one? Why?"

Chapter 9

Percent Problems

⌐⌐

This chapter contains examples of percent problems solved by students using procedures they assumed to be correct. These students do get correct answers sometimes, but their understanding is inadequate. Their error patterns need to be found and appropriate instruction to correct those errors provided.

As you identify patterns, remember that students sometimes overgeneralize. They remember what was true in a limited number of situations and apply it more generally. Take time to study each example completed by the student.

After finding the pattern, verify your hypothesis by completing the additional examples. As you suggest instructional activities to help the student, remember that when you are thinking about percent, you are thinking about hundredths or parts per 100. Also recall that a proportion is a statement that two ratios name the same number.

Be sure to suggest at least two instructional activities, then compare your suggestions with those provided in this book.

IDENTIFYING PATTERNS

Error Pattern P-P-1

Sara correctly solves some percent problems, but many answers are incorrect. Can you find an error pattern?

Name *Sara*

A. On a test with 30 items, Mary worked 24 items correctly.
What percent did she have correct?

$$\frac{24}{30} = \frac{x}{100}$$

Answer: *80 %*

B. Twelve students had perfect scores on a quiz. This is 40% of
the class. How many students are in the class.

$$\frac{12}{40} = \frac{x}{100}$$

Answer: *30 students*

C. Jim correctly solved 88% of 50 test items. How many items
did he have correct?

$$\frac{50}{88} = \frac{x}{100}$$

Answer: *57 items*

When you think you have found Sara's error pattern, use it to
solve these problems.

D. Brad earned $400 during the summer and saved $240 from
his earnings. What percent of his earnings did he save?

Answer:_____

E. Barbara received a gift of money on her birthday. She spent
80% of the money on a watch. The watch cost her $20. How
much money did she receive as a birthday gift?

Answer:_____

F. The taffy sale brought in a total of $750, but 78% of this was
used for expenses. How much money was used for expenses?

Answer:_____

Next, turn to page 205 to see if you identified the pattern correctly. Why might Sara or any student adopt such a procedure?

Error Pattern P-P-2

Steve is having difficulty solving percent questions. Can you find an error pattern in his paper?

Name *Steve*

A. What number is 30% of 180?

$$
\begin{array}{r}
1\,8\,0 \\
\times\ .3\,0 \\
\hline
0\,0\,0 \\
5\,4\,0 \\
\hline
5\,4.0\,0
\end{array}
$$

Answer: __54__

B. Fifteen percent of what number is 240?

$$
\begin{array}{r}
2\,4\,0 \\
\times\ .1\,5 \\
\hline
1\,2\,0\,0 \\
2\,4\,0 \\
\hline
3\,6.0\,0
\end{array}
$$

Answer: __36__

C. What percent of 40 is 28?

$$
\begin{array}{r}
4\,0 \\
\times.2\,8 \\
\hline
3\,2\,0 \\
8\,0 \\
\hline
1\,1.2\,0
\end{array}
$$

Answer: __11.2__

When you find Steve's error pattern, use it to solve these examples.

D. What number is 80% of 54?   ANSWER:_____

E. Seventy is 14% of what number?   Answer:_____

F. What percent of 125 is 25?   Answer:_____

Now, turn to page 206 to learn if you found Steve's procedure. How would you help a student who computes in this way?

Describing Instruction

Error Pattern P-P-1
(from Sara's paper on page 203)

If you used Sara's error pattern, you completed the three percent problems as shown.

D. Brad earned $400 during the summer and saved $240 from his earnings. What percent of his earnings did he save?

$$\frac{240}{400} = \frac{X}{100}$$ Answer: 60%

E. Barbara received a gift of money on her birthday. She spent 80% of the money on a watch. The watch cost $20. How much money did she receive as a birthday gift?

$$\frac{20}{80} = \frac{X}{100}$$ Answer: $25

F. The taffy sale brought in a total of $750, but 78% of this was used for expenses. How much money was used for expenses?

$$\frac{78}{750} = \frac{X}{100}$$ Answer: $10.40

Sara successfully solved percent problems when the class first solved them, but as different types of problems were encountered she began to have difficulty.

Sara *is* solving correctly the proportion she writes for the problem. However, she uses a procedure that often does not accurately represent the ratios described in the problem. She is using the following proportion for every problem encountered:

$$\frac{\text{lesser number in the problem}}{\text{greater number in the problem}} = \frac{x}{100}$$

She may have created her procedure from initial experiences with problems like A and D, although the procedure also seems to work with problems of the type illustrated by B and E. The procedure does *not* provide a correct solution with problems of the type illustrated by C and F.

How would you help Sara? Describe at least two instructional activities you believe would help her correctly solve percent problems.

1. _____

2. _____

After you have described at least two activities, turn to page 207 and compare your suggestions with those listed there.

Error Pattern P-P-2
(from Steve's paper on page 204)

If you found Steve's error pattern, your results are as follows.

D. What number is 80% of 54?

5 4
1 . 8 0
0 0
4 3 2
4 3 . 2 0

Answer: 43.2

E. Seventy is 14% of what number?

7 0
X . 1 4
2 8 0
7 0
9 . 8 0

Answer: 9.8

F. What percent of 125 is 25?

$$
\begin{array}{r}
1\ 2\ 5 \\
\times\ .2\ 5 \\
\hline
6\ 2\ 5 \\
2\ 5\ 0\ \ \\
\hline
3\ 1.2\ 5
\end{array}
$$

Answer: 31.25

Steve's solutions are correct when he is finding the percent of a specified number (Problems A and D). However, his solutions are incorrect when the percent is known and he needs to find a number (Problems B and E) or when he needs to find what percent one number is of a specified number (Problems C and F).

Usually, the first percent problems a student encounters involve finding the percent of a number. Steve probably developed his procedure while solving such problems, and he is using a version of it when he attempts to solve other types of percent problems. When the percent is given, he changes it to a decimal then multiplies this number times the other number given. When the percent is not given, he treats the lesser of the two given numbers as if it were a decimal and proceeds similarly.

How would you help Steve? Describe at least two instructional activities you believe would help him correctly solve percent problems.

1. _____

2. _____

After you have written at least two descriptions, turn to page 209 and check your suggestions against those listed there.

CONSIDERING ALTERNATIVES

Error Pattern P-P-1
(from pages 203 and 205)

Sara solved percent problems as shown in Examples D, E, and F.

D. Brad earned $400 during the summer and saved $240 from his earnings. What percent of his earnings did he save?

$$\frac{240}{400} = \frac{x}{100}$$

Answer: 60%

E. Barbara received a gift of money on her birthday. She spent 80% of the money on a watch. The watch cost $20. How much money did she receive as a birthday gift?

$$\frac{20}{80} = \frac{x}{100}$$

Answer: __$25__

F. The taffy sale brought in a total of $750, but 78% of this was used for expenses. How much money was used for expenses?

$$\frac{78}{750} = \frac{x}{100}$$

Answer: __$10.40__

Note: When you assign percent problems, ask to see all of the work done on each problem. You need to see what ratios are derived from the problem, and whether the proportion itself is correctly developed. This particular student is correctly processing the proportion once it is determined and does *not* need instruction concerning cross multiplication. For this student, corrective instruction should focus on the concepts of percent, relating data in a problem to ratios (to fractions), and possibly equal ratios.

What instructional activities did you suggest to help Sara correctly solve percent problems? See if your suggestions are among the following.

1. *Use 10 × 10 squares of graph paper.* Redevelop the meaning of percent as "per 100." Therefore, n% is always $\frac{n}{100}$. For example:

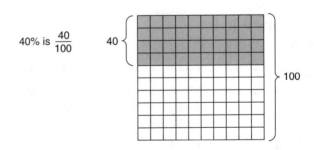

40% is $\frac{40}{100}$

2. *Use base-ten blocks.* To redevelop the meaning of percent, a flat block for 100 can be partially covered with long blocks for

10 and with unit blocks. But if this is done, it must be emphasized that the flat block (for 100) now represents *one*, and
part of that whole (a certain percent of it) has been covered.
3. *Identify what is being "counted."* Ask, "Do I know how many
there are in the whole set? Do I know how many are in part of
the set?" Show these numbers with a fraction:

$$\frac{\text{number in part of the set}}{\text{number in the whole set}}$$

In Problem B, for example, you are counting students. You
know there are 12 students in part of the class, but you do
not know how many students are in the whole class. Therefore, the fraction is:

$$\frac{12}{n}$$

4. *Use number lines to show equivalent ratios.* Sketch a number
line for the fraction in which both numbers are known.

$$40\% = \frac{40}{100}$$

Then sketch another number line just below it for the other
fraction. Because the two fractions are equal, you can align the
terms of one fraction with the counterparts in the other fraction. See if the student can estimate the unknown number.

$$\frac{12}{n}$$
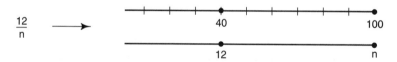

Error Pattern P-P-2
(from pages 204 and 206)

Steve solved percent problems as shown in Examples D, E, and F.

  D. What number is 80% of 54?

$$\begin{array}{r} 5\,4 \\ \times\ \ .8\,0 \\ \hline 0\,0 \\ 4\,3\,2\ \ \\ \hline 4\,3.2\,0 \end{array}$$

Answer: <u>43.2</u>

E. Seventy is 14% of what number?

$$
\begin{array}{r}
70 \\
\times .14 \\
\hline
280 \\
70 \\
\hline
9.80
\end{array}
$$

Answer: ___9.8___

F. What percent of 125 is 25?

$$
\begin{array}{r}
125 \\
\times .25 \\
\hline
625 \\
250 \\
\hline
31.25
\end{array}
$$

Answer: ___31.25___

Note: Emphasizing a rule like "percent times a number equals percentage" is not likely to be helpful because this is actually the rule Steve is attempting to apply. Many students find it difficult to identify the three types of percent problems; they also confuse the terms *percent* and *percentage*. Instead, it may be helpful to develop a strategy that is basically the same for all three types of percent problems—possibly the proportion method.

What activities did you suggest to help Steve correctly solve percent problems of different types? See if your suggestions are among those that follow.

1. *Show equal fractions.* Write a proportion for each problem with one fraction equal to another. With one fraction show what the problem tells about percent, and with the other show what the problem tells about the number of things. Use n whenever you are not told a number. For example:

Seventy is 14% of what number?

$$
\text{percent} \begin{cases} \dfrac{14}{100} = \dfrac{70}{n} & \leftarrow \text{part of the amount} \\ & \leftarrow \text{the whole amount} \end{cases}
$$

2. *Cross multiply.* When the student is able to write a correct proportion for a percent problem, suggest that there is a pattern that can help us find the unknown number. Have the student

supply several pairs of fractions known to be equal, fraction pairs like $\frac{1}{2} = \frac{2}{4}$. Then draw an X as illustrated on each pair and ask the student to compare the products of numbers within each line of an X. For $\frac{1}{2} = \frac{2}{4}$, compare the product of 1 and 4 with the product of 2 and 2. When something like "their products are equal" is noted, have the student test the observation with other pairs of fractions. Then apply cross multiplication to percent problems.

$$\frac{1}{2} = \frac{4}{8} \qquad \begin{array}{l} 1 \times 8 = 2 \times 4 \\ 8 = 8 \end{array} \qquad \frac{14}{100} = \frac{70}{n} \qquad \begin{array}{l} 14\,n = 100 \times 70 \\ 14\,n = 7000 \\ n = 500 \end{array}$$

CONCLUSION

If students are taught specific procedures when they lack sufficient understanding of related concepts, they are apt to adopt error patterns similar to those encountered in this chapter.

Percent problems challenge many students. Before your students practice solving percent problems, make sure they can relate percents to other expressions for rational numbers (fractions and decimals). Further, make sure they understand equivalent fractions and proportions. You may also want to determine whether they understand the equivalence of two special products within a proportion: if $\frac{a}{b} = \frac{c}{d}$, then a × d = b × c. Solving percent problems requires all of these understandings, so make sure your students have the prior knowledge they need.

As in other chapters, with some examples the student obtained a correct answer even though he was using an inappropriate procedure. Do not be fooled into thinking that such students are merely careless when answers are incorrect. Keep alert for the error patterns students use.

The student experiencing difficulty may profit from being a part of a group of students who create a number line or a unit region diagram to illustrate a percent problem and its solution. Many percent problems can be illustrated graphically. Frequently, graphic representations can help students estimate a reasonable answer.

Chapter **10**

Geometry and Measurement

You have observed that learning computational procedures involves looking for patterns, but so does much of learning in other areas of mathematics. Each student paper in this chapter contains examples focusing on a particular aspect of geometry or measurement.

In some cases a student has inferred an erroneous concept, possibly overgeneralizing from limited experiences. In other cases the student may have created a procedure that uses bits and pieces of information heard from time to time; the procedure gives the student an answer, but it does not make mathematical sense and it does not always provide correct answers.

While you are identifying the error pattern, be sure to consider each example given. Then use the student's procedure to complete the additional examples.

As you suggest instructional activities, remember the resources that are available for teaching geometry and measurement—materials like geoboards, dot paper, and cutout shapes.

As students sort, build, draw, model, trace, measure, and construct, their capacity to visualize geometric relationships will develop.[1]

Finally, compare your suggested activities with those of the author.

IDENTIFYING PATTERNS

Error Pattern G-M-1

Sometimes Martha names geometric figures correctly, but she often seems confused. Look carefully at her written work. Can you find the error pattern she is following?

Name **Martha**

A. Which of these are squares? Make an X under each square.

B. Which of these are triangles?
   Make an X under each triangle.

Clearly, Martha is experiencing difficulty. In constructing her own understanding of these figures, has she inferred something that is not actually true?

Make sure you found Martha's procedure by using her error pattern for the following exercise.

Which of these are rectangles?
Make an X under each rectangle.

Why might Martha be using this procedure? Turn to Pattern G-M-1 on page 222 and see if you identified her error pattern correctly. Can you think of a way to help Martha?

Error Pattern G-M-2

Oliver seems confused when right angles are discussed in class. Look carefully at his written work. Can you find the error pattern he followed?

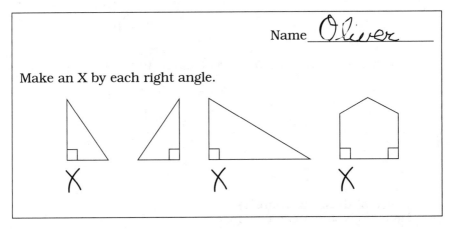

Did you determine what he is doing? In Oliver's thinking, what distinguishes a right angle? Why might he have come to that conclusion?

Make sure you found Oliver's pattern by using the error pattern to respond to this exercise.

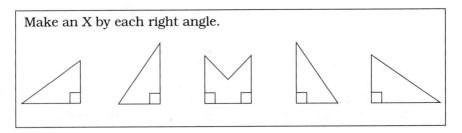

Now turn to Pattern G-M-2 on page 223 and compare your response. Do you think of a way to help Oliver?

Error Pattern G-M-3

Charlene is confident she knows how to determine the altitude of a triangle. Does she really?

Look carefully at her written work. Can you determine the procedure she used when responding in this exercise?

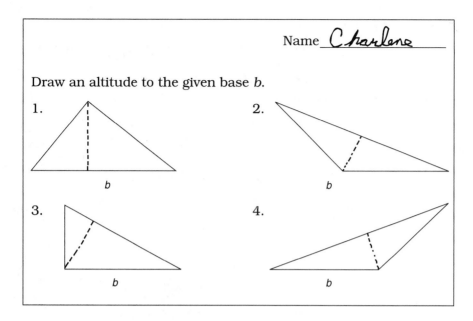

Did you determine what Charlene is doing? In her thinking, what is an altitude? Why might she have come to that conclusion?

Make sure you found her procedure by using the error pattern to respond to this exercise.

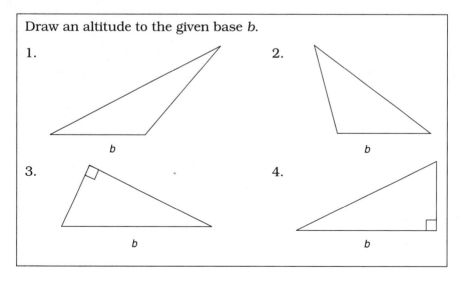

Now turn to Pattern G-M-3 on page 224 and compare your response. Can you think of a way to help Charlene or other students with a similar misconception?

Error Pattern G-M-4

Denny quickly determines the perimeter for a given figure. Sometimes he is correct, but other times he is not.

    Look carefully at his written work. Can you determine the procedure he used in this exercise?

Name _Denny_

Determine the perimeter of each of these rectangular regions:

1.

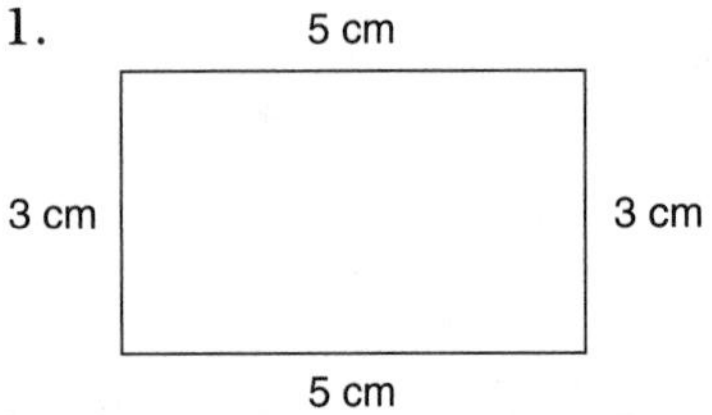

5 cm

3 cm   3 cm

5 cm

Answer _____ 16 cm

2.

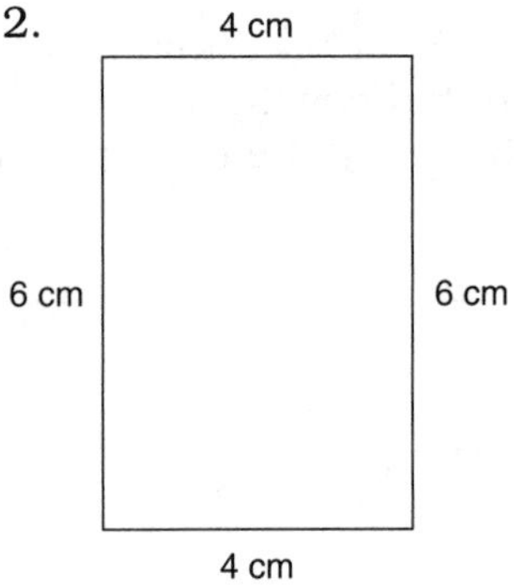

4 cm

6 cm   6 cm

4 cm

Answer _____ 20 cm

3.

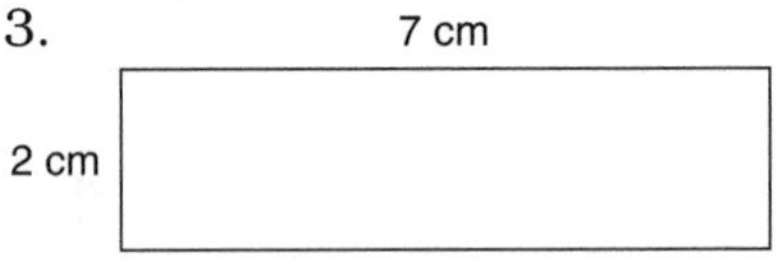

7 cm

2 cm

Answer _____ 14 cm

4.

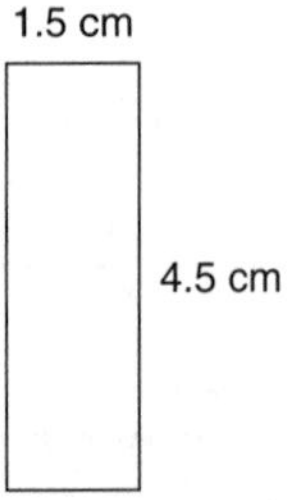

1.5 cm

4.5 cm

Answer _____ 6.75 cm

Did you determine what Denny is doing? What does he understand about *perimeter*? What does he not yet understand?

Make sure you found his procedure by using the error pattern to respond to the following exercise.

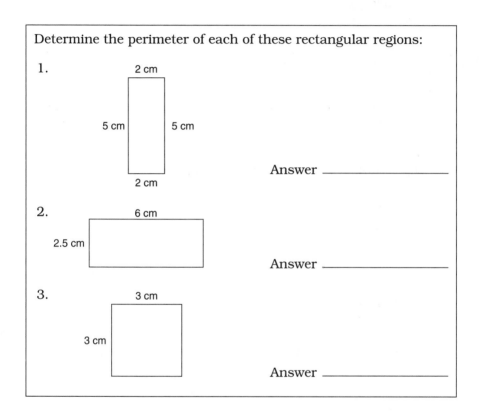

Determine the perimeter of each of these rectangular regions:

1.
2 cm
5 cm   5 cm
2 cm

Answer _____

2.
6 cm
2.5 cm

Answer _____

3.
3 cm
3 cm

Answer _____

Has Denny learned another concept or procedure that he is confusing with this situation?

Turn to Pattern G-M-4 on page 225 and compare your response. Can you think of a way to help Denny?

Error Pattern G-M-5

The teacher hoped that after studying ratios and proportions students would apply what they had learned to the study of similar figures, but Teresa is experiencing difficulty. Look carefully at her written work. Can you find the procedure she is following?

Name _Teresa_

1. The two pentagons are similar. Find the length of side X.

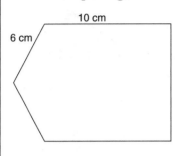

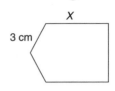

Answer ___5___

2. The two triangles are similar. Find the measure of angle Y.

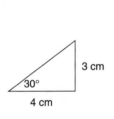

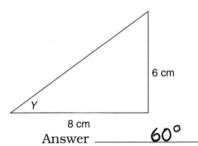

Answer ___60°___

3. The two trapezoids are similar. Find the measure of angle Z.

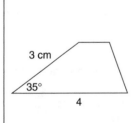

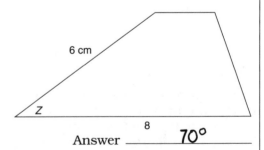

Answer ___70°___

Did you determine what Teresa is doing? What does she understand about similar figures that is correct? What does she believe to be true about similar figures that is *not* correct? Make sure you found her error pattern by using her procedure to respond to this exercise.

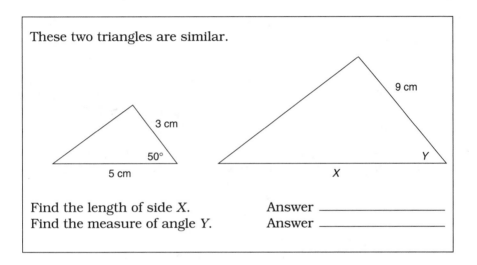

These two triangles are similar.

3 cm

9 cm

50°

Y

5 cm

X

Find the length of side X.   Answer _____
Find the measure of angle Y.   Answer _____

Turn to Pattern G-M-5 on page 226 and compare your response. Can you think of a way to help Teresa?

Error Pattern G-M-6

Even though the teacher hoped each student would apply what had been learned about ratios and proportions to the study of similar figures, Nick developed his own procedure to respond to the exercises. Look carefully at his written work. Can you find his pattern?

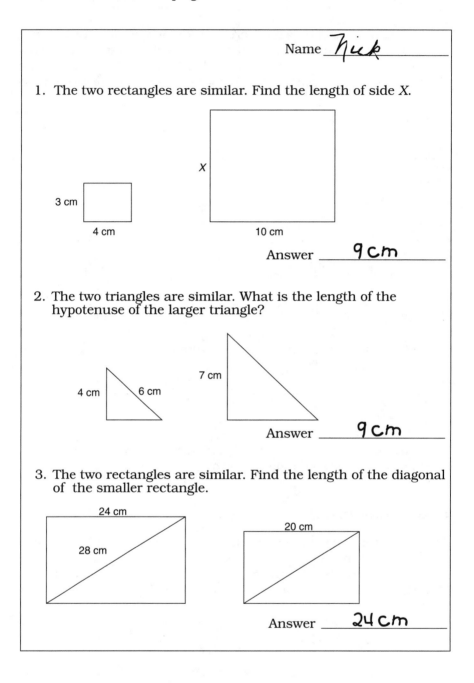

Name _Nick_

1. The two rectangles are similar. Find the length of side X.

3 cm

4 cm

X

10 cm

Answer ___9 cm___

2. The two triangles are similar. What is the length of the hypotenuse of the larger triangle?

4 cm   6 cm

7 cm

Answer ___9 cm___

3. The two rectangles are similar. Find the length of the diagonal of the smaller rectangle.

24 cm

28 cm

20 cm

Answer ___24 cm___

Did you determine what Nick is doing? Make sure you found his error pattern by using his procedure to respond to this exercise.

1. The two triangles are similar. Find the length of side *X*.

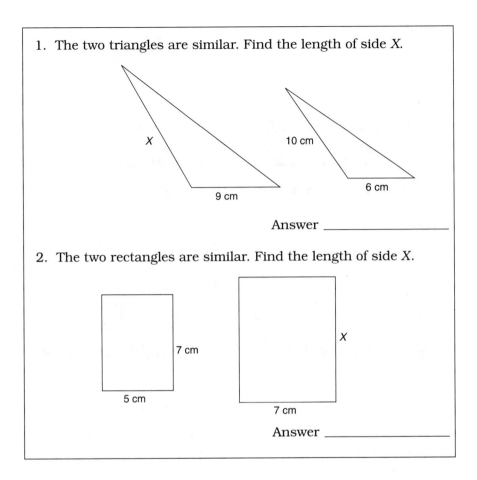

Answer _____

2. The two rectangles are similar. Find the length of side *X*.

Answer _____

Now turn to Pattern G-M-6 on page 226 and compare your response. How could you help Nick?

Error Pattern G-M-7

The refrigerator contained 5 gallons and 1 quart of punch before the party. Three gallons and 3 quarts of punch were served at the party. How much punch remained after the party?

Margaret found that 1 gallon and 8 quarts remained, which is not correct. She is having difficulty when computing with measurements. Can you find an error pattern in her work?

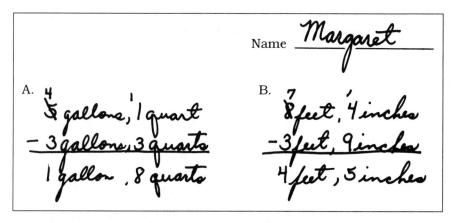

Name *Margaret*

A.
$$\overset{4}{\cancel{5}} \text{ gallons}, \overset{1}{\text{1}} \text{ quart}$$
$$- 3 \text{ gallons}, 3 \text{ quarts}$$
$$1 \text{ gallon}, 8 \text{ quarts}$$

B.
$$\overset{7}{\cancel{8}} \text{ feet}, \overset{'}{4} \text{ inches}$$
$$- 3 \text{ feet}, 9 \text{ inches}$$
$$4 \text{ feet}, 5 \text{ inches}$$

Check yourself by using Margaret's erroneous pattern to complete these examples.

C.
$$6 \text{ yards}, 1 \text{ foot}$$
$$- 2 \text{ yards}, 2 \text{ feet}$$

D.
$$3 \text{ quarts}, 1 \text{ cup}$$
$$- 1 \text{ quart}, 3 \text{ cups}$$

Why is Margaret computing this way? What does she not yet understand?

After you finish Examples C and D, turn to page 228 to see if you accurately identified Margaret's error pattern.

DESCRIBING INSTRUCTION

Error Pattern G-M-1
(from Martha's paper on page 213)

If you discovered what Martha was doing, you probably completed the exercise as shown.

Which of these are rectangles?
Make an *X* under each rectangle.

[shapes: rectangle, triangle, rectangle with X below, small rectangle with X below, rectangle]

Martha's understanding of what a square is, what a triangle is, and what a rectangle is, includes a specific orientation. It is as if she said, "If you turn a square and make a diamond, it's not a square anymore."

Students often see examples of squares, triangles, and rectangles with one particular orientation (often with a horizontal base). Martha probably associated the name of each figure with that configuration. She does not appear to have been taught the name of each figure while observing examples with different orientations.

It may also be true that squares and rectangles were presented to her as completely different configurations.

If you were Martha's teacher, what help would you provide?

Briefly describe two instructional activities you believe would provide the understanding needed.

1. _____

2. _____

After you describe at least two activities, turn to page 228 to see if your suggestions are among those listed.

Error Pattern G-M-2
(from Oliver's paper on page 214)

If you discovered Oliver's error pattern, you probably completed the exercise as shown.

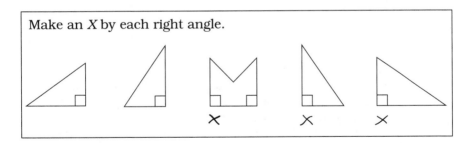

Make an *X* by each right angle.

To Oliver, a *right angle* goes to the right. (It is possible he also believes that some angles are *left angles.*)

It may be that when the term *right angle* was introduced, the examples that he observed actually did have a horizontal leg going to the right. He assumed that this was part of what makes a right angle.

If you were Oliver's teacher, how would you help him correct his understanding?

Briefly describe two instructional activities you would provide for him.

    1. _____

    2. _____

   After you describe at least two activities, turn to page 230 to see
if your suggestions are among those listed.

Error Pattern G-M-3
(from Charlene's paper on page 215)

If you discovered what Charlene is doing, you probably completed the
exercise as shown.

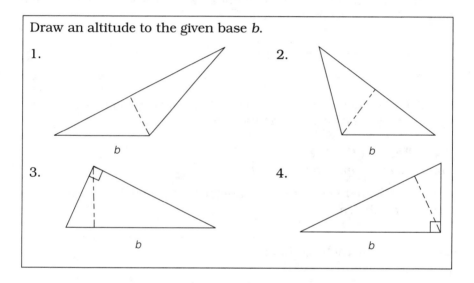

Draw an altitude to the given base *b*.

1.   2.

3.   4.

   Charlene appears to believe that an altitude is a line segment
from the angle opposite the longest leg of the triangle *to* the longest
leg, and that line segment is perpendicular to the longest leg. (This often works with altitudes presented in examples.)

   She does not appear to consider "to the given base" in the question for the exercise; she just draws the altitude as she understands it.

   Briefly describe two instructional activities you believe would
help Charlene understand what an altitude is and be able to draw
them correctly.

    1. _____

    2. _____

   Next, turn to page 231 to see if your suggestions are among those
listed.

Error Pattern G-M-4

(from Denny's paper on page 216)

If you discovered what Denny is doing, you probably completed the exercise as shown.

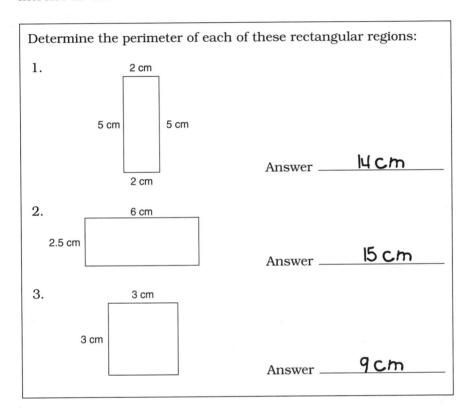

Determine the perimeter of each of these rectangular regions:

1.
2 cm
5 cm   5 cm
2 cm
Answer __14 cm__

2.
6 cm
2.5 cm
Answer __15 cm__

3.
3 cm
3 cm
Answer __9 cm__

Denny appears to have constructed his own procedural definition for perimeter, something like: "If all four sides have numbers, add; if only two sides have numbers, multiply."

He may be confusing this situation with procedures he used when finding the area of a rectangle.

Briefly describe two instructional activities you believe would help Denny more adequately understand what a perimeter is, and be able to determine the length of each perimeter more accurately.

1. _____

2. _____

Next, turn to page 232 to see if your suggestions are among those listed.

Error Pattern G-M-5
(from Teresa's paper on page 218)

If you discovered Teresa's error pattern, you probably completed the exercise as shown.

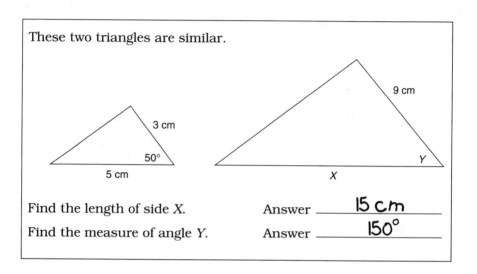

These two triangles are similar.

3 cm

9 cm

50°

5 cm

X

Y

Find the length of side *X*.   Answer _____ **15 cm** _____

Find the measure of angle *Y*.   Answer _____ **150°** _____

Teresa appears to have overgeneralized as she constructed her own rule for exercises involving similar figures. She thinks something like, "Do the same thing to everything. If one thing is twice as much, everything is twice as much." She does not seem to distinguish between comparing sides in similar triangles and comparing angles in similar triangles.

Briefly describe two instructional activities you believe would help Teresa more adequately understand similar figures and be able to complete such exercises as this correctly.

1. _____

2. _____

Turn to page 233 to see if your suggestions are among those listed.

Error Pattern G-M-6
(from Nick's paper on page 220)

If you discovered Nick's error pattern, you probably completed the exercise as shown.

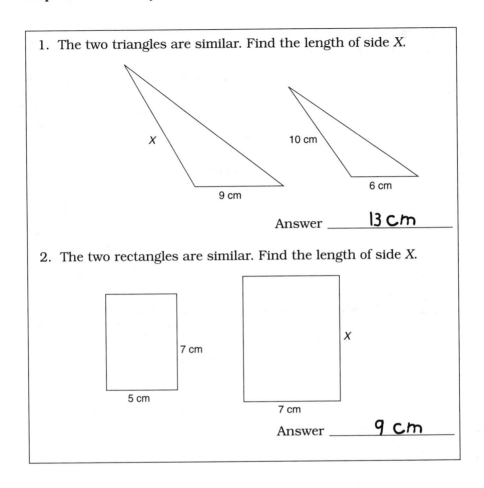

1. The two triangles are similar. Find the length of side X.

X   10 cm

9 cm   6 cm

Answer ____13 cm____

2. The two rectangles are similar. Find the length of side X.

7 cm

5 cm

X

7 cm

Answer ____9 cm____

Nick appears to believe that measures of related sides of similar figures differ by the same number. Therefore, if the difference between two related sides is known, addition or subtraction can often be used to determine missing lengths. Clearly, his understanding of similar figures and equivalent ratios (proportions) is not adequate.

Briefly describe two instructional activities you believe might help Nick more adequately understand relationships in similar figures and be able to complete exercises such as this correctly.

1. _____

2. _____

Next, turn to page 234 to see if your suggestions are among those listed.

Error Pattern G-M-7
(from Margaret's paper on page 222)

Using Margaret's error pattern, Examples C and D would be completed as shown.

Margaret is regrouping in order to subtract, just as she does when subtracting whole numbers expressed with base-ten numeration. She crosses out the left figure and writes one less above it, then places a one in front of the right figure. This technique produces a correct result when the relationship between the two measurement units is a base-ten relationship, but the results are incorrect whenever other relationships exist.

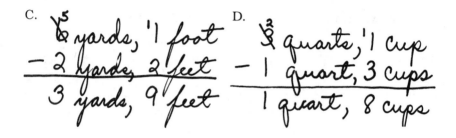

How would *you* help Margaret? Describe at least two instructional activities you believe would make it possible for Margaret to subtract correctly in measurement situations.

1. _____

2. _____

After you have written at least two descriptions, turn to page 236 and see if any of your activities are among the suggestions listed there.

CONSIDERING ALTERNATIVES

Error Pattern G-M-1
(from pages 213 and 222)

This error pattern suggests that the student's understanding of these figures includes a specific orientation. Furthermore, the relationship between squares and rectangles may not be understood.

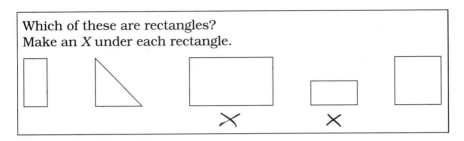

You suggested instructional activities that may help the student. Are any of the activities you suggested similar to those described here?

1. *Turn the figure.* Let the student make a rectangle on a geoboard, copy it on geoboard dot paper, then turn the geoboard and copy the rectangle again. This can be done several times. Emphasize that this is the same rectangle turned different ways.
2. *Classify with Venn diagrams.* Provide small groups of students with cutouts for selected two-dimensional shapes as shown. Also provide a response paper with overlapping loops labeled *Four Sides with Square Corners* and *Equal Sides.* Have students sort the shapes appropriately and listen as students state their reasons for placing individual cutouts where they do. Then in the discussion that follows say, "We have another name for a shape with four sides and square corners; it is called a *rectangle.* Is a square a rectangle? Always? Why?"

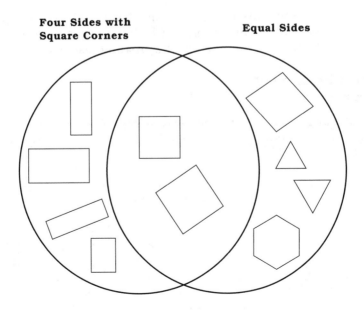

3. *Make concept cards.* For each specified polygon, let students make a concept card patterned after the Creature Cards. Provide cards with three headings. For rectangles, the completed concept card might look like this:

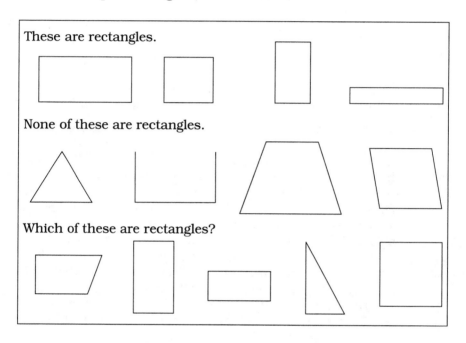

Students can give completed cards to other students to identify rectangles in the last row. Orientation of figures is likely to be included in the ensuing discussion.

Error Pattern G-M-2
(from pages 214 and 223)

A right angle may be understood as a "square corner" or 90-degree angle, but apparently a right angle is also understood as "going to the right."

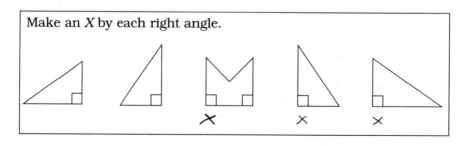

Are any of the instructional activities you suggested for this student similar to these?

1. *Use a square corner.* Let the student use the (square) corner of an object to find right angles. Emphasize that any triangle with a square corner is a right triangle.
2. *Make a tesselation.* Will a right triangle tesselate? Let the student repeatedly trace around a cutout right triangle to make a tesselation if she can. Emphasize the need to turn the right triangle different directions. Then let the student mark the right angle in each right triangle.
3. *Make a concept card.* Let the student make a concept card for the concept *right triangle,* as described for G-M-1.
4. *Relate the right angle to the hypotenuse.* Show the student several right triangles with varied configurations and orientations. For each triangle, let the student identify the right angle and the hypotenuse. Then the student can write a sentence that describes the relationship between the right angle and the hypotenuse.

Error Pattern G-M-3
(from pages 215 and 224)

Apparently, this student thinks an altitude is the line segment that goes from the angle opposite the longest leg of the triangle, perpendicular to the longest leg. Sometimes she draws it correctly.

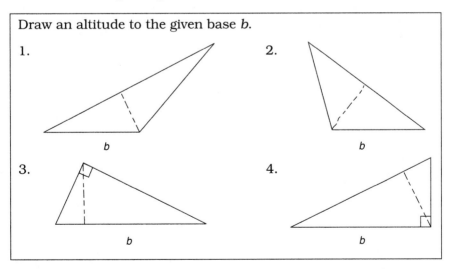

The instructional activities you suggested probably focused, in part, on the idea of "the base of a triangle." Were any of the instructional activities you suggested similar to these?

1. *Investigate.* Let the student investigate these questions:

   • How many altitudes does a triangle have?
   • Do all triangles have the same number of altitudes? Why?

   The student can write about what she found and draw triangles and altitudes to illustrate her paragraph.

2. *Use cutouts of triangles.* For each specified triangle cutout, let the student trace around the shape three times, with three different orientations, so that each of the legs serves as the base. Then the student can construct an altitude for each triangle. Note that three different altitudes can be drawn from the same cutout triangle.

Error Pattern G-M-4
(from pages 216 and 225)

This student's procedure for finding the length of the perimeter of a rectangle seems to be dependent upon the number of sides actually labeled. If only two sides are labeled, he multiplies, even though a perimeter is the *sum* of the measures of the four sides.

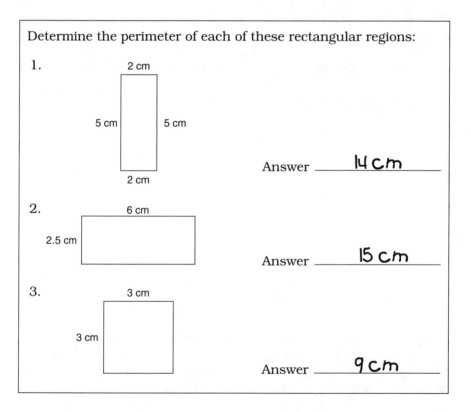

Determine the perimeter of each of these rectangular regions:

1. 2 cm · 5 cm · 5 cm · 2 cm   Answer _____ 14 cm _____

2. 6 cm · 2.5 cm   Answer _____ 15 cm _____

3. 3 cm · 3 cm   Answer _____ 9 cm _____

You suggested activities that should help this student. Are any of your suggestions similar to these?

1. *Trace around the figure.* Let the student trace around the figure with his finger, and say the measure (the length) of each side as he does. He can then add to find the total perimeter.
2. *Relate to a fence.* Let the student determine how long a fence is that goes around the figure. He will need to make sure he has a measurement for each side before finding the total length.
3. *Copy and label.* Let the student copy or trace the figure, then label every side. If some measurements are not given, he will have to think about what he already knows about figures like these.
4. *Study regular polygons with only one side labeled.* Let the student write out how to find the perimeter of any regular polygon. If he can, he should describe more than one way.

Error Pattern G-M-5
(from pages 218 and 226)

This student apparently thinks that *all* corresponding parts of similar triangles are proportional. That is, if one corresponding part is three times as great, all corresponding parts are three times as great. In truth, corresponding *legs* of similar triangles are proportional, but not corresponding *angles*—they are equal in measure.

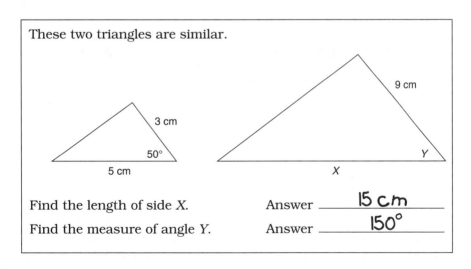

These two triangles are similar.

3 cm

9 cm

50°

Y

5 cm

X

Find the length of side X.   Answer _____ 15 cm _____

Find the measure of angle Y.   Answer _____ 150° _____

Are any of the instructional activities you suggested for this student similar to these?

1. *Use a geoboard.* Can the student make this triangle on her geoboard?

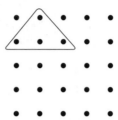

Challenge her to make a second triangle with all three sides two times as long. The triangles should be the same shape, but different sizes. The two triangles can be copied on geoboard dot paper, cut out, and the student can compare the angles.

2. *Compare what is alike and different.* Examine cut out shapes of pairs of similar polygons. Place one on top of the other to determine what is the same (angle measure) and what is different (lengths of sides).

3. *Construct pairs of shapes.* Let the student construct cutouts of similar shapes that are different sizes. Before she draws them and cuts them out, is she able to tell how she will know that her shapes are similar? Stress that the cutouts will need to be the same shape but different sizes, and that the angles will be the same size.

4. *Make a journal entry.* After investigating, the student can make a journal entry about what is alike and what is different about two similar figures.

Error Pattern G-M-6
(from pages 220 and 226)

This student appears to have made an incorrect inference regarding the relationship between corresponding legs of similar figures. The student uses addition and subtraction to determine missing lengths.

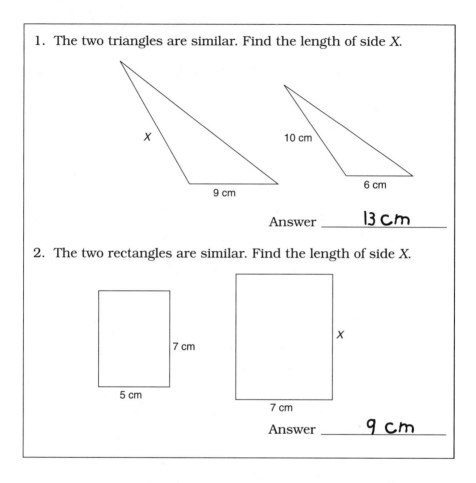

1. The two triangles are similar. Find the length of side X.

   X

   10 cm

   9 cm

   6 cm

   Answer _____ 13 cm _____

2. The two rectangles are similar. Find the length of side X.

   7 cm

   5 cm

   X

   7 cm

   Answer _____ 9 cm _____

You suggested activities which should help this student. Are any of your suggestions similar to these?

1. *A group investigation.* Let students examine many pairs of carefully selected similar figures, and measure and record measurements for corresponding sides. They can reflect on the relationship between corresponding sides. Is it an addition-subtraction relationship? Is it a multiplication-division relationship? Students can write about what they did and what they decided.

2. *Relate to equivalent ratios.* Do the measures of corresponding sides form equivalent ratios? That is, do the ratios of two pairs of corresponding sides make a proportion? Why? The student can measure examples of similar figures to investigate.

Error Pattern G-M-7

(from pages 222 and 228)

You suggested instructional activities for helping Margaret. Are any of your suggestions among those listed?

C.

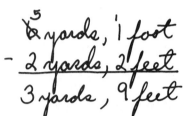

D.

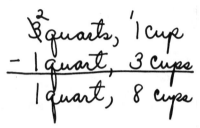

1. *Use measuring devices.* First, let the student show the minuend with measuring devices. In Example C it could be shown with yardsticks and foot rules. Let the student see if she can take away as much length (volume, and so on) as is suggested by the subtrahend. In the process it will be necessary to exchange. Be sure to point out that exchanges are not always a ten for ten ones; many other kinds of exchanges occur with measurement situations.

2. *Regroup in many different number bases.* Use multibase blocks, chip trading activities, place-value charts, or sticks and bundles of sticks to learn to regroup in different number bases. A game-rule orientation in which the rule for exchanging changes from game to game may help the student generalize the regrouping pattern. For base-four games and activities, the rule would be "Exchange a 4 for ones"; in base-12 games, the rule would be "Exchange a 12 for ones," and so on. Follow such activities with computation that involves measurement. Help students connect regrouping within computation with exchanges that were encountered when working in other number bases.

3. *Identify number-base relationships.* For several examples of computation that involve measurements, let the student determine the number-base relationship for each example, and also state the rule for exchanging (or regrouping) she would use when computing. (Pairs of students could work on this activity together.)

CONCLUSION

Whenever some students need to get correct answers they are inclined to develop error patterns, even while studying geometry and measurement. They think about what they observe, but they also make invalid assumptions or overgeneralize.

This suggests there is a need to provide varied instructional experiences during which students reflect on and sometimes write about what they are observing. Many useful manipulatives and diagrams are available for modeling geometric concepts, including drawings, cut out shapes, geoboards, and dot paper. Frequently it is helpful to provide both examples and nonexamples of a concept.

Sometimes students can be challenged to create models of what they are studying. For example: "How could you show subtraction of these measurements? Could you use base-ten blocks? Why?"

Geometry and measurement are areas where making an investigation is a particularly useful instructional strategy. "What is the relationship between two similar triangles? between their sides? between their angles?"

Throughout the study of geometry and measurement, be alert for students who overgeneralize and form other error patterns.

REFERENCE

1. National Council of Teachers of Mathematics. (2000). *Principles and standards for school mathematics*. Reston, VA: The Council, p. 165.

Chapter 11

Integers

ᓚᘏᗢ

In this chapter you will find examples of papers on which students practiced adding and subtracting with integers. These papers may be like some you will encounter in your own classroom.

Consider all examples on the paper as you look for a student's error pattern. Check your findings by using the student's procedure with the examples provided for that purpose.

After you read about each student's procedure, suggest needed instruction. Keep in mind the relation of subtraction to addition, and different models for addition of integers such as number-line models and counting models. Try to suggest at least two different activities to help each student. Then compare your suggestions with the author's.

In Appendix A, papers numbered 19 and 20 also illustrate error patterns with integers.

IDENTIFYING PATTERNS

Error Pattern A-I-1

> Acme stock decreased in value 8 points on Monday, then increased in value 6 points on Tuesday. What was the total change in value for the two days?

Karl is enjoying some success when adding with integers. However, he frequently gets incorrect sums that are not even reasonable. Can you determine the error pattern he is using?

Name _Karl_

A. $^-8 + 6 =$ _$^-2$_   C. $7 + ^-2 =$ _5_

B. $5 + ^-9 =$ _4_   D. $^-4 + 10 =$ _$^-6$_

Karl may have constructed his procedure while working with examples that have a common characteristic. Make sure you found his error pattern by using his procedure to complete these examples.

E. $10 + ^-6 =$ _____   F. $10 + ^-14 =$ _____

Would it help Karl if he estimated before adding? Turn to page 240 and see if you identified his procedure correctly.

Error Pattern A-I-2

Daphne gets some correct sums. Even so, many of her sums are incorrect.

She constructed her own rule for adding integers, and it is not an easy error pattern to determine. Can you find her procedure?

Name **Daphne**

Write the sum.

A. $^-6 + ^-8 =$ _2_   C. $4 + ^-3 =$ _7_

B. $^-8 + ^-3 =$ _$^-5$_   D. $^-2 + ^-5 =$ _3_

Daphne may have constructed her procedure while working with examples that have one thing in common. Make sure you found her error pattern by using her procedure to complete these examples.

E. $^-6 + 10 =$ _____   F. $10 + ^-6 =$ _____

Turn to page 241 and see if you identified her procedure correctly. How would you help Daphne or any student with this kind of error pattern?

Error Pattern S-I-1

From time to time, Nicole subtracts integers and gets the correct difference. Very frequently, however, her answer is incorrect.

She appears to have learned a phrase or rule in another context, and she is applying it inappropriately. Can you find her error pattern?

> Name **Nicole**
>
> Write the sum.
>
> A. $3 - (^-4) = \underline{\textbf{7}}$ C. $7 + {}^-2 = \underline{\textbf{5}}$
>
> B. $^-6 + 2 = \underline{\textbf{8}}$ D. $^-5 - 4 = \underline{\textbf{9}}$

Make sure you found Nicole's procedure by using it to subtract these examples.

E. $^-6 - 3 = \underline{\hspace{2cm}}$ F. $^-2 - {}^-5 = \underline{\hspace{2cm}}$

What phrase (or "rule") has Nicole learned that she appears to be applying inappropriately? Turn to page 241 and see if you identified Nicole's procedure correctly.

DESCRIBING INSTRUCTION

Error Pattern A-I-1
(from Karl's paper on page 239)

If you discovered Karl's error pattern, you probably completed the exercise as shown below.

E. $10 + {}^-6 = \underline{\textbf{4}}$ F. $10 + {}^-14 = \underline{\textbf{4}}$

As Karl was considering addition and subtraction of integers—with all the negative and minus signs as well as plus signs—he apparently concluded that in order to add you find the difference between what we would call the absolute values of the two integers. But where does he get the sign he attaches to his sum? He seems to use the sign of the first addend.

Karl's procedure *does* produce the correct sum at times, thereby reinforcing his conviction that he is adding integers.

Describe two instructional activities you believe might help Karl more adequately understand integers and addition of integers.

1. _____

2. _____

Next, turn to page 242 to see if your suggestions are among those listed.

Error Pattern A-I-2
(from Daphne's paper on page 239)

If you discovered Daphne's error pattern, you probably completed the exercise as shown.

E. ⁻6 + 10 = __*4*__   F. 10 + ⁻6 = __*16*__

Daphne may picture a number line in her mind and begin at the place where the first addend is located. In order to add, she apparently moves to the right as indicated by the second addend. However, she seems to ignore the sign of the second addend. She uses the absolute value of the second addend with the effect that she uses the second addend as a positive number, even when it is negative.

As indicated in Exercise E above, Daphne's procedure *does* produce the correct sum at times. This suggests to her that she actually does understand how to add integers.

Describe two instructional activities you believe would help Daphne more adequately understand integers and addition of integers.

1. _____

2. _____

Turn to page 243 to see if your suggestions are among those listed.

Error Pattern S-I-1
(from Nicole's paper on page 240)

If you discovered Nicole's error pattern, you probably completed the exercise as shown below.

E. ⁻6 − 3 = __*9*__   F. ⁻2 − ⁻5 = __*3*__

Nicole is confusing signs of operations and signs of numbers. She is also inappropriately applying something she must have learned by rote: "Two negatives make a positive."

She counts the plus/positive and minus/negative symbols (symbols for operations and for numbers). If there are two minus/negative symbols, she adds the absolute values. If the number of minus/negative symbols is odd, she subtracts the absolute values. Surprisingly, Nicole's procedure *does* produce the correct difference at times.

Describe two instructional activities you believe would help Nicole more adequately understand positive and negative integers and operations on integers (including subtraction).

1. _____

2. _____

Turn to page 245 to see if your suggestions are among those listed.

CONSIDERING ALTERNATIVES

Error Pattern A-I-1
(from pages 239 and 240)

This student apparently adds two integers by subtracting absolute values then using the sign of the first addend as the sign of the sum. We may well question how much the student actually understands about the numbers we call integers and the operation we call addition.

$$\text{E. } 10 + {}^-6 = \underline{\quad 4 \quad} \qquad \text{F. } 10 + {}^-14 = \underline{\quad 4 \quad}$$

Which of the activities you suggested to help this student are similar to these?

1. *Use checkers.* Discrete objects such as black and red checkers can be used to show addition of integers. Let each black checker represent a positive one and each red checker a negative one. Given an addition example, have the student show the two integers by creating a set for each. To show addition, match the two sets one-to-one. A black-and-red combination is worth zero, and it is ignored or discarded because $(+1) + (-1) = 0$; that is, they cancel out each other. The number and color of nonmatching checkers shows the sum.

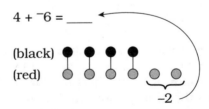

2. *Use a number line.* Arrows for integers are drawn on the number line as follows:

- Length is determined by the absolute value of the number.
- Direction is determined by the sign of the number:
    Arrows for positive numbers go to the right.
    Arrows for negative numbers go to the left.

To add, start at zero, and draw the arrow for the first addend.

$^-3 + {}^+2 =$ ____

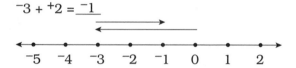

Begin the arrow for the second addend at the tip of the first arrow.

$^-3 + {}^+2 = \underline{{}^-1}$

The sum is indicated by the tip of the second arrow.

   Note: A more accurate modeling for *equals* is suggested by letting the sum be shown by another arrow going from zero to the tip of the second arrow. That is, addition with the two addend arrows produces the same number as the sum arrow.

3. *Focus on the sign of the sum.* For a set of examples, do not have the student compute sums. Instead, have the student determine *only* the sign of each sum. She may want to use checkers to help her decide.

4. *Write a rule.* Have the student write out his own rule for adding two integers. He then needs to test his rule to see if it always produces the correct sum, possibly by using checkers.

Error Pattern A-I-2
(from pages 239 and 241)

This student can probably locate an integer on a number line, but she does not seem to have an adequate understanding of numbers (integers) and operations (addition in these examples).

   E. $^-6 + 10 =$ ___*4*___   F. $10 + {}^-6 =$ ___*16*___

   Here are some instructional activities which may help this student. Are any of your suggestions among these?

1. *Focus on the four possible combinations.* Let the student examine the four possible combinations, those with like signs

and those with unlike signs. Provide examples of each combination and let the student use checkers (see Error Pattern A-I-1) to determine correct sums. What patterns does the student observe?

$$3 + 5 = ? \qquad \quad ^-3 + {}^-5 = ?$$
$$3 + {}^-5 = ? \qquad \quad ^-3 + 5 = ?$$

2. *Focus on the sign of the sum.* Instead of computing sums, let the student determine the sign of each sum for a set of examples you provide. She may want to use checkers to help decide.
3. *Use cutout arrows.* Cutout arrows can be used in a manner similar to the way a number line is used in Error Pattern A-I-1. Prepare a set of cutout arrows varying in length from one unit to five units long. Also prepare a mat to use with the arrows.

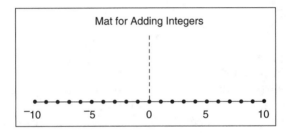

Arrows are selected for each integer as follows:

- Choose an arrow of the length suggested by the absolute value of the integer.
- Turn the arrow as suggested by the sign of the integer by placing the point to the right if it is positive, the point to the left if it is negative.

To add, place the heel of the first arrow at zero. Then place the heel of the second arrow at the tip of the first arrow.

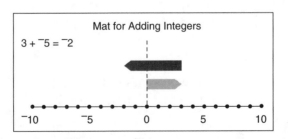

The sum is indicated by the tip of the second arrow. (See note in A-I-1.)

4. *Make a journal entry.* Let the student describe her experiences adding integers. She should illustrate her journal entry with examples and include any patterns or rules she has observed. Make sure she tests any rule to see if it always produces the correct sum, possibly by using checkers.

Error Pattern S-I-1
(from pages 240 and 241)

This error pattern was explained, "Two negatives make a positive. There are two negatives in E (a negative sign and a minus sign) so you add the numbers. There are three negatives in F so you subtract."

E. $^-6 - 3 =$ _____**9**_____   F. $^-2 - {}^-5 =$ _____**3**_____

You suggested instructional activities to help this student. Are any of your ideas among those listed?

1. *Distinguish numbers and operations.* For several examples let the student circle the sign of the operation, then tell you the two numbers that are to be added. Emphasize that the word *negative* is used with numbers; a *minus* sign indicates subtraction.

2. *Make equivalent expressions.* Explain how to show the same as $^-5 - 7$ by changing it to an equivalent addition expression: $^-5 + {}^-7$. Add the inverse (or opposite) of the addend (the second number). Let the student make equivalent addition expressions for many subtraction expressions, including examples of all four combinations of positive and negative numbers. Are any patterns observed?

3. *Subtract by adding.* Remind the student that an open number sentence (usually an equation) asks a question, and there are different ways of asking the same question. A question using subtraction can be changed into an equivalent question using addition. Checkers and arrows and number lines are most useful for adding, and they can be used for subtraction if we change the subtraction example into an equivalent addition example. Provide subtraction examples and let the student rename each as an addition example, then find the sum using whatever method makes most sense to the student.

CONCLUSION

When you help students learn to add and subtract with integers, be especially alert for error patterns. As they develop their procedures, students sometimes overgeneralize from a limited number of experiences or focus on irrelevant attributes.

Symbols are often a source of confusion. Help students distinguish between symbols or signs for numbers, and symbols for operations. Numbers can be represented with sets or locations on a number line, while operations are represented in other ways.

The meaning of the equals sign is very important for students to understand. For example, an expression indicating addition of two numbers (e.g., 2 + ⁻3) is itself a name for a number, and their sum (⁻1) is a name for a number. They are names for *the same* number, and that is what the equals sign indicates. This is as true for integers as it is for whole numbers and rational numbers.

Most students will find it helpful to experience both models for addition and subtraction of integers: the number-line model and the counting-sets model. When using a model, be sure to relate the model to a number sentence, numbers to their numerals, and operations to the sign for the operation. Remember the meaning of the equals sign.

Diagnosis is a continuous process. It continues even during instructional activities as you observe students at work. Keep looking for patterns.

Chapter 12

Algebra

Algebra is a powerful system that uses symbols to communicate patterns and generalizations that are used throughout much of mathematics. Clearly, it is important that students begin with an accurate understanding of how the symbols are used.

This chapter contains examples of papers on which students practiced working with variables in simplifying and evaluating expressions. Look for a pattern in each paper, and verify your conclusions by using the erroneous procedure with the examples provided for that purpose.

Accompanying some of the patterns is a discussion that focuses on reasons a student may learn the particular error pattern. There are evidences of purely mechanical procedures with symbols, and operations are misunderstood. These students practiced concepts and procedures that are not correct, and it is important they do not reinforce them further.

After you read about each student's erroneous procedure, suggest needed instruction, then compare your ideas with the author's suggestions.

IDENTIFYING PATTERNS

Error Pattern ALG-1

The error pattern in Ivette's paper is all too common. Can you find it?

Name _Ivette_

1. $(a^2)^2 = $ _a^4_

2. $(b^2)^3 = $ _b^5_

3. $(a^3b^4)^2 = $ _a^5b^6_

Did you find Ivette's procedure? Check yourself by using her procedure to complete Examples 4 and 5.

4. $(x^3)^2 = $ _____

5. $(xy^2)^2 = $ _____

Turn to page 250 to see if you identified the procedure correctly. Why might Ivette be using such a procedure?

Error Pattern ALG-2

Can you find Juan's error pattern?

Name _Juan_

1. $6(1+4x)+2 = 6(5x)+2$
$= 30x+2$

2. $7+5(2+3x) = 7+5(5x)$
$= 7+25x$

Did you find Juan's procedure? Check yourself by using his procedure to complete Examples 3 and 4.

3. $3(2x+1) = $ _____

4. $2(3+2x)+4 = $ _____

Turn to page 250 to see if you identified the procedure. Why might Juan be doing this?

Error Pattern ALG-3

Can you find the error pattern in Tina's paper? It may surprise you.

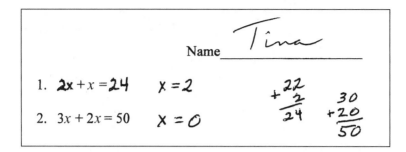

Did you find Tina's procedure? Check yourself by using her procedure to complete Examples 3 and 4.

> 3. $3x + x = 32$
> 4. $4x + 2x = 66$

Turn to page 251 to see if you identified the procedure. Why might Tina be doing this?

Error Pattern ALG-4

Can you find the error pattern in Booker's paper?

Name $Booker$

A. $(2x^3y^3)^2$ $\underline{2x^5y^5}$ B. $(^-4x^2y^3)^2$ $\underline{-4x^4y^5}$

C. $(3x^4y^2)^2$ $\underline{3x^6y^4}$ D. $(^-2x^4y^2)^2$ $\underline{-2x^6y^4}$

Did you find Booker's procedure? Check yourself by using his procedure to complete Examples E and F.

> E. $(2\,x^2y^2)^2$ _____   F. $(-3x^2y^3)^2$ _____

Now turn to page 251 to see if you identified the procedure. Why might Booker be doing this?

DESCRIBING INSTRUCTION

Error Pattern ALG-1

(from Ivette's paper on page 248)

Did you find Ivette's error pattern?

$$4.\ (x^3)^2 = \underline{x^5}$$

$$5.\ (xy^2)^2 = \underline{x^3 y^4}$$

When simplifying such expressions, Ivette adds the exponents as the parentheses are removed. Sometimes students verify a procedure by substituting a particular number and making sure the two expressions are equal, but apparently Ivette has not done this.

What *does* Ivette understand? What does she *not* yet understand? Ivette should not continue to practice her procedure. How would you help her? Describe two instructional activities that you believe would help her.

1. _____

2. _____

After you complete your two descriptions, turn to page 252 and compare what you have written with the suggestions presented there.

Error Pattern ALG-2

(from Juan's paper on page 248)

Did you find Juan's error pattern?

$$3.\ 3(2x+1) = 3(3x)$$
$$= 9x$$

$$4.\ 2(3+2x)+4 = 2(5x)+4$$
$$= 10x+4$$

When simplifying such expressions, Juan adds (incorrectly) before he removes parentheses. He does not distinguish between numbers that are and are not coefficients.

What *does* Juan understand? What does he *not* yet understand? How could you help Juan so he does not continue to practice such a procedure? Describe two instructional activities you believe would help.

1. _____

2. _____

After you describe two activities, turn to page 252 and compare what you have written with the suggestions presented there.

Error Pattern ALG-3
(from Tina's paper on page 249)

Did you find her error pattern?

3. $3x + x = 32$ $x = 1$

$$\begin{array}{r} 3\,1 \\ +\,1 \\ \hline 3\,2 \end{array}$$

4. $4x + 2x = 66$ $x = 3$

$$\begin{array}{r} 43 \\ +23 \\ \hline 66 \end{array}$$

Variables are treated as if they are digits *within* whole numbers—a mechanical process ignoring place values. (Her computations at the right help identify her thought processes.)

Apparently there is much Tina does not yet understand. What *does* she understand? Describe two instructional activities you believe would help her.

1. _____

2. _____

After you describe two instructional activities, turn to page 253 and compare what you have written with the suggestions presented there.

Error Pattern ALG-4
(from Booker's paper on page 249)

Did you find his error pattern?

E. $(2x^2y^2)^2 = 2x^4y^4$ F. $(^-3x^2y^3)^2 = ^-3x^4y^5$

When Booker simplifies expressions like these he makes two errors. First, he does not square the numerical coefficient. Second, he adds exponents when he should multiply them.

How would you go about helping him? Describe two appropriate instructional activities.

1. _____

2. _____

After you describe two activities, turn to page 254 and compare what you have written with the suggestions presented there.

CONSIDERING ALTERNATIVES

Error Pattern ALG-1
(from pages 248 and 250)

What instructional activities did you suggest to help Ivette correct the error pattern illustrated? See if your suggestions are among those listed below.

$$4.\ (x^3)^2 = X^5$$
$$5.\ (xy^2)^2 = X^3 y^4$$

1. *Focus on the total number of factors.* Explain that such an expression involves multiplying; for example, $(b^2)^3$ means $b^2 \times b^2 \times b^2$, which includes three sets of two factors: $(b \times b) \times (b \times b) \times (b \times b)$. Altogether, b is a factor *six* times. Ask, "How can we find the total number of factors (the product in this case) without so much writing?" (You multiply exponents.)
2. *Substitute a small number and compute the amount.* Substitute a number like 2 or 3, and compute the amount. Begin within the parentheses, then continue. Have the student examine the written work and reflect on what was done. For $(b^2)^3$, the number was written as a factor six times: three pairs of factors is six factors, so $(b^2)^3$ is $(b)^6$ and the exponents 2 and 3 can be multiplied. Would this also be true if a different number were substituted for b?

Error Pattern ALG-2
(from pages 248 and 250)

What instructional activities did you suggest to help Juan correct the error pattern illustrated? See if your suggestions are among those listed.

4. $3(2x + 1) =$ $3(3x)$
$= 9x$

5. $2(3 + 2x) + 4 =$ $2(5x) + 4$
$= 10x + 4$

1. *Use an array to represent the product.* For a product like $3(2z + 1)$, represent the multiplication with an array.

$$2z + 1$$
$$3 \boxed{}$$

Then partition the array much as you would for multiplication with whole numbers.

For 3×14:

$$10 + 4$$

$$3 \boxed{3 \times 10 \quad | \quad 3 \times 4} \rightarrow 30 + 12 \rightarrow 42$$

Similarly:

$$2z + 1$$

$$3 \boxed{3 \times 2z \quad | \quad 3 \times 1} \rightarrow 6z + 3$$

Have Juan compare the result with his error pattern and discuss (possibly write out) a procedure that produces the correct product.

2. *Substitute a small number and compute the amount.* For instance, for $3(2z + 1)$, assume that $z = 4$. Then $3(2z + 1) = 3(8 + 1)$. But $8 + 1$ is 9, and 3×9 is 27. (Using the erroneous pattern with $z = 4$, the result is 36.) Compare the procedures and note that there are not three *z*s; there are only two *z*s before multiplication by 3.

Error Pattern ALG-3

(from pages 249 and 251)

What instructional activities did you suggest to help Tina correct the error pattern illustrated? See if your suggestions are among those listed.

3. $3x + x = 32$ $x = 1$

$$\begin{array}{r} 31 \\ + \ 1 \\ \hline 32 \end{array}$$

4. $4x + 2x = 66$ $x = 3$

$$\begin{array}{r} 43 \\ +23 \\ \hline 66 \end{array}$$

1. *Explain a coefficient as shorthand.* Explain that when there are several of one variable, the amount might be written as "three *x*s" or "four *y*s." But it is shorter and easier to write it as "3*x*" and "4*y*."

Not three *x*s, but 3*x*.
Not four *y*s, but 4*y*.

2. *Let the expression represent a mathematical situation.* What could "4*x*" represent? Let the student, or a small group of students, describe several situations that could be represented by 4*x*. For example, "*x* could be the number of trading cards in each of 4 packages."

3. *Focus on the meaning of expressions like "3B."* Ask the student, "Which of these are equal to 3*B*: 3 + *B*, 30 + *B*, 3 × *B*, or *B*+*B*+*B*? Why?" As you discuss the matter, emphasize that a variable and its coefficient are always two different numbers.

Error Pattern ALG-4

(from pages 249 and 251)

What instructional activities did you suggest to help Booker correct the error pattern illustrated? See if your suggestions are among those listed below.

E. $(2x^2y^2)^2$ $\underline{\ 2x^4y^4\ }$ $(^-3x^2y^3)^2$ $\underline{\ -3x^4y^5\ }$

1. *Write out all factors and rearrange them.* An expression like $(2\ a^2\ b^3)^2$ represents one number named by a long string of factors multiplied together, so rewrite the number as a string of factors, then rearrange the factors by like terms.

$(2a^2b^3)^2 = (2a^2b^3) \times (2a^2b^3)$
$= (2 \times a \times a \times b \times b \times b) \times (2 \times a \times a \times b \times b \times b)$
$= (2 \times 2) \times (a \times a \times a \times a) \times (b \times b \times b \times b \times b \times b)$
$= 4 \times a^4 \times b^6$

Have the student examine the result and reflect, "How can the result be obtained without writing out all of the factors?"

2. *Determine the frequency of each term as a factor.* Altogether, how many times is 2 a factor? How many times is *a* a factor? And *b?*

CONCLUSION

Algebra is a powerful system that uses symbols, but the symbols must be used correctly. Be alert to error patterns in students' early work with symbols. Do not focus instruction only on procedures and getting correct answers. Students need a good foundation if they are to learn algebra. They need a well-developed number sense and knowledge of the properties of operations on numbers.

It is often helpful for students to be reminded that a particular expression is simply a name for a number. Sometimes that name is itself a sum or a difference. At other times it is a product, and it can be broken down into a string of factors.

By examining parts of an expression, and sometimes by using analogies from prior work with whole numbers, students can be helped to make sense out of algebraic expressions. Be sure you take time to discuss alternatives and make relationships clear. Sometimes a standard procedure can be seen as a shortcut to a much more time-consuming, but sensible, process.

Glossary

Algorithms are step-by-step procedures for accomplishing a task, such as solving a problem. In this text the term usually refers to paper-and-pencil procedures for finding a sum, difference, product, or quotient.

Alternative assessments are nontraditional means of collecting information about student learning. They are often contrasted with more traditional paper-and-pencil tests.

Arithmetic is a branch of mathematics that is concerned with nonnegative real numbers and applications of the operations addition, subtraction, multiplication, and division.

Assessment refers to gathering information about student learning. When methods or strategies for assessment are varied, more satisfactory judgments can be made about past learning and about instruction that is appropriate.

Basic number combinations (or **basic facts**) of arithmetic are simple equations or number sentences involving two one-digit whole numbers and their sum or product. Examples include $6 + 7 = 13$, $13 - 7 = 6$, $6 \times 8 = 48$, and $48 \div 8 = 6$. Altogether there are 390 basic facts for the four operations, and they can be written either horizontally or vertically.

Buggy algorithms are step-by-step procedures with at least one erroneous step. As a result, the procedure does not accomplish the intended task. When used to refer to paper-and-pencil computational procedures, buggy algorithms are often computational procedures with an error pattern.

Computation is the process of making a calculation. An estimate is sufficient for some situations. At other times, when an exact

256

number is required, computation can be done mentally, with a calculator (or computer), or by means of a paper-and-pencil algorithm—whichever is most appropriate.

Conceptual learning in mathematics focuses on ideas and on generalizations that make connections among ideas, in contrast to learning that focuses only on skills and step-by-step procedures without explicit reference to mathematical ideas.

Conceptual maps are graphic organizers that show the inter-relationships of ideas and processes for a particular area of content.

Concrete materials are instructional materials that can be handled and moved about as mathematical ideas and processes are modeled. They are often three-dimensional, but may be two-dimensional. Concrete materials are often called manipulatives.

Cooperative groups are small groups of students who work together on tasks. Students communicate mathematical ideas and help each other learn.

Corrective instruction may be similar to developmental instruction; however, it is not initial teaching of the concept or procedure. A student has somehow failed to learn or has learned misconceptions, and corrective instruction is needed.

Developmental instruction usually refers to the initial teaching of a concept or procedure such as an algorithm. It is planned, sequential instruction that gives careful attention to learning concepts as well as procedures. Developmental instruction for paper-and-pencil procedures usually involves the use of manipulatives.

Diagnosis is the process of investigating a student's condition in regard to learning mathematics. Data are collected to determine what the student knows and can do, and what concepts and processes are yet to be learned. Typically, a judgment is made about appropriate next steps for instruction.

Diagnostic interviews are conducted one-on-one with individuals. The interviewer presents opportunities to demonstrate mathematical understanding and skill, and attempts to determine how the student is thinking. Modeling of mathematical concepts or procedures is often involved.

Diagnostic teaching responds frequently, even within a single lesson, to evidences that individual students are or are not learning particular concepts and skills. Diagnostic teaching moves back-and-forth between collecting data about students and providing instruction.

Digits are the symbols we use to create numerals. In our Hindu-Arabic numeration system we use 0, 1, 2, 3, 4, 5, 6, 7, 8, and 9. *Multi*digit numerals are composed of two or more digits. The term digit comes from the Latin *digitus* for finger.

Equivalent expressions are names for the same idea. For example, equivalent numerical expressions are names for the same number: $6 + 7$ and 13 name the same number, as do $\frac{1}{2}$ and $\frac{2}{4}$.

Error patterns are observed within student work whenever an action is taken regularly which does not lead, in every case, to a correct result. Some error patterns produce correct results part of the time. Error patterns are most commonly observed within the written work of students.

Evaluation is the process of making judgments about student achievement or about instruction needed. Evaluations should be based on data collected during assessment.

Formative evaluation occurs when assessment data are gathered before completion of a particular lesson or unit of instruction, and decisions are made about how instruction should continue.

Graphic organizers are graphic representations that help learners organize information in their thinking. Examples include charts, diagrams, webs, conceptual maps, and number lines. They help students connect mathematical concepts and procedures.

Informal assessment refers to assessment without the planning which typically precedes tests, performance tasks, and many interviews. Unplanned observations and incidental notations are examples of informal assessment.

Invented algorithms usually refers to paper-and-pencil computational procedures invented by students, often with encouragement and guidance from a teacher while students are solving problems with the aid of concrete materials.

Low-stress algorithms are paper-and-pencil computational procedures that involve only minimal information held in memory while executing the procedure. Typically, recall of number combinations is straightforward, and renaming is facilitated through nonstandard notation.

Manipulatives are concrete materials used during instruction.

Mental computation is the process of making a calculation mentally, without the aid of a calculator, a computer, or a paper-and-pencil procedure. Mental computation relies heavily on important mathematical understandings. Examples include the distributive property and principles related to numeration.

Models represent concepts and principles to be understood, processes to be learned, and problems to be solved. Concrete materials can be used to model mathematical ideas such as numerical concepts, spatial concepts, principles of numeration, and operations. Mathematical statements can model complex relationships and problem situations.[1]

Number combinations. See **basic number combinations.**

Number sense can be thought of as the informal "feel" for quantities that students develop.

Numeracy suggests the disposition and ability to use mathematical knowledge and skills appropriately and effectively in everyday situations.

Numeration refers to systems of counting or numbering, especially symbol systems used to represent numbers. Patterns among place values are a major focus of the study of our own Hindu-Arabic numeration system for recording whole numbers. Decimals are an extension of the system.

Operations on numbers are mathematical processes whereby one number is derived from others. Arithmetic is concerned with four operations: addition, subtraction, multiplication, and division.

Overgeneralizing is the process of deriving conclusions that can be applied more broadly than justified. Students over-generalize when they jump to a conclusion before they have adequate data at hand.

Overspecializing is the process of deriving conclusions that are restricted inappropriately. This may happen because students focus on irrelevant attributes of a limited number of instances.

Peer assessment occurs when students thoughtfully consider examples of work by other students, keeping specific criteria in mind.

Peer tutoring occurs when students instruct one another by questioning, explaining, and demonstrating concepts and procedures.

Portfolios are collections of student work over time that can be used to aid student self-assessment. Typically, they provide varied sources of information for evaluating student learning.

1. For a discussion of modeling, see National Council of Teachers of Mathematics. (2000). *Principles and standards for school mathematics*. Reston, VA: The Council, pp. 70–71.

Proceduralization is the process whereby a practiced procedure becomes more automatic over time; increasingly, less conceptual knowledge is used and more procedural knowledge is used as the procedure is executed.

Procedural learning in mathematics focuses on learning skills and step-by-step procedures. In practice, it does not always include understanding of mathematical concepts and principles involved. However, procedural learning should be tied to conceptual learning and to real life applications.

Rational numbers are numbers that can be expressed in the form $\frac{a}{b}$, in which a and b are integers and $b \neq 0$. In this text rational numbers are expressed with fractions, decimals, and percents.

Rubrics are criteria for scoring a product or performance, usually organized so that levels are designated and indicators are described.

Self-assessment occurs when individuals reflect on their learning, examine what they have done, and thoughtfully evaluate their own learning. Self-assessment should note accomplishments as well as make comparisons with standards and criteria.

Standards tell what students should know and be able to do. They are statements about what is valued in mathematics teaching and learning.

Summative evaluation occurs when assessment data are gathered after completion of a particular unit of instruction and judgments are made about student learning. It usually involves a test, completion of projects, or a culminating performance task. Summative evaluations can point to the effectiveness of the instructional unit itself.

Whole numbers are nonnegative integers: {0, 1, 2, 3, . . . }.

Selected Resources

ᒥ ᒧ

The annotated listing of resources that follows is divided into two categories: *Assessment and Diagnosis* and *Instruction*. Many of the resources listed in one category contain implications for the other.

Assessment and Diagnosis

BABBIT, B. C. (1990). *Error patterns in problem solving.* (ERIC Document Reproduction Service No. ED 338 500). Babbit used data on error frequencies from the Fourth National Assessment of Educational Progress and a study of problem-solving performance to compile a listing of common errors for traditional one-step word problems. Teacher knowledge of student error patterns was also examined.

BEHR, M. J., WACHSMUTH, I., POST, T. R., & LESH, R. (1984). Order and equivalence of rational numbers: A clinical teaching experiment. *Journal for Research in Mathematics Education, 15,* 323–341. The authors describe correct and erroneous strategies used by students, with implications for instruction.

BOOTH, L. R. (1988). Children's difficulties in beginning algebra. In A. Coxford & A. Schulte (Eds.), *The ideas of algebra* (pp. 20–32). Reston, VA: National Council of Teachers of Mathematics. Booth uses sample dialogue to illustrate difficulties some students have in conceptualizing the use of variables.

BROWN-HERBST, K. (1999). So math isn't just answers. *Mathematics Teaching in the Middle School, 4*(7), 448–455. The author presents a scoring guide for K–12 students developed to reflect Alaska's state mathematics standards. Students were involved in the process of developing the scoring guide.

BUSH, W. S., & GREER, A. S. (Eds.). (1999). *Mathematics assessment: A practical handbook for grades 9–12.* Reston, VA: National Council of Teachers of Mathematics. This handbook explains how to find, modify, and create assessment tasks, and how to plan a classroom assessment program. Tips on scoring, grading, reporting, and using assessment data are included.

BUSH, W. S., & LEINWAND, S. (Eds.). (2000). *Mathematics assessment: A practical handbook for grades 6–8.* Reston, VA: National Council of Teachers of Mathematics. This handbook addresses: tools for assessment, implementing an assessment system for grades 6–8, and using the results of assessment. Exemplary assessment tasks are illustrated.

CAI, J., MAGONE, M. E., WANG, N., & LANE, S. (1996). Describing student performance qualitatively. *Mathematics Teaching in the Middle School, 1,* 828–835. The authors discuss and illustrate scoring by levels and present a framework for qualitative analysis of student work.

CAWLEY, J. F., & PARMAR, R. S. (1996). Arithmetic computation abilities of students with learning disabilities: Implications for instruction. *Learning Disabilities Research & Practice 11*(4), 230–237. The authors compare data from learning disabilities students and normally achieving students, and make observations concerning error patterns.

CLARKE, D. J. (1992). Activating assessment alternatives in mathematics. *The Arithmetic Teacher, 39*(6), 24–29. Clarke describes several assessment and record-keeping procedures for classroom situations, including annotated class lists, work folios, student-constructed tests, and student self-assessment.

COLE, K., COFFEY, J., & GOLDMAN, S. (1999). Using assessments to improve equity in mathematics. *Educational Leadership 56*(6), 56–58. The authors argue that assessment that is open, explicit, and accessible helps all students achieve the goals of standards-based learning.

COX, L. S. (1975). Systematic errors in the four vertical algorithms in normal and handicapped populations. *Journal for Research in Mathematics Education, 6,* 202–220. Cox documents the fact that many children use specific erroneous procedures. Data on the frequency of selected error patterns are included.

DRAKE, B. M., & AMSPAUGH, L. B. (1994). What writing reveals in mathematics. *Focus on Learning Problems in Mathematics, 16*(3), 43–50. The authors discuss diagnostic information that can be gained from students' writing and they present examples, including error patterns.

ENRIGHT, B. E. (1989). *Basic mathematics: Detecting and correcting special needs.* Boston: Allyn & Bacon. This is a resource for detecting and correcting mathematical needs of exceptional students. Analysis of error patterns is stressed, and suggestions are made for corrective instruction.

ENSIGN, J. (1998). Parents, portfolios, and personal mathematics. *Teaching Children Mathematics 4*(6), 346–351. Ensign reports an attempt to connect in-school mathematics with out-of-school experiences for children in grades K–5. Out-of-school mathematics was often richer and more complex than concurrent in-school mathematics.

FARRELL, M. A. (1992). Implementing the professional standards for teaching mathematics: Learning from your students. *Mathematics Teacher, 85,* 656–659. In her discussion of student feedback, Farrell includes analyses of students' error patterns as a way of understanding why students develop misconceptions in mathematics.

FUSON, K. C., WEARNE, D., HIEBERT, J. C., MURRAY, H. G., HUMAN, P. G., OLIVIER, A. I., CARPENTER, T. P., & FENNEMA, E. (1997). Children's conceptual structures for multidigit numbers and methods of multidigit addition and subtraction. *Journal for Research in Mathematics Education 28*(2), 130–162. Researchers describe a problem-solving approach used to teach multidigit number concepts, and the conceptual structures constructed by the children. These structures are linked to addition and subtraction methods used by the children. Errors that may arise with each method are identified.

GINSBURG, H. P., LOPEZ, L. S., MUKHOPADHYAY, S., YAMAMOTO, T., WILLIS, M., & KELLEY, M. S. (1992). Assessing understanding of arithmetic. In R. Lesh & S. J. Lamon (Eds.), *Assessment of authentic performance in school mathematics* (pp. 265–289). Washington, DC: AAAS Press. The authors address the nature of understandings as well as their assessment. They discuss the interview and a variety of tests for use with individuals as well as larger groups of students.

GRAEBER, A. O., & BAKER, K. M. (1991, summer). Curriculum materials and misconceptions concerning multiplication and division. *Focus on Learning Problems in Mathematics, 13,* 25–38. The authors analyze student texts in relation to common misconceptions regarding multiplication and division.

GRAEBER, A. O., & BAKER, K. M. (1992, April). Little into big is the way it always is. *The Arithmetic Teacher, 39,* 18–21. The authors conclude that many children believe you "always take the little into the big" and "all operations are commutative." They also observe that children do not connect what they know about fractions with division of whole numbers. Suggestions for instruction in grades 4 and above are included.

GRAEBER, A. O., & TIROSH, D. (1990). Insights fourth and fifth graders bring to multiplication and division with decimals. *Educational Studies in Mathematics, 21,* 565–588. The authors describe conceptions held by children that may impede their work with decimals, and they discuss implications of their findings.

HARVEY, J. G. (1992). Mathematics testing with calculators: Ransoming the hostages. In T. A. Romberg (Ed.), *Mathematics assessment and evaluation: Imperatives for mathematics educators* (pp. 139–168). Albany, NY: State University of New York Press. Harvey discusses and illustrates different approaches to testing that might be used with calculators. Research studies on calculator-based mathematics tests are also summarized.

JITENDRA, A. K., & KAMEENUI, E. J. (1996). Experts' and novices' error patterns in solving part-whole mathematical word problems. *Educational Research 90*(1), 42–51. The authors found that experts tend to use a schemadriven approach to solve problems in well-defined domains, but novices search for a solution procedure and work backward.

KAMII, C., & LEWIS, B. A. (1991). Achievement tests in primary mathematics: Perpetuating lower-order thinking. *The Arithmetic Teacher 38*(9), 4–9. The authors caution that we can get misleading information from achievement tests. Limitations of achievement tests are described, and the value of interviews is highlighted.

KAUR, B., & SHARON, B. H. P. (1994). Algebraic misconceptions of first-year college students. *Focus on Learning Problems in Mathematics 16*(4), 43–58. From their analysis of misconceptions and errors, the authors list 12 problematic areas in the teaching of algebra, and discuss implications for instruction.

LAMBDIN, D. V., & WALKER, V. L. (1994). Planning for classroom portfolio assessment. *The Arithmetic Teacher 41*(6), 318–324. The authors distinguish between folders and portfolios, and provide tips for getting started with portfolio assessment. They emphasize the need for students to reflect on their work in mathematics and the need for teachers to provide guidance in being reflective.

LANKFORD, F. G. JR. (1992). What can a teacher learn about a pupil's thinking through oral interviews? *Arithmetic Teacher 40*(2), 106–111. Lankford compares computational strategies and examines errors. The article is a classic, republished from the January 1974 issue of the *Arithmetic Teacher* (pp. 26–32).

LESH, R. (1992). Computer-based assessment of higher order understandings in elementary mathematics. In T. A. Romberg (Ed.), *Mathematics assessment and evaluation: Imperatives for mathematics educators* (pp. 81–110). Albany, NY: State University of New York Press. Lesh stresses the close link between instruction and assessment. He notes that alternative models may be available to interpret a given situation.

LESH, R., & LAMON, S. (Eds.). (1992). *Assessment of authentic performance in school mathematics.* Washington, DC: AAAS Press. In this book, which addresses many difficult issues in assessment, most chapters focus on the content of assessment while some illustrate varied modes of delivery.

LIEDTKE, W. (1988). Diagnosis in mathematics: The advantages of an interview. *The Arithmetic Teacher 36*(3), 26–29. Liedtke includes interview strategies and specific interview protocols.

LOCKHEAD, J., & MESTRE, J. (1988). From words to algebra: Mending misconceptions. In A. Coxford & A. Schulte (Eds.), *The ideas of algebra, K–12* (pp. 127–135). Reston, VA: National Council of Teachers of Mathematics. The authors illustrate difficulties students have translating word problems into mathematical statements, then describe an instructional approach in which students identify inconsistencies inherent in their misconceptions.

LONG, M. J., & BEN-HUR, M. (1991). Informing learning through the clinical interview. *The Arithmetic Teacher 38*(6), 44–46. The authors demonstrate the value of interviews as a tool for classroom teachers to uncover learning difficulties, even among students who get correct answers on test papers.

MACGREGOR, M., & STACEY, K. (1993). Cognitive models underlying students' formulation of simple linear equations. *Journal for Research in Mathematics Education 24*(3), 217–232. The authors examine students' errors and note the effects of misinterpreting algebraic letters and thinking that the equals sign denotes correspondence or association rather than equality.

MADDEN, M., & HOPE, J. A. (1993). An analysis of an adult's struggle with innumeracy. *Focus on Learning Problems in Mathematics 75*(4), 7–17. The authors report an interview with a 31-year-old interviewed in an attempt to help him perform routine numerical tasks associated with daily life. Analysis of the results has implications for instruction in general.

MARKOVITS, Z., EYLON, B. S., & BRUCKHEIMER, M. (1988). Difficulties students have with the function concept. In A. Coxford & A. Schulte (Eds.), *The ideas of algebra, K–12* (pp. 43–60). Reston, VA: National Council of Teachers of Mathematics. The authors describe difficulties and misconceptions students experience with reference to the function concept, and suggest remedies.

MARQUIS, J. (1988). Common mistakes in algebra. In A. Coxford & A. Schulte (Eds.), *The ideas of algebra, K–12* (pp. 204–205). Reston, VA: National Council of Teachers of Mathematics. Marquis uses her own test with students to find common mistakes in algebra. The test is presented.

MCDONALD, J., BEAL, J., & AYERS, F. (1992). Details of performance on computer and paper administered versions of a test of whole number computation skills. *Focus on Learning Problems in Mathematics 14*(3), 15–27. The authors compare student performance on a computer administered test with a paper-and-pencil test.

NORWOOD, K. S., & CARTER, G. (1994). Journal writing: An insight into students' understanding. *Teaching Children Mathematics 1*(3), 146–148. The authors describe several journal-writing activities that can assess student understanding of specific mathematical ideas.

OPPENHEIMER, L. & HUNTING, R. P. (1999). Relating fractions and decimals: Listening to students talk. *Mathematics Teaching in the Middle School 4*(5), 318–321. The authors describe specific difficulties students have relating fractions and decimals, and they encourage teachers to investigate the level of understanding by listening to students explain how they solved routine problems.

RESNICK, L. B., NESHER, P., LEONARD, F., MAGONE, M., OMANSON, S., & PELED, I. (1989). Conceptual bases of arithmetic errors: The case of decimal fractions. *Journal for Research in Mathematics Education 20*(1), 8–27. The authors document major categories of errors as children learn decimal fractions, and establish conceptual sources for the children's errors. They suggest that error patterns cannot be avoided during instruction and encourage educators to use them as diagnostic tools to determine children's understanding.

ROMBERG, T. A. (Ed.). (1992). *Mathematics assessment and evaluation: Imperatives for mathematics educators.* Albany, NY: State University of New York Press. This book stresses the need for valid data and implications of the NCTM Standards for test development. Assessment alternatives are explored in the hope that authentic performance can be determined.

RON, P. (1998). My family taught me this way. In L. J. Morrow & M. J. Kenney (Eds.), *The Teaching and Learning of Algorithms in School Mathematics* (pp. 115–119). Reston, VA: National Council of Teachers of Mathematics. Ron illustrates difficulties, and errors, common among European and Latin American students when learning algorithms taught in the United States.

SAMMONS, K. B., KOBETT, B., HEISS, J., & FENNELL, F. (1992). Linking instruction and assessment in the mathematics classroom. *The Arithmetic Teacher 39*(6), 11–16. The authors describe and illustrate both formative and summative assessment techniques. Investigations based on problem-solving and at-home connections are included.

SANTEL-PARKE, C., & CAI, J. (1997). Does the task truly measure what was intended? *Mathematics Teaching in the Middle School 3*(1), 74–82. The authors encourage the development of more open-ended assessment tasks with realistic contexts.

SCHOENFELD, A. H. (1985). Making sense of "out loud" problem-solving protocols. *The Journal of Mathematical Behavior 4*, 171–191. Schoenfeld argues that the circumstances in which people generate "out loud" solutions often affect those solutions in a variety of ways.

SCHULMAN, L. (1996). New assessment practices in mathematics. *Journal of Education 178*(1), 61–71. Schulman discusses assessment practices that incorporate NCTM's standards for assessment. Strategies for gathering evidence and documenting student learning are described and illustrated.

SCHULMAN, L. & MOON, J. (1995). *Finding the connections: Linking assessment, instruction and curriculum in elementary mathematics.* Portsmouth, NH: Heinemann. The authors describe varied forms of data gathering and documentation, and also the context in which to diagnose error patterns and plan needed instruction.

SGROI, L. A., GROPPER, N., KILKER, M. T., RAMBUSH, N. M., AND SEMONITE, B. (1995). Assessing young children's mathematical understandings. *Teaching Children Mathematics 1*(5), 275–277. The authors describe instructional tasks in a kindergarten that enable teachers to infer understanding of concepts.

STEFANICH, G. P., & ROKUSEK, T. (1992). An analysis of computational errors in the use of division algorithms by fourth-grade students. *School Science and Mathematics 92*(4), 201–205. The authors classify incorrect responses of fourth graders (division algorithm for whole numbers) and study the effects of instruction for the systematic errors identified.

STENMARK, J. K. (Ed.). (1991). *Mathematics assessment: Myths, models, good questions, and practical suggestions.* Reston, VA: National Council of Teachers of Mathematics: This very useful publication provides mathematics educators with a handbook for alternative forms of assessment.

TONACK, D. A. (1996). A teacher's views on classroom assessment. *Mathematics Teaching in the Middle School 2*(2), 770–773. Tonack uses instructional and assessment tasks involving computation of volume to emphasize that instruction and assessment cannot really be separated.

TUCKER, B. F. (1989). Seeing addition: A diagnosis-remediation case study. *The Arithmetic Teacher 36*(5), 10–11. Tucker provides an illustration of how diagnosis can lead to specific instructional tasks that get results.

WILDE, S. (1991). Learning to write about mathematics. *The Arithmetic Teacher 38*(6), 38–43. Wilde illustrates the diagnostic value of writing within the mathematics classroom.

WOODWARD, J., & HOWARD, L. (1994). The misconceptions of youth: Errors and their mathematical meaning. *Exceptional Children 61*(2), 126–136. The authors discuss a technology-based diagnostic system and related research. In view of the frequency of misconceptions among students with learning disabilities and the widespread use of technology, they suggest much more emphasis on conceptual understanding.

Instruction

ALBERT, L. R., & ANTOS, J. (2000). Daily journals connect mathematics to real life. *Mathematics Teaching in the Middle School 5*(8), 526–531. The authors emphasize description during student projects, and then focus on assessment of mathematics learning.

ANDERSON, A. (1995). Effects of the implicit or explicit use of 1 on students' responses when multiplying monomials $(ax^n)(bx^m)$ where n or $m = 1$. *Focus on Learning Problems in Mathematics 17*(1), 34–48. The author found that use of an explicit 1 helped many students.

ASHLOCK, R. B., & WASHBON, C. A. (1978). Games: Practice activities for the basic facts. In M. S. Suydam & R. E. Reys (Eds.), *Developing computational skills* (pp. 39–50). Reston, VA: National Council of Teachers of Mathematics. The use of games for practice with number combinations is discussed. Games are described in relation to the guidelines presented.

ASHLOCK, R. B., JOHNSON, M. L., WILSON, J. W., & JONES, W. L. (1983). *Guiding each child's learning of mathematics: A diagnostic approach to instruction.* New York: Merrill/Macmillan. In their cognitively oriented methods text, the authors present models for guiding both diagnosis and instruction.

BARONE, M. M., & TAYLOR, L. (1996). Peer tutoring with mathematics manipulatives: A practical guide. *Teaching Children Mathematics 3*(1), 8–15. The authors illustrate sample activities for peer tutoring, including structured journal pages for both tutor and tutee.

BAROODY, A. J., & BARTELS, B. H. (2000). Using concept maps to link mathematical ideas. *Mathematics Teaching in the Middle School 5*(9), 604–609. The authors describe concept maps and their roles in instruction. Illustrations are included, as are teaching tips on getting started.

BLEY, N. S., & THORNTON, C. A. (1995). *Teaching mathematics to students with learning disabilities* (3rd ed.). Austin, TX: Pro-Ed. This methods text has many practical suggestions for helping students with learning disabilities to learn number combinations and algorithms.

BORASI, R. (1994). Capitalizing on errors as "springboards for inquiry:" A teaching experiment. *Journal for Research in Mathematics Education 25*(2), 166–208. This report examines how errors among secondary students can be used instructionally.

BUSCHMAN, L. (1995). Communicating in the language of mathematics. *Teaching Children Mathematics 1*(6), 324–329. Buschman describes varied communication activities: journals, a mathematician's chair, cooperative learning, a family newsletter, and 14 "communication structures."

BYRENES, J. P., & WASIK, B. A. (1991). Role of conceptual knowledge in mathematical procedural learning. *Developmental Psychology 27*(5), 777–786. The authors report on an experiment comparing two approaches to eliminating errors in computation: simultaneous activation and dynamic interaction. Their results favor dynamic interaction, in which there is progressive independence of procedural knowledge as expertise is gained.

CAI, J. (1998). Developing algebraic reasoning in the elementary grades. *Teaching Children Mathematics 5*(4), 225–229. Cai emphasizes the need to help students make the transition from visual representations to abstract understandings, and shows how discussions of alternatives can facilitate this transition.

CALIANDRO, C. K. (2000). Children's inventions for multidigit multiplication and division. *Teaching Children Mathematics 6*(6), 420–426. Caliandro describes the experiences of third-grade students with strong mathematical ability who invented algorithms and challenged one another.

CAPPS, L. R., & PICKREIGN, J. (1993). Language connections in mathematics: A critical part of mathematics instruction. *The Arithmetic Teacher 41*(1), 8–12. Among many interesting observations is the fact that the meaning of a mathematical symbol may vary with the context, as do words in language.

CAREY, D. A. (1991). Number sentences: Linking addition and subtraction word problems and symbols. *Journal for Research in Mathematics Education 22*(4), 266–280. Carey found that the first-grade children she studied focused on the semantic structure of word problems, rather than on part-whole relationships that indicate the operation to be used to find the missing number.

CARROLL, W. M., & PORTER, D. (1997). Invented strategies can develop meaningful mathematical procedures. *Teaching Children Mathematics 3*(7), 370–374. The authors argue that invented procedures promote understanding and describe ways to encourage algorithm invention.

CAWLEY, J. F. (1987). Specially designed instruction and arithmetic computation for the learning disabled. *Reading, Writing, and Learning Disabilities 3*, 85–92. Cawley warns against practices dominated by rule-governed approaches, and illustrates more concept-rooted methods for learning disabled students.

CAWLEY, J. F., BAKER-KROCZYNSKI, S., & URBAN, A. (1992). Seeking excellence in mathematics education for students with mild disabilities. *Teaching Exceptional Children 24*(2), 40–43. The authors explore the possibility of adapting NCTM standards for use among special educators.

CAWLEY, J. F., HAYES, A. M. F., & SHAW, R. A. (1988). *Mathematics for the mildly handicapped.* Newton, MA: Allyn & Bacon. This methods text focuses on diagnostic instruction of disabled learners.

CHAMBERS, D. L. (1996). Direct modeling and invented procedures: Building on students' informal strategies. *Teaching Children Mathematics 3*(2), 92–95. Chambers notes that when students use strategies they understand they gain confidence in their ability to do mathematics—whether the strategies are informal, invented procedures, or more conventional algorithms. More efficient conventional procedures, when taught without understanding, lead to both errors and lack of confidence.

CLARK, F. B., & KAMII, C. (1996). Identification of multiplicative thinking in children in grades 1–5. *Journal for Research in Mathematics Education 27*(1), 41–51. The authors found that multiplicative thinking appears early and develops slowly, and conclude that the introduction of multiplication in second grade is appropriate for some students, but not for all of them.

CORWIN, R. B., STOREYGARD, J., & PRICE, S. (1996). *Talking mathematics: Supporting children's voices.* Portsmouth, NH: Heinemann. The authors discuss why mathematical talk is important, and describe practical ways to encourage and support that talk.

CRAMER, K., & KARNOWSKI, L. (1995). The importance of informal language in representing mathematical ideas. *Teaching Children Mathematics 1*(6), 332–335. The authors describe teaching strategies based on a model by Lesh, strategies which introduce words and symbols so that students can informally record what they have observed and already know.

CURCIO, F. R., & SCHWARTZ, S. L. (1998). There are no algorithms for teaching algorithms. *Teaching Children Mathematics 5*(1), 26–30. The authors argue for a balance between student invention of computational procedures and the development of traditional (and alternative) algorithms.

DRISCOLL, M. (1999). *Fostering algebraic thinking: A guide for teachers, grades 6–10.* Newton, MA: Education Development Center, Inc. Driscoll describes strategies to cultivate habits of thinking associated with successful learning of algebra and its use. Samples and analyses of student work are included.

ENGLEHARDT, J. M., & USNICK, V. (1991). When should we teach regrouping in addition and subtraction? *School Science and Mathematics 91*(1), 6–9. From their exploratory studies, the authors conclude that more attention may need to be given to alternate sequences of instruction that begin with more general cases and examples that involve regrouping, and that the traditional emphasis on mastery of number combinations and numeration concept knowledge may need to be reexamined.

FALKNER, K. P., LEVI, L., & CARPENTER, T. P. (1999). Children's understanding of equality: A foundation for algebra. *Teaching Children Mathematics 6*(4), 232–236. Noting that elementary school students generally think that an equals sign means to carry out the operation that precedes it, the authors describe instruction in which early grade students came to understand the equals sign as expressing the relationship "is the same as."

FENNEL, F. (1991). Diagnostic teaching, writing and mathematics. *Focus on Learning Problems in Mathematics 13*(3), 39–50. Fennell explores the role of student writing for diagnosing student knowledge and skills. A math pals letter project is described, and many suggestions are made for diagnostic teaching.

FISCHER, F. E. (1990). A part-part-whole curriculum for teaching numbers in the kindergarten. *Journal for Research in Mathematics Education 21*(3), 207–215. Fischer found that kindergarten children were more successful with addition and subtraction word problems and with place-value concepts when set-subset relationships were taught.

FUSON, K. C. (1990). Issues in place-value and multidigit addition and subtraction learning and teaching. *Journal for Research in Mathematics Education 21*(4), 273–280. Fuson argues for a sequence for teaching and learning about place-value and multidigit addition and subtraction in which problems with and without trades are presented at the same time.

FUSON, K. C. (1992). Research on whole number addition and subtraction. In D. A. Grouws (Ed.), *Handbook of Research on Mathematics Teaching and Learning* (pp. 243–275). New York: Maxwell/Macmillan. In her summary of research, Fuson focuses on children's conceptual structures for the operations and for addition and subtraction multidigit computation. She also stresses the variety of real-world situations in addition and subtraction.

FUSON, K. C., & BRIARS, D. J. (1990). Using a base-ten blocks learning/teaching approach for first- and second-grade place-value and multidigit addition and subtraction. *Journal for Research in Mathematics Education 21*(3),

180–206. Two studies were conducted in which base-ten blocks were used to carry out steps in computation. Each step in the procedure was immediately recorded with numerals. Activities focused on four-digit numbers, but included practice with five- to eight-digit addition and subtraction.

GOLEMBO, V. (2000). Writing a PEMDAS story. *Mathematics Teaching in the Middle School* 5(9), 574–579. Golembo illustrates a creative context in which to teach seemingly arbitrary content such as the order of operations.

GRAEBER, A. O., & CAMPBELL, P. F. (1993). Misconceptions about multiplication and division. *Arithmetic Teacher* 40(7), 408–411. The authors focus on the fact that many students believe "multiplication makes bigger," and they make suggestions for instruction to help students make sense of the situation.

GROUWS, D. A. (Ed.), (1992). *Handbook of research on mathematics teaching and learning.* New York: Macmillan. This extensive volume is a major resource to consult if you want to know what research tells us about the teaching and learning of mathematics. Articles on operations include conceptual structures required by learners, with implications for both diagnosis and instruction.

HANKES, J. E., (1996). An alternative to basic-skills remediation. *Teaching Children Mathematics* 2(8), 452–457. Hankes applies cognitive-based instruction to remedial situations and to the learning disabled student.

HANSELMAN, C. A. (1997). Stop using foul language in the mathematics classroom. *Mathematics Teaching in the Middle School* 3(2), 143–160. Hanselman argues against use of terms like *reduce, cancel,* and *invert* which cause students to focus only on the procedure, with no conceptual understanding.

HIEBERT, J., & LEFEVRE, P. (1986). Conceptual and procedural knowledge in mathematics: An introductory analysis. In J. Hiebert (Ed.), *Conceptual and procedural knowledge: The case of mathematics.* Hillsdale, NJ: Lawrence Erlbaum Associates. The authors define conceptual and procedural knowledge in mathematics, and discuss relationships between the two.

HUINKER, D. (1998). Letting fraction algorithms emerge through problem solving. In L. J. Morrow & M. J. Kenney (Eds.), *The teaching and learning of algorithms in school mathematics* (pp. 170–182). Reston, VA: National Council of Teachers of Mathematics. After presenting guiding principles, Huinker addresses computational procedures for each of the four operations and notes advantages of student-invented algorithms for fractions.

HUTCHINGS, B. (1978). Low-stress algorithms. In D. Nelson & R. E. Reys (Eds.), *Measurement in school mathematics.* Reston, VA: National Council of Teachers of Mathematics. Hutchings describes and illustrates low-stress procedures for whole-number computation, algorithms that are especially useful with students experiencing difficulty with standard procedures.

ISAACS, A. C., & CARROLL, W. M. (1999). Strategies for basic-fact instruction. *Teaching Children Mathematics* 5(9), 508–515. The authors describe instructional strategies and caution that neglecting number combinations may undermine reforms.

JOHNSON, A. (1999). Krystal's method. *Mathematics Teaching in the Middle School* 5(3), 148–150. Johnson illustrates how one student invented her own procedure for subtracting mixed numbers with regrouping.

KAMII, C., LEWIS, B. A., & LIVINGSTON, S. J. (1993). Primary arithmetic: Children inventing their own procedures. *Arithmetic Teacher* 41(4), 200–204. The authors describe experiences with early grade children inventing their own computational procedures, and discuss advantages of such procedures.

KAZEMI, E. (1998). Discourse that promotes conceptual understanding. *Teaching Children Mathematics* 4(7), 410–414. Kazemi emphasizes the need to expect students to justify procedures—not just to state them—and discusses how this relates to the way teachers react to student errors.

KIDD, D. H., & LAMB, C. E. (1993). Mathematics vocabulary and the hearing-impaired student: An anecdotal study. *Focus on Learning Problems in Mathematics 15*(4), 44–52. Difficulties in learning and understanding mathematics vocabulary were observed in high school hearing-impaired students. Anecdotes are discussed along with possible causes and recommendations.

LAPPAN, G., & BOUCK, M. K. (1998). Developing algorithms for adding and subtracting fractions. In L. J. Morrow & M. J. Kenney (Eds.), *The teaching and learning of algorithms in school mathematics* (pp. 183–197). Reston, VA: National Council of Teachers of Mathematics. The authors describe experiences that enable students to learn about addition and subtraction with fractions in contexts that make sense to them.

LEUTZINGER, L. P. (1999). Developing thinking strategies for addition facts. *Teaching Children Mathematics 6*(1), 14–18. Leutzinger illustrates how students can use number combinations they know to determine ones they do not know.

MACGREGOR, M., & STACEY, K. (1999). A flying start to algebra. *Teaching Children Mathematics 6*(2), 78–85. The authors emphasize the need for students to understand numbers and know the properties of operations with numbers if they are to enjoy success with algebra. The relationships of problem structures and various operations must be made explicit.

MACK, N. K. (1998). Building a foundation for understanding the multiplication of fractions. *Teaching Children Mathematics 5*(1), 34–38. Mack stresses the need to help students build on their informal knowledge and solve real-world problems.

MADSEN, A. L., SMITH, P., & LANIER, P. (1995). Does conceptually oriented instruction enhance computational competence? *Focus on Learning Problems in Mathematics 17*(4), 42–64. The authors provide data from general mathematics classes as evidence that conceptually-oriented instruction does indeed result in computational mastery as well as understanding of mathematical concepts.

MCCLAIN, K., COBB, P., & BOWERS, J. (1998). A contextual investigation of three-digit addition and subtraction. In L. J. Morrow & M. J. Kenney (Eds.), *The teaching and learning of algorithms in school mathematics* (pp. 141–150). Reston, VA: National Council of Teachers of Mathematics. The authors describe a sequence of instruction used with third graders, a sequence designed to help students develop increasingly sophisticated and meaningful algorithms.

MIDDLETON, J. A., VAN DEN HEUVEL-PANHUIZEN, M., & SHEW, J. A. (1998). Using bar representations as a model for connecting concepts of rational number. *Mathematics Teaching in the Middle School 3*(4), 302–312. The authors illustrate varied uses of the bar as a mathematical model, including several examples of problems that involve sharing submarine sandwiches.

MILLER, J. L., & FEY, J. T. (2000). Proportional reasoning. *Mathematics Teaching in the Middle School 5*(5), 310–313. The authors illustrate how understanding and strategies for proportional reasoning can be built through guided collaborative work on authentic problems.

MOON, C. J. (1993). Connecting learning and teaching through assessment. *The Arithmetic Teacher 41*(1), 13–15. Moon emphasizes the role of criteria in linking teaching and assessment; students need to know what assessment criteria are to be applied.

MOON, J., & SCHULMAN, L. (1995). *Finding the connections: Linking assessment, instruction, and curriculum in elementary mathematics*. Portsmouth, NH:

Heinemann. The authors focus on classroom practices in grades K–6 as they emphasize conceptual links among assessment, instruction, and curriculum.

MORROW, L. J. (1998). Whither algorithms? Mathematics educators express their views. In L. J. Morrow & M. J. Kenney (Eds.), *The teaching and learning of algorithms in school mathematics* (pp. 1–6). Reston, VA: National Council of Teachers of Mathematics. Morrow addresses five issues related to algorithms in school mathematics.

MORROW, L. J. & KENNEY, M. J. (Eds.). (1998). *The teaching and learning of algorithms in school mathematics.* Reston, VA: National Council of Teachers of Mathematics. This Council yearbook focuses on issues and history, and also on curriculum and instruction at the elementary, middle, and high school levels.

MOSS, J., & CASE, R. (1999). Developing children's understanding of the rational numbers: A new model and an experimental curriculum. *Journal for Research in Mathematics Education 30*(2), 122–147. The authors report a study in which children taught an experimental curriculum were compared with a control group using "instruction of a more classic nature." Although the control group continued to make typical mistakes, students using the experimental curriculum gave evidences of deep conceptual understanding.

MULLIGAN, J. T., & MITCHELMORE, M. C. (1997). Young children's intuitive models of multiplication and division. *Journal for Research in Mathematics Education 28*(3), 309–330. The authors identify 12 distinct calculation strategies they group into categories of intuitive models. They conclude that children acquire an expanding repertoire of intuitive models for multiplication and division.

NATIONAL COUNCIL OF TEACHERS OF MATHEMATICS (2000). *Principles and standards for school mathematics.* Reston, VA: The Council. This publication replaces earlier NCTM standards documents. Six foundational principles are established, then 10 standards for grades PreK–12 are set forth and illustrated for each of four grade bands: PreK–2, 3–5, 6–8, and 9–12. There are five content standards and five process standards. The document is available online at www.standards.nctm.org (select E-Standards).

NOWLIN, D. (1996). Division with fractions. *Mathematics Teaching in the Middle School 2*(2), 116–119. Nowlin describes activities that can be helpful when establishing a conceptual basis for dividing with fractions.

NUNES, T., SCHLIEMANN, A. D., & CARRAHER, D. W. (1993). *Exploring the nature of street mathematics.* New York: Cambridge University Press. Research done in Brazil is reported with interesting findings. For example, individuals focused on meanings while learning mathematics outside of school in order to perform specific tasks, but when learning mathematics in schools they focused on numbers and disregarded meaning within problems.

OBERDORF, C. D., & TAYLOR-COX, J. (1999). Shape up! *Teaching Children Mathematics 5*(6), 340–345. The authors describe typical misconceptions in the elementary grades, and make suggestions for instruction that can avoid such misconceptions.

ORTON, A. (Ed.). (1999). *Pattern in the teaching and learning of mathematics.* New York: Cassell. Contributors report research on perception, conception, and the use of pattern in learning mathematics. Students of varied ages are the focus of these studies conducted at the University of Leeds.

PARKER, J., & WIDMER, C. C. (1992). *The Arithmetic Teacher 40*(1), 48–51. The authors make many suggestions for teaching computation within problem-solving contexts.

PHILIPP, R. A. (1996). Multicultural mathematics and alternative algorithms. *Teaching Children Mathematics 3*(3), 128–133 . Alternative algorithms for operations with whole numbers are the focus; they are often associated with specific cultures.

RATHMELL, E. C. (1978). Using thinking strategies to teach the basic facts. In M. N. Suydam & R. E. Reys (Eds.), *Developing Computational Skills* (pp. 13–38). Reston, VA: National Council of Teachers of Mathematics. Thinking strategies are described for use when organizing instruction in number combinations for addition and multiplication.

REYS, B. J. (1985). Mental computation. *Arithmetic Teacher 32*(6), 43–46. Reys presents many ideas for developing skill with mental computation.

REYS, B. J., & REYS, R. E. (1998). Computation in the elementary curriculum: Shifting the emphasis. *Teaching Children Mathematics 5*(4), 236–241. The authors propose a sequence for instruction in computation, specifying emphases for grades K–2, 3–5, and 6–8. Efficient paper-and-pencil algorithms for whole number computation are introduced in grades 3–5, and efficient algorithms for fraction and decimal computation are introduced in grades 6–8.

RUBENSTEIN, R. N. (2000). Word origins: Building communication connections. *Mathematics Teaching in the Middle School 5*(8), 493–497. Rubenstein illustrates how roots, meanings, and related words can make confusing mathematical terms easier to understand and remember.

RUSSELL, S. J. (2000). Developing computational fluency with whole numbers. *Teaching Children Mathematics 7*(3), 154–158. Russell stresses connections between understanding and computational procedures as she defines computational fluency and discusses its assessment.

SCHOEN, H. L., & ZWENG, M. J. (Eds.). (1986). *Estimation and mental computation*. Reston, VA: National Council of Teachers of Mathematics. This Council yearbook focuses on instruction. Varieties of estimation are described, as is research on teaching and learning estimation.

SGROI, L. (1998). An exploration of the Russian peasant method of multiplication. In L. J. Morrow & M. J. Kenney (Eds.), *The teaching and learning of algorithms in school mathematics* (pp. 81–85). Reston, VA: National Council of Teachers of Mathematics. The algorithm is described and student explanations are examined.

SHARP, J. (1998). A constructed algorithm for the division of fractions. In L. J. Morrow & M. J. Kenney (Eds.), *The teaching and learning of algorithms in school mathematics* (pp. 198–203). Reston, VA: National Council of Teachers of Mathematics. Sharp describes activities with manipulatives that lead to the invention of a common denominator algorithm for division of fractions.

SOWDER, J. (1992). Estimation and number sense. In D. A. Grouws (Ed.), *Handbook of Research on Mathematics Teaching and Learning* (pp. 371–389). New York: Maxwell/Macmillan. Included in Sowder's summary of research are sections on computational estimation, mental computation, and number sense.

STEELE, D. F. (1999). Learning mathematical language in the zone of proximal development. *Teaching Children Mathematics 6*(1), 38–42. Steele emphasizes the need for teachers to use students' oral language in classroom activities, and cautions against moving them too quickly toward new mathematical language.

SUTTON, J. T., & URBATSCH, T. D. (1991). Transition boards: A good idea made better. *The Arithmetic Teacher 38*(5), 4–9. The authors describe how base-ten blocks can be used with addition and subtraction transition boards when teaching multidigit computation procedures.

SWEENEY, E. S., & QUINN, R. J. (2000). Concentration: Connecting fractions, decimals, & percents. *Mathematics Teaching in the Middle School 5*(5), 324–328. The authors describe a series of lessons. A game is created, and there are assessments.

TRAFTON, P. R., & THIESSEN, D. (1999). *Learning through problems; number sense and computational strategies: A resource for teachers.* Portsmouth, NH: Heinemann. Number sense and computation can be learned within a problem-centered framework.

USISKIN, Z. (1998). Paper-and-pencil algorithms in a calculator-and-computer age. In L. J. Morrow & M. J. Kenney (Eds.), *The teaching and learning of algorithms in school mathematics* (pp. 7–20). Reston, VA: National Council of Teachers of Mathematics. Usiskin lists principles for teaching algorithms of all types. Algorithms are valuable, but have inherent dangers.

USNICK, V. E. (1992). Multidigit addition: A study of an alternative sequence. *Focus on Learning Problems in Mathematics 14*(3), 53–62. Usnick studied the effects of two instructional sequences for the standard addition algorithm: a traditional sequence in which examples with no regrouping are introduced and practiced before examples with regrouping, and an alternative sequence with regrouping introduced initially. The alternative sequence was as effective as the traditional sequence.

USNICK, V., & ENGELHARDT, J. M. (1988). Basic facts, numeration concepts, and the learning of the standard multidigit addition algorithm. *Focus on Learning Problems in Mathematics 10*(2), 1–14. From the authors' study it is not clear that actual mastery of basic number combinations and relevant numeration concepts is necessary before introducing the addition algorithm.

WEARNE, D., & HIEBERT, J. (1994). Place value and addition and subtraction. *The Arithmetic Teacher 41*(5), 272–274. The authors emphasize the importance of understanding place value as they discuss what they have learned from having students develop their own algorithms for adding multidigit numbers.

WHITIN, D. J., & WHITIN, P. E. (1998). The "write" way to mathematical understanding. In L. J. Morrow & M. J. Kenney (Eds.), *The teaching and learning of algorithms in school mathematics* (pp. 161–169). Reston, VA: National Council of Teachers of Mathematics. The authors describe how writing about base-ten blocks and writing personal stories can be used to assess students' understanding of computational procedures.

WITHERSPOON, M. J. (1999). And the answer is . . . Symbolic literacy. *Teaching Children Mathematics 5*(7), pp. 396–399. The author discusses symbols, both their assigned meanings and their use within algorithms. Implications for instruction are discussed.

WOOD, T., & SELLERS, P. (1997). Deepening the analysis: Longitudinal assessment of a problem-centered mathematics program. *Journal for research in Mathematics Education 28*(2), 163–186. From their research on teaching and learning computation in the early grades, the authors conclude that two years of beginning instruction using a problem-centered approach is significantly better than either two years of textbook instruction or one year of problem-centered instruction followed by one year of textbook instruction.

Appendix A

Selected Student Papers and Key

The following pages supplement Part II. They contain excerpts from the written work of students who are using procedures that do not provide correct answers, at least not in every case. Identify the patterns; in each paper find the procedure used. Note how these students tend to manipulate symbols, apparently without thinking about numbers and operations on numbers.

Briefly describe each pattern then check the key on page 281 if you wish.

PAPER 1

$$8 + 8 = 16 \qquad 7 + 6 = 15$$
$$5 + 6 = 13 \qquad 9 + 8 = 19$$

Description of Pattern _____

_____

PAPER 2

1. $57 = \underline{5}$ tens $+ \underline{7}$ ones
2. $483 = \underline{4}$ ones $+ \underline{8}$ hundreds $+ \underline{3}$ tens
3. $270 = \underline{2}$ hundreds $+ \underline{7}$ ones $+ \underline{0}$ tens

Description of Pattern _____

_____

PAPER 3

7875 → *7900*   6349 → *6400*

4743 → *4700*   5361 → *5400*

Description of Pattern _____

_____

PAPER 4

A.	B.	C.
35	2 4	4 3
+ 2 8	+ 1 7	+ 2 6
1 8	1 4	1 5

Description of Pattern _____

_____

PAPER 5

A.	B.	C.
4 7	6 5	7 8
− 3	− 2	− 4
1 4	4 3	3 4

Description of Pattern _____

_____

PAPER 6

A.   B.   C.

$$
\begin{array}{r}
\overset{5}{6}'4\,8 \\
-\,3\,9\,7 \\
\hline
8\,5\,1
\end{array}
\qquad
\begin{array}{r}
4\overset{2}{3}'6 \\
-\,2\,1\,8 \\
\hline
2\,4\,8
\end{array}
\qquad
\begin{array}{r}
\overset{4}{5}'2\,9 \\
-\,3\,8\,5 \\
\hline
6\,4\,4
\end{array}
$$

Description of Pattern _____

PAPER 7

A.   B.   C.

$$
\begin{array}{r}
\overset{13}{3}\,6 \\
\times\,2\,5 \\
\hline
1\,8\,0 \\
1\,0\,2 \\
\hline
1\,2\,0\,0
\end{array}
\qquad
\begin{array}{r}
\overset{32}{7}\,8 \\
\times\,4\,3 \\
\hline
2\,3\,4 \\
3\,3\,2 \\
\hline
3\,5\,5\,4
\end{array}
\qquad
\begin{array}{r}
\overset{13}{6}\,5 \\
\times\,3\,7 \\
\hline
4\,5\,5 \\
2\,2\,5 \\
\hline
2\,7\,0\,5
\end{array}
$$

Description of Pattern _____

PAPER 8
Find the average for each set of numbers

A. 26, 74, 83   Answer __45__

B. 73, 98, 65   Answer __57__

C. 57, 62, 95, 81   Answer __59__

Description of Pattern _____

PAPER 9

1. John spent $4.50 at the fair. Now he has $2.75 remaining. How much money did he have before the fair?

   $1.75

2. The store had a sale of red and blue shirts. There were 46 red shirts left after the sale, and 28 blue shirts were left. How many shirts were left after the sale?

   18

Description of Pattern _____

_____

PAPER 10

A.

$$\frac{1}{3} + \frac{2}{9} = \frac{3}{9}$$

B.

$$\frac{3}{4} + \frac{3}{2} = \frac{6}{4}$$

C.

$$\frac{5}{6} + \frac{1}{2} = \frac{6}{6}$$

Description of Pattern _____

_____

PAPER 11

A.

$$1\frac{3}{5} = 1\frac{8}{15}$$
$$+ 2\frac{1}{3} = 2\frac{7}{15}$$
$$\overline{\qquad 3\frac{15}{15}}$$

B.

$$4\frac{2}{4} = 4\frac{18}{4}$$
$$+ 1\frac{1}{2} = 1\frac{3}{4}$$
$$\overline{\qquad 5\frac{21}{4}}$$

C.

$$6\frac{2}{3} = 6\frac{20}{6}$$
$$+ 3\frac{1}{6} = 3\frac{19}{6}$$
$$\overline{\qquad 9\frac{39}{6}}$$

Description of Pattern _____

_____

PAPER 12

A.
$$\frac{7}{8} \times \frac{3}{7} = \frac{7}{8} \times \frac{6}{8} = \frac{42}{8}$$

B.
$$\frac{1}{6} \times \frac{2}{3} = \frac{1}{6} \times \frac{4}{6} = \frac{4}{6}$$

C.
$$\frac{5}{12} \times \frac{1}{4} = \frac{5}{12} \times \frac{3}{12} = \frac{15}{12}$$

Description of Pattern _____

_____

PAPER 13

A. $5\frac{1}{3} \times 6\frac{3}{4} = 30\frac{3}{12}$

B. $7\frac{2}{5} \times 2\frac{1}{8} = 14\frac{2}{40}$ C. $1\frac{7}{8} \times 4\frac{2}{3} = 4\frac{14}{24}$

Description of Pattern _____

_____

PAPER 14

A. $\frac{5}{6} \div \frac{2}{3} = \frac{5}{6} \div \frac{4}{6} = \frac{1}{6}$

B. $\frac{1}{2} \div \frac{3}{4} = \frac{2}{4} \div \frac{3}{4} = \frac{1}{4}$ C. $\frac{7}{8} \div \frac{1}{5} = \frac{35}{40} \div \frac{8}{40} = \frac{4}{40}$

Description of Pattern _____

_____

PAPER 15

A.   B.   C.

$$.4 + .3 = .07$$

$$\begin{array}{r} 1.32 \\ +3.46 \\ \hline .0478 \end{array}$$

$$\begin{array}{r} 27.5 \\ + 8.9 \\ \hline 3.64 \end{array}$$

Description of Pattern _____

_____

PAPER 16

A.   B.   C.

7.7 + 13.2 = ?   2.5 + 4.32 = ?   15.4 + 8.69 = ?

$$\begin{array}{r} 7.7 \\ +13.2 \\ \hline 20.9 \end{array}$$ $$\begin{array}{r} 2.\ 5 \\ +4.32 \\ \hline 6.37 \end{array}$$ $$\begin{array}{r} 15.\ 4 \\ +\ \ 8.69 \\ \hline 23.73 \end{array}$$

Description of Pattern _____

_____

PAPER 17

A. 25% of 100   *2500*

B. ½ of 20% of 100   *1000*

C. ⅕ of 1% of 40   *8*

Description of Pattern _____

_____

PAPER 18

A.

$$0.5\overline{)60} \rightarrow 0.5\overline{)60}^{12}$$
$$\underline{5}$$
$$10$$
$$\underline{10}$$

B.

$$60\overline{)2.4} \rightarrow 60\overline{)2.40}^{0.04}$$
$$\underline{240}$$

C.

$$0.4\overline{)18} \rightarrow 0.4\overline{)18.0}^{4.5}$$
$$\underline{16}$$
$$20$$
$$\underline{20}$$

Description of Pattern _____

_____

PAPER 19

1. $^{-}8 + 6 =$ __−2__   3. $7 + ^{-}2 =$ __5__
2. $5 + ^{-}9 =$ __4__   4. $^{-}4 + 10 =$ __−6__

Description of Pattern _____

_____

PAPER 20

1. $3 - (^{-}4) =$ __7__   3. $7 + ^{-}2 =$ __5__
2. $^{-}6 - 2 =$ __8__   4. $^{-}5 - 4 =$ __9__

Description of Pattern _____

_____

PAPER 21

a. $\sqrt{3} + \sqrt{20} = $ __$\sqrt{23}$__   b. $\sqrt{5} + \sqrt{8} = $ __$\sqrt{13}$__

Description of Pattern _____

_____

KEY TO ERROR PATTERNS IN ADDITIONAL STUDENT PAPERS

1. All near doubles are answered by doubling the greater number and adding one.
2. The first digit is copied in the first blank, the second digit is copied in the second blank, and the third digit is copied in the third blank—regardless of the arrangement of values.
3. The student rounds up if *either* the tens digit *or* the ones digit is five or greater.
4. The sum of all digits is determined, regardless of place value.
5. The minuend is subtracted from both the ones and the tens.
6. After renaming, the two top digits are *added* before subtracting.
7. When multiplying by the tens digit, both reminder numbers are added.
8. This student begins by adding the tens. The sum is divided by the number of addends and the remainder is ignored. The process is repeated for the ones. Numbers resulting from this process are recorded right to left to show the "average."
9. This student appears to use key words like *remaining* and *left* to indicate he should subtract; but the unknown in these problems is the total amount, and addition should be used to find the total amount.
10. The numerators are added and recorded as the new numerator. The greater denominator is used as the new denominator because the lesser denominator "will go into" the greater denominator.
11. After the least common denominator is determined, the student computes the numerator by multiplying the original denominator times the whole number and then adding the original numerator.
12. This student renames unlike fractions so they have a common denominator before multiplying the numerators. The common denominator is used for the denominator in the product. The student's procedure is very similar to the correct procedure for *adding* unlike fractions.

13. The whole numbers and common fractions are multiplied independently.
14. After common denominators are determined, one numerator is divided by the other (with the remainder ignored) to determine the resulting numerator.
15. The rule for placing the decimal point in a product is applied to a sum.
16. The student is careful to do two things he has been taught: line up the digits on the right, and line up the decimal points. It would be better to align place values instead of decimal points.
17. This student multiplies all of the "top numbers" (whole numbers and numerators) as if they were all whole numbers, then divides by the "bottom number" (denominator).
18. This student copies the example, but without any decimal points, and then divides as if both numbers were whole numbers. After dividing, decimal points are placed within the dividend and the divisor as they were originally. Finally, a point is placed within the quotient above the decimal point in the dividend.
19. In these examples, the student *always* found the difference using absolute values; then if the first addend was negative, the student affixed a negative sign.
20. All minus signs and signs of negation are counted. If there is an even number of signs, the absolute values are added. If there is an odd number of signs, absolute values are subtracted.
21. Rather than adding square roots, the student adds numbers under square root signs.

Appendix B

Research on Errors in Computation

⌐⌐

Many early researchers attempted to identify categories of errors. Brueckner did extensive work as early as the 1920s; his studies were reported in his classic 1930 text[1] and in yearbook articles.[2] Throughout his writings he emphasized the need to supplement analysis of written work with interviews. Typical of his research is his 1928 report, which includes almost 9,000 errors tabulated into 114 categories.[3] Many of his categories would be questioned today; for example, he listed the annexation of unnecessary zeros as an error.

Interest in categories of errors continued. In a study of high school students published in 1950, Arthur pointed to adding denominators and failing to invert the divisors as types of errors.[4] Roberts' study, published in 1968, identified four categories of "failure strategies:" wrong operation, obvious computational error, defective algorithm, and random response.[5] The largest number of errors was due to erroneous or incorrect algorithm techniques in all achievement groups except the lowest quartile; they made more random responses. Clearly, practice papers of *all* students must be considered carefully. By the mid-1970s, Burrows was able to publish an extensive review of literature on computational errors with whole numbers.[6] Englehardt listed eight categories in his study published in 1977.[7] He found that basic fact error, grouping error, and inappropriate inversion accounted for 61% of errors made.

In his 1978 analysis, Backman used four categories for procedural errors: errors in sequencing steps within a procedure, errors in selecting information or procedures, errors in recording work, and errors in conceptual understanding.[8] In 1980, Kilian and others reported types of errors made during multiplication; they distinguished between procedural errors that involve zeros and carrying, and calculation errors that involve basic multiplication combinations of tables over five.[9] Clements focused on careless errors in his study published in 1982.[10] But in their study published in 1994 Cumming and Elkins cast doubt on the notion of carelessness as an explanation, for they were able to identify systematic underlying causes of errors.[11]

In their analysis of errors published in 1992, Stefanich and Rokusek focused on division.[12] The causes of errors they observed were attributed to lack of an adequate concept of place value, poor handwriting (misaligned digits in numerals), and a lack of knowledge of basic number combinations.

Several studies have focused on the frequency with which specific types of errors occur. For example, Guiler noted that in division of decimals, more than 40% of the children placed the decimal point three or more places too far to the right.[13] Such studies remind us of the value of a thorough understanding of numeration and the ability to estimate.

A classic study of the frequency of different error patterns is Lankford's study of seventh graders.[14] He conducted diagnostic interviews of 176 students in six schools located in different parts of the United States. He noted that "unorthodox strategies were frequently observed—some yielding correct answers and some incorrect ones."[15]

Cox's study focused on whole number algorithms and compared the work of students in regular classrooms with computation done by students placed in special education classrooms.[16] A study reported by Graeber and Wallace examined addition, subtraction, and multiplication of whole numbers.[17] In both the Cox study and the Graeber and Wallace study, an erroneous procedure was not classified as systematic unless it occurred at least three times.

Bransford and Vye cautioned that research on errors should be distinguished from research on misconceptions.[18] They noted that whereas errors are typically associated with performance after instruction, misconceptions include inaccurate conceptions before instruction.

A research and development project at the University of Maryland focused on both misconceptions and error patterns common among secondary school students. The investigators classified misconceptions they observed into four categories: overgeneralizations, overspecializations, mistranslations, and limited conceptions.[19] They found that many of the misconceptions had logical explanations but did not have adequate frames of reference. Interestingly, many experienced teachers did not acknowledge that there actually were logical explanations for the misconceptions.

Some studies of errors have focused on verbal problem solving. Babbitt used data from the Fourth National Assessment of Educational Progress along with a study of problem-solving performances of fifth- and sixth-grade students. She sorted errors into four categories: computation errors, operational errors, nonattempt errors, and miscellaneous errors, and concluded that error analysis of student work can actually reveal underlying conceptual misunderstandings and a lack of appropriate strategies for problem solving.[20] Clarkson also studied student performance with word problems.[21]

Sadowski and McIlveen studied error patterns in sentence-solving.[22] They found that some inadequate procedures used by students produce a correct solution quite frequently, thereby reinforcing continued use of the error pattern. Davis and Cooney reported a study in which they describe categories of errors made by algebra students.[23] From his study of high school algebra errors, Matz suggested that "errors are the results of reasonable, although unsuccessful, attempts to adapt previously acquired knowledge to a new situation."[24] From her study that focused on implicit use of "1" as an exponent, Anderson noted that "students interpret mathematical language differently and we should not take for granted that students understand the symbolism."[25]

Noting the similarity of errors across studies, Bright suggested the following categories for future studies of errors in solving linear equations: arithmetic errors, combination errors, transposition errors, operation errors, incomplete solutions, and execution errors.[26]

A number of studies have focused on difficulties in learning computation procedures. Resnick made a helpful distinction: she contrasted what she called the syntax of a computational procedure with the semantics of the procedure.[27] Syntax includes the arrangement of symbols and the mechanics or procedural rules of the algorithm, whereas semantics refers to the mathematical meanings or principles involved. She determined that students who develop error patterns often focus on the syntax; they tend to manipulate digits and ignore the quantities involved.

Cox concluded from her research that not only did children make systematic errors but, without instructional intervention they also continued with the error patterns for long periods of time.[28] In his study of students in Grades 5–8, MacKay reported that many children actually had a high degree of confidence in their erroneous procedures.[29]

Siegler viewed the result of a student using an error pattern as a rule-governed error, and asserted that "associative knowledge is considerably more important than people frequently acknowledge."[30] From their study, Byrnes and Wasik concluded that conceptual knowledge is a necessary but not sufficient condition for acquiring procedural skill; a process known as "proceduralization" needs to take place in which procedures become fluid and automatic."[31]

The similarity of error patterns to bugs in a computer program has been noted and, as a result, systematic errors are sometimes called *bugs* in professional literature. Attempts have been made to construct computer programs for diagnosing systematic student errors. One such attempt, DEBUGGY, was found to be a valuable research tool though some error patterns were not diagnosed. Repair Theory was developed to explain many of the remaining patterns. While describing his work with Repair Theory, VanLehn reported that the bugs or error patterns of some students are unstable from one test to the next. It appeared that error patterns are sometimes used as "problem-solving strategies," but only long enough to get the student through the test.[32] Woodward and Gersten described TORUS, a computer-based program for students with learning disabilities in which student work samples in addition and subtraction are analyzed and profiles of misconceptions and weaknesses are provided.[33]

Orey and Burton studied how error patterns and clinical assessment interrelate as a basis for designing a computer diagnostic system for subtraction.[34] In designing a program to diagnose errors in whole number computation, Janke and Piley attempted to include desired features mentioned in recent professional literature.[35] Student achievement actually improved when feedback on errors from the computer program was given to teachers.

A comparison of computer testing with paper-and-pencil was made by Ronau and Battista.[36] They found that the tests for diagnosing ratio and proportion errors, though designed to be equivalent, were *not* actually equivalent; the computer version proved to be more difficult. As a result, the two tests provided different profiles of student knowledge. In contrast, McDonald, Beal, and Ayers found almost identical performance in testing with computer and paper-and-pencil tests.[37] However, they found that students took longer to complete the computer test; students used more mental computation strategies when taking the computer test.

In a longitudinal study published in 1997, Carpenter and others found that a substantial number of students in all groups used buggy algorithms, even the invented-strategy group.[38]

Other research is noted in the list of resources for assessment and diagnosis, beginning on page 261.

REFERENCES

1. Bruekner, L. J. (1930). *Diagnostic and remedial teaching in arithmetic.* Philadelphia: John C. Winston.
2. For example: (1935). Diagnosis in arithmetic, pp. 269–302 in *Educational Diagnosis.* 34th yearbook of the National Society for the Study of Education. Bloomington, IL: Public School Publishing.
3. Brueckner, L. J. (1928, September). Analysis of difficulties in decimals. *Elementary School Journal 29,* 32–41.
4. Arthur, L. E. (1950, May). Diagnosis of disabilities in arithmetic essentials. *Mathematics Teacher 43,* 197–202.

5. Roberts, G. H. (1968). The failure strategies of third grade arithmetic pupils. *Arithmetic Teacher 15*(5), 442–446.
6. Burrows, J. K. (1976). *A review of the literature on computational errors with whole numbers. Mathematics Education Diagnostic and Instructional Centre (MEDIC)*. Vancouver: British Columbia University, Faculty of Education. (ERIC No. ED 134 468).
7. Engelhardt, J. M. (1977). Analysis of children's computational errors: A qualitative approach. *British Journal of Educational Psychology 47*, 149–154.
8. Backman, C. A. (1978). Analyzing children's work procedures. In M. Suydam (Ed.), *Developing computational skills* (pp. 177–195). Reston, VA: National Council of Teachers of Mathematics.
9. Kilian, L., Cahill, E., Ryan, C., Sutherland, D., & Taccetta, D. (1980). Errors that are common in multiplication. *Arithmetic Teacher 27*(5), 22–25.
10. Clements, M. A., (1982). Careless errors made by sixth-grade children on written mathematical tasks. *Journal for Research in Mathematics Education 13*(2), 136–144.
11. Cumming, J. J., & Elkins, J. (1994). Are any errors careless? *Focus on Learning Problems in Mathematics 16*(4), 21–30.
12. Stefanich, G. P., & Rokusek, T. (1992). An analysis of computational errors in the use of division algorithms by fourth-grade students. *School Science and Mathematics 92*(4), 201–205.
13. Guiler, W. S. (1946). Difficulties in decimals encountered in ninth-grade pupils. *Elementary School Journal (46)*, 384–393.
14. Lankford, F. G. Jr. (1972). *Some computational strategies of seventh grade pupils*. U.S. Department of Health, Education, and Welfare, Office of Education, National Center for Educational Research and Development (Regional Research Program) and The Center for Advanced Study, The University of Virginia. (Project Number 2-C-013, Grant Number OEG-3, 72-0035).
15. Ibid., 40.
16. Cox, L. S. (1975). Systematic errors in the four vertical algorithms in normal and handicapped populations. *Journal for Research in Mathematics Education 6*(4), 202–220.
17. Graeber, A. O., & Wallace, L. (1977). *Identification of systematic errors: Final report*. Philadelphia: Research for Better Schools, Inc. (ERIC Document Reproduction Service No. ED 139 662).
18. Bransford, J. D., & Vye, N. J. (1989). A perspective on cognitive research and its implications for instruction. In L. B. Resnick & L. E. Klopfer (Eds.), *Toward the thinking curriculum: Current cognitive research* (pp. 173–205). Alexandria, VA: Association for Supervision and Curriculum Development.
19. Graeber, A. O. (1992). *Methods and materials for preservice teacher education in diagnostic and prescriptive teaching of secondary mathematics* (NSF Project Final Report). College Park, MD: University of Maryland.
20. Babbitt, B. C. (1990). *Error patterns in problem solving*. Paper presented at the International Conference of the Council for Learning Disabilities, Austin, TX. (ERIC Clearinghouse No. SE 052 356).
21. Clarkson, P. C. (1992). Unknown/careless errors: Some implications for traditional test procedures. *Focus on Learning Problems in Mathematics 14*(4), 3.
22. Sadowski, B. R., & McIlveen, D. H. (1984). Diagnosis and remediation of sentence-solving error patterns. *Arithmetic Teacher 31*(5), 42–45.
23. Davis, E. J., & Cooney, T. J. (1977). Identifying errors in solving certain linear equations. *The MATYC Journal 11*(3), 170–178.

24. Matz, M. (1982). Towards a process model for high school algebra errors. In D. Sleeman & J. S. Brown (Eds.), *Intelligent tutoring systems* (pp. 25–50). London: Academic Press.

25. Anderson, A. (1995). Effects of the implicit or explicit use of 1 on students' responses when multiplying monomials $(ax^n)(bx^m)$ where n or $m = 1$. *Focus on Learning Problems in Mathematics 17*(1), 34–48.

26. Bright, G. W. (1981). Student errors in solving linear equations. *RCDPM Newsletter 6*(2), 3–4.

27. Resnick, L. B. (1984). Beyond error analysis: The role of understanding in elementary school arithmetic. In H. N. Cheek (Ed.), *Diagnostic and prescriptive mathematics: Issues, ideas, and insights* (pp. 2–14). Kent, OH: Research Council for Diagnostic and Prescriptive Mathematics.

28. Cox, L. S. (1975). Diagnosing and remediating systematic errors in addition and subtraction computations. *Arithmetic Teacher 22*(2), 151–157.

29. MacKay, I. D. (1975). *A comparison of students' achievement in arithmetic with their algorithmic confidence.* Vancouver, BC: University of British Columbia, Mathematics Education Diagnostic and Instructional Centre. (ERIC Documentation Reproduction Service No. ED 128 228).

30. Siegler, R. (1985). Research on learning. In T. Romberg & D. Stewart (Eds.), *School mathematics: Options for the 1990s* (pp. 75–80). Reston, VA: National Council of Teachers of Mathematics.

31. Byrnes, J. P. & Wasik, B. A. (1991). Role of conceptual knowledge in mathematical procedural learning. *Developmental Psychology 27*(5), 777–786.

32. VanLehn, K. (1981). *Bugs are not enough: Empirical studies of bugs, impasses and repairs in procedural skills.* Palo Alto, CA: Palo Alto Research Center, Cognitive and Instructional Sciences Group, Xerox.

33. Woodward, J., & Gersten, R. (1992). *The TORUS Project: An innovative-assessment technology program: Final report.* Eugene, OR: Eugene Research Institute. (ERIC Reproduction Service No. ED 385 968).

34. Orey, M. A., & Burton, J. K. (1992). The trouble with error patterns. *Journal of Research on Computing in Education 25*(1), 1–17.

35. Janke, R. W., & Pilkey, P. J. (1985). Microcomputer diagnosis of whole number computational errors. *Journal of Computers in Mathematics and Science Teaching 5*(1), 45–51.

36. Ronau, R. N., & Battista, M. T. (1988). Microcomputer versus paper-and-pencil testing of student errors in ratio and proportion. *Journal of Computers in Mathematics and Science Teaching 7*(3), 33–38.

37. McDonald, J., Beal, J., & Ayers, F. (1992). Details of performance on computer and paper administered versions of a test of whole number computation skills. *Focus on Learning Problems in Mathematics 14*(3), 15–27.

38. Carpenter, T. P., Franke, M. L., Jacobs, V. R., Fennema, E., & Empson, S. B. (1997). A longitudinal study of invention and understanding in children's multidigit addition and subtraction. *Journal for Research in Mathematics Education 29*(1), 3–20.

Appendix C

Gamelike Activities with Base Blocks
⌐⌐

Gamelike activities using base blocks and a pattern board can be incorporated into developmental instruction as a bridge between having students informally work out solutions with manipulatives and providing more direct instruction in conventional algorithms. The activities also can be used for corrective instruction when a student has not successfully learned an algorithm taught by other means.

The pattern board serves as an organizing center for materials. It is the place where the "game is played" because each activity has a goal analogous to winning a game. Each activity also has rules much as a game has rules: rules about how to interpret the problem by placing base-ten blocks on the pattern board. There also are rules about how to proceed with the activity toward the goal.

Initially the activity should be completed without any paper record being made; but when students have learned to do the activity, that which is done on the pattern board can be recorded step by step. That record, a mathematical representation of what the student observes, will be the conventional algorithm.

After initial experiences with the activity, one student can manipulate the blocks on the pattern board while another student intervenes and records what is done step by step. Then the two students can exchange roles. Eventually, have students use only the paper-and-pencil computation procedure to find the needed number, visualizing the pattern board and activity as they do so. The computation procedure makes sense to students because they have observed relationships and patterns, giving them a visual referent for the algorithm itself.

As students are involved with such gamelike activities, encourage them not only to talk about things that are observed repeatedly but also to look beyond simple repetitions for more complex structures.

Observe and discuss structures such as our numeration system ("Each place to the left has a value that is ten times as great.") and *repeated* sequences of steps that are observed within an algorithm. If the gamelike activity for addition is played with other number-base blocks before base-ten blocks are used, students can observe that the games for different bases are structured alike, except for the trading rule.

The gamelike activities that follow use base-ten blocks. Activities are described for addition, subtraction, and division of whole numbers.

ADDITION OF WHOLE NUMBERS

The purpose of this gamelike activity is to obtain the sum of two numbers in a manner that will picture the conventional computation procedure.

The Pattern Board

This is a grid with four columns for materials. It also has four rows: three rows above a heavy line and one row below the line. (You may want to lightly shade the top row because it has a special use.) Label columns right to left: Units (or Ones), Tens, Hundreds, and Thousands.

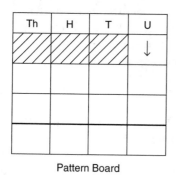

Pattern Board

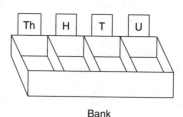

Bank

Materials for Quantities

Base-ten blocks usually are used, although there is value in using blocks for other bases initially—before written records are made. Other bases help students focus on the trading pattern.

Bank

This is wherever materials for quantities are stored and sorted. It is where trades for *equal* quantities are executed (e.g., 10 tens for one 100).

Goal of the Activity

The goal (with base-ten blocks) is to show the total amount of wood (or plastic) with as few pieces as possible. This will indicate the standard numeral for the sum.

Rules

1. Show the two quantities in the problem (the two addends) on the two rows above the heavy line. The top row of the pattern board should be empty as you start. For 618 + 782, the pattern board would look similar to this.

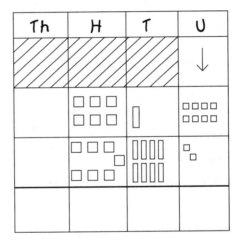

2. Within a column, move the total quantity of materials *below* the heavy line.
3. Start with the ones column and proceed to the left.
4. As you move materials below the heavy line, *trade 10 ones for one ten* **if you can.** If you do trade, place the one ten in the top row in the tens column. Note: When using another number base, trade *that* number "if you can." E.g., in base three, trade three ones for one three if you can.

Example

Beginning with the units (at the arrow), the child collects 10 units if she can (for this is a base-ten game) and moves all remaining units below the heavy line. If she has been able to collect 10 units, they are traded at the bank for one ten. The ten is then placed above the other tens in the shaded place. (At first, many students want to verify the equivalence of what goes into the bank and what comes out by placing the 10 units in a row and matching them with one ten.) As the student continues, she collects 10 tens if she can, and then moves all remaining tens below the heavy line. If she has been able to collect 10 tens, they are traded at the bank for one hundred, and the hundred is placed above the other hundreds in the shaded place. Finally, the child collects 10 hundreds if she can and moves all remaining hundreds below the heavy line. If she has been able to collect 10 hundreds they are traded at the bank for one thousand, and the thousand is placed in the shaded area at the top of the column for thousands. It is not possible to collect 10 thousands, so the one remaining thousand is brought below the heavy line. As the student computes the sum on paper, she records the number of blocks in each region every time trading is completed. (Making the record can be likened to writing a story.) When the record is finished, the algorithm is completed.

SUBTRACTION OF WHOLE NUMBERS

The purpose of this gamelike activity is to obtain the difference between two numbers in a manner that will picture the conventional decomposition computation procedure for subtraction.

The Pattern Board

This grid is identical to the pattern board described for the addition activity.

Materials for Quantities

Base ten blocks are recommended.

Bank

Materials for quantities are stored and sorted at the bank. It is where trades for *equal* quantities are executed (e.g., one ten for 10 ones).

Goal of the Activity

The goal is to show the amount of wood in the unknown part. Think of subtraction as finding the unknown amount in one part of a quantity whenever the total amount and the amount in the other part are known.

> **Note:** It is important for developing the decomposition algorithm that the verbal problem setting be a "take-away" problem rather than a comparison problem. The two addend quantities should be parts of the given quantity for the sum. An example:
>
> **Gary hopes to sell a total of 243 baseball cards at the fair. He has already sold 185 cards. How many remain to be sold?**

Rules

1. Show the total quantity (the sum or minuend) in the second row above the heavy line. The top row of the pattern board should be empty as you start.
2. Use numeral cards to show the known addend on the first row above the heavy line. *Do not use base blocks* because this amount is really part of the amount already shown for the sum. Place numeral cards to show the number of ones, tens, and so on. For 243 − 185, the pattern board would look similar to this.

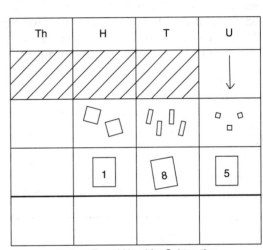

$$\begin{array}{r} 243 \\ -185 \\ \hline \end{array}$$

Pattern Board Used for Subtraction

3. Within a column, move the total quantity of base blocks to the two parts below—one above the heavy line (known addend) and one below it (unknown addend). Place the amount indicated on the numeral card, and the remaining amount below the heavy line.
4. Start with the ones column and proceed to the left.
5. If there are not enough blocks in the column to place on the numeral card, *trade one ten for 10 ones* or *one hundred for 10 tens*, and so on so you will have enough. Then place blocks on the numeral card and any remaining blocks below the heavy line.

Note: When the student is ready to record the computation, proceed with the activity step by step. Let the student trade and remove blocks while you make a step-by-step record of the student's moves in an evolving algorithm. Then reverse the process: While you trade and remove blocks (thinking aloud), let the student make the record. Two students can take turns being manipulator and recorder.

DIVISION OF WHOLE NUMBERS

The purpose of this gamelike activity is to obtain the quotient of a three- or four-digit number divided by a one-digit number in a manner that will picture the conventional computation procedure.

The Pattern Board or Play Area

The play area may or may not be a "board" as such. A space is needed to display base-ten blocks for the dividend of the problem, and a number of collecting spaces are needed as determined by the divisor. For example, if the divisor is four then four collecting spaces are needed. These can be blank sheets of paper, box lids, and so on.

For 1412 ÷ 4 the play area might look similar to the following.

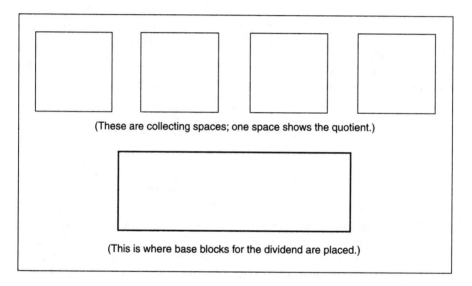

(These are collecting spaces; one space shows the quotient.)

(This is where base blocks for the dividend are placed.)

Materials for Quantities

Base-ten blocks are recommended.

Bank

This is wherever materials for quantities are stored and sorted. It is where trades for *equal* quantities are executed (e.g., two hundreds for 20 tens).

Goal of the Activity

The goal (with base-ten blocks) is to show the amount for the unknown factor; that is, the amount in each equivalent set.

Rules

1. Show the total amount (dividend, product) with base-ten blocks.
2. Provide collecting spaces as determined by the divisor.
3. Begin with the largest available block of wood, then work progressively with smaller blocks.
4. For a given block size, parcel out an equal number of blocks in each collecting space. **Parcel out only once.**[1] Think: *What is the greatest number of blocks I can put in each collecting space and still have enough for all the spaces?*
5. If there are not enough blocks of a given size to put even one block in each collecting space, then trade those blocks for an equal amount of wood of the next smaller size. For example, trade two hundreds for 20 tens.
6. When you have proceeded as far as you can, the blocks in one collecting space indicate the quotient. Undistributed blocks indicate the remainder.

Example

$$4\overline{)1412}$$

Show 1412 by placing these blocks in the dividend pile: one thousand-block, four hundreds-blocks, one ten-block, and two units-blocks. Interpret the problem as a parceling out or partitioning of the blocks into four sets of equal number—sets indicated by the collecting spaces.[2]

It is not possible to put even one thousand-block in each collecting place, so exchange the one thousand-block for an equal amount of wood, i.e., for 10 hundreds-blocks. Then, before you parcel out the 14 hundreds-blocks, think something like, "What is the greatest number of hundreds-blocks I can put in each of the four collecting places? Two in each of the four places is OK, but more can be parceled out. Three in each of the four places is OK. Four in each of the four places is 16, more than I have. I will put three in each place." Parcel out the blocks; two hundreds-blocks remain.

---

[1] If the student deals out blocks one at a time much as they would deal out playing cards, then only a mechanical procedure for getting an answer is learned; it will not picture the algorithm. Emphasize the need to think about the greatest number, for you only parcel out once.

[2] Any accompanying verbal problem should be a partitive problem; that is, a problem in which the known factor indicates the number of equivalent subsets. The verbal problem should *not* be a measurement problem, a problem in which the known factor indicates the number for each subset.

Exchange the two hundreds-blocks for 20 tens-blocks; there are now 21 tens-blocks altogether. Proceed similarly, placing five tens-blocks in each of the four places, with one tens-block remaining. Exchange the tens-block for 10 units, for a total of 12 units. This time place three units in each of the four collecting places. The quotient is 353.

The algorithm can be recorded as this activity is observed—step by step.

Appendix D

Sample Activities for Cooperative Groups

⌐⌐

Following are examples of activities for two or more students to complete cooperatively. Most activities focus on some aspect of a specific computational procedure, though they can often be adapted to other algorithms. Interact with your students as they work, and prompt them to reflect on what they are doing.

A. WHOLE NUMBER NUMERATION

Show 352 with a set of wooden base-ten blocks. Also show the same amount of wood using one less ten rod. Explain how you know the two sets of blocks contain the same amount of wood. (Similar tasks can be designed with decimals.)

B. WHOLE NUMBER COMPUTATION

1. How many digits are in each answer? Write why there are that many digits. Use estimation or mental computation, *not* paper-and-pencil or a calculator.
   a. 347 + 642
   b. 479 − 183
   c. 67 × 98
   d. 3688 ÷ 7

2. Find the missing digits in each of these.

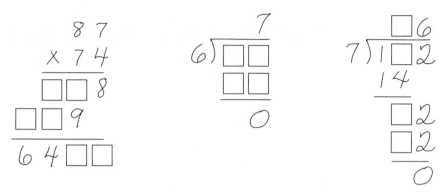

3. Are A, B, and C done correctly?
Decide how Brenda subtracted.

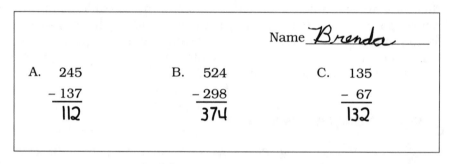

Use your subtraction procedure to subtract D and E correctly.

D.   458   E.   241
     −372   −96

Write what you observed in Brenda's paper.

Write how your subtraction procedure is different.

4. Sometimes it is easier to multiply two whole numbers in your head instead of using paper. Many students find it easier to multiply 40×600 in their heads than using paper, but they would use paper or a calculator for 47×618. Some students would also multiply 4×198 in their heads.

   Write how you can know it will be easier to multiply in your head when you are to multiply two whole numbers.

5. Solve this puzzle by finding missing digits. Solve the puzzle in at least two different ways.

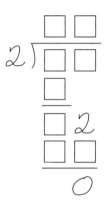

C. COMPUTATION WITH FRACTIONS

1. Which is larger? Write why you believe it is larger.
   a. $\frac{1}{2}$ or $\frac{5}{8}$
   b. $\frac{1}{3}$ or $\frac{3}{8}$
   c. $\frac{3}{4}$ or $\frac{7}{8}$

2. Find the missing number.

$$\frac{3}{8} + \frac{\square}{8} = \frac{1}{2}$$

3. In two different ways, show that

$$4\frac{1}{4} \times 4 \quad \text{does } \textbf{not} \text{ equal} \quad 16\frac{1}{4}.$$

4. Study these examples and decide how the subtraction was done.

A. $\begin{array}{r} \cancel{6}\,5\frac{3}{3} \\ -\ \ \frac{1}{3} \\ \hline 5\frac{2}{3} \end{array}$

B. $\begin{array}{r} \cancel{8}\,7\,\,5\frac{\pm}{4} \\ -\ \ \frac{3}{4} \\ \hline 7\frac{2}{4} \end{array}$

C. $\begin{array}{r} \cancel{10}\,9\,\,\frac{\cancel{5}}{8}\,\frac{11}{8} \\ -\ 2\frac{7}{8} \\ \hline 7\frac{4}{8} \end{array}$

When you know how the subtraction was done, complete Examples D and E the same way.

D. $9\frac{1}{3}$ E. $12\frac{1}{4}$

   $-\ 2\frac{2}{3}$ $-\ 4\frac{3}{4}$

Now write out a description of the procedure. Be sure to tell *how* to do it, and also *why* it gives the correct answer.

D. PROBLEM SOLVING

1. Give each group a collection of at least 10 clippings; each clipping is an advertisement for an item selling for less than $10. Have each group select exactly six items that have a total cost of more than $15 and less than $20. They must prove to you that they have completed the task correctly.
2. Each group needs a chart with a four-by-three grid, labeled as shown below. Make sure each cell on the chart measures at least four-by-six inches. Also provide each group of students with about 10 blank four-by-six-inch cards.

	Estimate	Paper	Mental Computation
Add			
Subtract			
Multiply			
Divide			

Students assume a calculator is not available, and create word problems for each cell in the grid. They write each problem on a four-by-six-inch card and fasten it within the appropriate cell.

Before you assign this task, you may want to review how we know when estimation is the appropriate way to compute a needed number, and (when an exact answer is needed) how we know that mental computation would be more appropriate than using a paper-and-pencil procedure.

3. Give each group of students a different word problem to solve. After they have solved the problem, they are to make a poster to explain
   - how they decided what operation to use, and
   - how they computed the answer.

E. ASSESSMENT OF GROUP ACTIVITIES

1.

About Our Group	Name_____		
	😊	😐	🙁
1. We listened to each other.			
2. We worked together.			
3. There were good ideas.			
4. We finished our task.			

What was well done?

What should have been different?

2. Have students write about their participation.
    - In my group, I am happy with the way I . . .
    - In my group, I can improve by . . .
    - My group should . . .